THE NARRATIVE OF THE LIFE OF A GENTLEMAN LONG RESIDENT IN INDIA

THE NARRATIVE OF THE LIFE OF A GENTLEMAN LONG RESIDENT IN INDIA

GEORGE FRANCOIS GRAND

GYAN

Published by

Gyan Publishing House
5, Ansari Road
Daryaganj, New Delhi-110002
Phone: 011-47034999, 9811692060
E-mail: books@gyanbooks.com

Distribution Network
gyanbooks.com
India, USA, Canada, UK, Australia

ISBN: 978-93-7169-362-2 (PB)

First Published, 1910

2nd Impression 2025

Printed at: Gyan Press, Delhi.

THE NARRATIVE OF THE LIFE OF A GENTLEMAN LONG RESIDENT IN INDIA
Author: GEORGE FRANCOIS GRAND

COL. MORDAUNT'S COCKFIGHT AT LUCKNOW IN THE PROVINCE OF OUDH, 1786.

THE NARRATIVE
OF THE
LIFE OF A GENTLEMAN
LONG RESIDENT IN INDIA.

BY G. F. GRAND.

A NEW EDITION

EDITED FOR

THE CALCUTTA HISTORICAL SOCIETY

WITH

INTRODUCTION, NOTES AND ADDITIONAL LETTERS

BY

WALTER K. FIRMINGER.

CALCUTTA HISTORICAL SOCETY,

28, DALHOUSIE SQUARE, CALCUTTA.

1910.

Printed by D. L. MONRO at THE CALCUTTA GENERAL PRINTING COMPANY, 300, Bowbazar Street, and Published by the CALCUTTA HISTORICAL SOCIETY at 28, Dalhousie Square, Calcutta.

THE NARRATIVE

OF THE

LIFE OF A GENTLEMAN

LONG RESIDENT IN INDIA.

COMPREHENDING A PERIOD OF THE MOST EVENTFUL IN THE HISTORY OF THAT COUNTRY, WITH REGARD TO THE REVOLUTIONS OCCASIONED BY EUROPEAN INTERFERENCE, AND INTERSPERSED WITH INTERESTING ANECDOTES, AND TRAITS CHARACTERISTICAL OF THOSE EMINENT PERSONS WHO DISTINGUISHED THEMSELVES AT THAT JUNCTURE.

CAPE OF GOOD HOPE:

PRINTED FOR THE AUTHOR.

1814.

CONTENTS.

LIST OF ILLUSTRATIONS.

INTRODUCTION.

It is not known whether or no this little book was, before this present edition, ever *published*. The title-page shows that it was "printed for the Author" at the Cape of Good Hope in 1814, and its circulation may, perhaps, like that of a previous book of Grand's on the Land Revenues of Bengal, have been intended for a limited circulation amongst the influential friends of the Author. In the original it forms a quarto volume of seventy-five pages and an Appendix of xxxi. Dr. Busteed notes that the copy in the British Museum has a pasted-in flyleaf "in which, written apparently in a senile hand, is this note signed Jno. Row—

'The annexed *Narrative* was the first book printed in the English language at the Cape of Good Hope, and was given me by Mr. Smith.'"

The India Office copy has been transcribed for me by Mr. T. Taplin. It is a copy presented to the India Office Library by Archibald Constable.

We may observe (p. 202) that Grand completed the book at the Cape on 1st February 1808, when blessed in his "second domestic attachment."* The incident of his first domestic attachment has its place

* This seems to show that the book could not have been written *pour faire chanter* in 1814 or 1815. The book, although completed in 1808, was not printed before 1814, a date, it might have seemed, when Napoleon's fall would have rendered the Princesse de Talleyrand amenable to unfavourable treatment by the restored Bourbons.

in the autobiography, but it is quite secondary to his complaints on the score of the ill-treatment he conceived himself to have received from Lord Cornwallis. Strangely enough, in Elijah Barwell Impey's *Memoirs of Sir Elijah Impey* (p. 308) there is a passage in which Grand's *Narrative* is spoken of as if it were intended by its author to serve as blackmail on the Princesse de Talleyrand. Impey's son (a most incompetent apologist) tells us that both Grand and his former wife came to England in 1815; "his object was to publish the particulars of that lady's life at Calcutta, in revenge for his disappointment at Batavia—her's to seek for riches for that publication." This passage is the only evidence that can be produced for the assertion that Grand after 1802 ever again revisited England, but Elijah Barwell Impey, not only asserts that Grand was in England in 1815 but that both Grand and his former wife were there and sought his advice.* "This advice," he says, "of course, was very unpalatable to both: the lady took a legal opinion, and the gentleman *took* himself off. What has become of him since, I know not." Impey *fils* tells us that he saw the book—"a paltry book, published at the Cape." It need hardly be pointed out that Grand had been a servant of the Batavian Republic, not at Batavia, but at the Cape of Good Hope. It is just possible that there is a chapter of the story for the present, and perhaps for a long time to come, doomed to oblivion. That the book completed in 1808, and printed in 1814, was not written

* The Princess was in England in 1815.

with a view to blackmail the unfortunate Princesse de Talleyrand seems to me to be apparent whether we read it from line to line or read it "between the lines." The question is whether or no the younger Impey's unsupported statements can be received with any credit whatever. He is a thoroughly inaccurate writer, and not the least reliance can be based on his unsupported assertions: and yet I scruple to believe him to be absolutely dishonest. He tells us, for instance, that in December 1801 or thereabouts he was present at a re-union at Neuilly of "Sir Elijah and Lady Impey, M. and Me. de Talleyrand, Sir Philip Francis, and Mr. Le Grand!" Grand, when the story of this alleged re-union reached him in South Africa, indignantly denied that he had ever seen his wife since 1778. But the fact remains that the younger Impey asserts that he met both Grand and his divorced wife in 1801 and again in 1815: and it is a question, therefore, not of Impey's accuracy, but of his veracity.

It cannot, however, be believed that this book was composed to serve as blackmail. If in 1815, Grand attempted to make use of it for a purpose so dishonourable, we may ask what is there in it that could have served such a purpose? By that date Madame de Talleyrand must have been quite prepared for the worst construction of her past history. It is far more likely that this book was written to set forth a tale of woe against Lord Cornwallis and his colleagues. It is an attack on Lord Cornwallis' administration in the two most vital points—the mismanaged war in Mysore with its weak termination, and the policy of the Permanent Settlement. The account of the war against Tipu Sultan is in reality no account at all; it is but a partisan representation of certain events in that war.

The lavish praise bestowed upon Warren Hastings in the *Narrative* would be remarkable were it not that Grand was so clearly Hastings's dependent. It is significant that Grand says not a word about the second Mrs. Warren Hastings, of whom he must have seen a great deal, and, when he goes home in 1773, on the *Marquis of Rockingham*, he does not tell us that one of his fellow passengers was the Baron Charles Von Imhoff.* It is fairly clear that Grand knew how to keep his tongue quiet. The humiliating account he gives of General Richard Smith's birth and failings might perhaps be ascribed to the fact the General was a close supporter of Francis, the professing political purist, and that Smith was one of the leaders in the Parliamentary proceedings for the impeachment of Hastings and Impey. Grand's review of Hastings' policy has a real claim to be considered of independent value.

It can hardly be doubted that the interest of this book to many who purchase it in the present edition will be centred in that lady who, despite spurious and unworthy portraits, over every generation of Calcutta antiquaries exercises an extraordinary charm. Dr. Busteed in the latest edition of the *Echoes from Old Calcutta* has thrown so much fresh light on

* Imhoff was deported from Calcutta by order of the Court. See *Bengal: Past and Present*, Vol. III., pp. 145-6.

the later history of Catherine Noel Verlée that it is now almost possible to write an independent biography of her. I shall not attempt to repeat even in the most brief manner the facts of the history which Dr. Busteed has revealed with enormous industry, and has set forth with a charm so well known to readers of his more than admirable work.* Having carefully considered the facts, I must, however, confess that I hold that although it is abundantly clear that on the night of the 8th December 1778, Philip Francis did, beyond all doubt, visit the Grands' house with a criminal intent, yet as Sir Robert Chambers—if *Hicky's Gazette* may be trusted—puts it.

"1. There is no proof, either positive or circumstantial, that Mrs. Grand knew of, or previously consented to his (Francis') coming for any purpose.

"2. There is no proof, either direct or founded on violent presumption, that they were actually together, much less that they committed any crime together."

There has been a great deal of careless writing on the subject. Even Sir James Fitzjames Stephen has said—"that in the case of *Grand* v. *Francis* 'it was proved that he (Francis) got into her (Mrs. Grand's) bedroom by a ladder.'† Nothing of the kind was asserted at the time. The ladder was not set up against the house, but against the wall running round the compound;

* In addition to the documents quoted by Busteed, see the papers printed in the Second Appendix to this Volume.

† *Nuncomar and Impey*, Vol. II., p. 112.

there is not only no proof to show that Francis reached Mrs. Grand's room, but good ground for believing that he never got upstairs. The only ground for believing that she and Francis ever met in the upper part of the house is Grand's statement, that she confessed her shame to him! That Francis was ever a successful lover of Mrs. Grand at all may even be doubted—that he was wildly enamoured is beyond question."*

Two things should be remembered about Mrs. Grand at this time. She was born on 21st November 1762, and therefore was at the time of Francis's trespass only a little over sixteen years of age. Secondly, war had broken out between England and France some few months before, and her relatives at Chandernagore had been reduced to a state of the greatest poverty. When, on 9th December, Grand sent the poor child back to her married half-sister's home at Chandernagore, he was sending her to a ruined household. In the year following we find her brother-in-law a prisoner of war in the newly opened jail on the Maidan and her aged father all but begging his bread at Balasore. That having lost her reputation, the girl ultimately went astray is unfortunately too true: but there is quite enough in the early stages of her history to win for her a sympathy, if indeed she would, either then or now, care to have it so.

---

* Lady Francis records that her husband always maintained that he had been an unsuccessful claimant to Mrs. Grand's affections. Francis's refusal to meet Grand in a duel points this way.

That in after years our Author did sponge on his wife is beyond doubt. Catherine Noel married Talleyrand on 9th September 1802.* Grand would lead us to suppose that his appointment by the Batavian Government was due to the influence of his own family, but Dr. Busteed has shown that Talleyrand was the suggester of the appointment and that the Princesse urged M. Van der Goes, the Minister for Foreign Affairs of the Batavian Republic, to get Grand, her real husband, "de s'embarquer sans délai." †

Since the appearance of the latest edition of Dr. Busteed's *Echoes from Old Calcutta* (4th edition, 1908), which threw so much new light on Mrs. Grand's career immediately following her departure from India, we have heard a good deal about her parentage and family from Mr. Lehuraux, the industrious historian of Chandernagore, and also a great deal from other writers about her later life in Paris. We have heard of her in the *Memoires de la Comtesse de Boigne* (where there is an unpleasant and incredible anecdote) and in the *Chronique de la Duchesse de Dino*. Monsieur R. Guyot gave several pictures of her in an article "Madame Grand á Paris" in the *Feuilles d'Histoire* of May 1909, and last year we have from M. Bernard de Lacombe a volume, which has already reached a third edition—*La Vie Privèe de Talleyrand—Son Emigration—Son marriage—Sa Retraite—Sa Conversion—Sa Mort.* That the closing

* Le 22 Fructidor An X.

† See for evidence the notes at the conclusion of this volume.

years of her life must have been sad ones we cannot doubt. She died on the 10th December 1839, as Dr. Busteed correctly says, and not the 9th, as the Duchesse de Dino records. On hearing of her death, the ex-Bishop of Autun (with a brutality characteristic of him) remarked "Ceci simplifie beaucoup ma position."

We have so long been asked to accept various pictures as portraits of Madame Grand (the Serampore daub for instance), that it is pleasing to know that the portrait by Mlde. Vigée Le Brun which we have been kindly permitted by Messrs. Thacker Spink to reproduce here, is undoubtedly genuine. Here is M. Lacombe's description of the picture : "Sa taille souple et gracieuse s'abandonne dans une attitude de repos. Elle songe ; ses grands yeux candides semblent suivre à travers l'espace un rêve heureux. Les traits du visage, éclairés de côté, sont d'une finesse exquise ; le mention est délicat ; les lèvres s'entr'ouvrent pour un sourire ; les chevaux, relevés et frisés, entourent le front d'une auréole légère, et retombent en boucles sompteuses sur la gorge nue. Enfin, pour compléter le sujet, une toilette d'úne élégance très sobre, où le bleu pâle, le gris et le blanc se foudent harmonieusement, et qui n'a, pour ornements, qu'un fichu des mousseline encadrant le décolletage, un large nœud de soie bleue des les cheveux, un autre sur là poitrine."* Yet the portrait strikes M. Lacombe, as it must strike us,

* Here is an account of a ball dress worn by Madame Grand on February 22nd, 1787 :—" Un fourreau de taffetas blanc bordé d'une frange de soie rose, une jupe de crêpe blanc rayé de ruban de

"Que dirait, devant le portrait de cette jeune femme, au regard doux et sentimental, qu'un orage avait déjà boulversé sa vie ?"

I have endeavoured to make the *Narrative* easier to read by breaking it up into chapters: in the original it is continuous. The footnotes in square brackets I have added myself: the others are from the original. I have occasionally inserted dates (in brackets) in order to fix the reader's attention. The index is a new feature. Grand is far from being an accurate writer, as will be observed from the comments supplied in the footnotes and the notes at the conclusion of this volume.

I am afraid the personality of the author of the *Narrative** will not impress the reader very favourably.

---

satin blanc pailleté en argent, bordé de même ruban, les parements bordés *idem* et fleurs de laurier : les manchettes à deux rangs de blonde bâtarde, les moignons de crêpe blanc pailetté rattachés par un bracelet de pied d'alouette rose, une guirlande de mêmes fleurs pour la taille, une ruche de tulle au bord du corset." Cost 264 *livres*.

* When the press lists of the Imperial Record Department for the Cornwallis period are published it will perhaps be possible to trace the whole story of Grand's troubles in Behar but the most essential documents are to be sought for at the Board of Revenue, Calcutta. See Hunter : *Bengal MS. Records*. In 1783 Grand brought charges against the Judge at Durbungah which the Governor-General and Council decided were "founded entirely on the misrepresentations of your servants." In connection with this dispute, Grand wrote a letter to the Chief Justice which is now among the Impey MSS. at the British Museum. Dr. Busteed says that the letter shows that "the writer was not only quarrelsome and self-important, but a sneaking sort of man also." *Echoes*, p. 278.

"A foreign adventurer with few scruples and with little sense of honour," writes Mr. O'Malley in his Gazetteer of Muzaffarpur. Yet, despite the many inaccuracies in this book, despite the enormous conceit which tempts us to place it aside with disgust, there is so much that reveals the story of men and manners in the days of Hastings and Cornwallis, that its publication, I feel sure, will be welcomed. In the latter portion of his narrative Grand is not telling us the whole truth, and yet no doubt Behar owes him a debt for its once flourishing indigo industry.

I have to express my gratitude to Mr. E. W. Madge who, in my absence from Calcutta, has taken many unselfish pains in hunting up for me the Registers at St. John's and references to books in the libraries; to Mr. Lehuraux I am indebted for information derived from the French archives at Chandernagore; to Mr. J. S. Davidson, J.P., for information about Grand's connections by marriage—the Ledlies; and finally to Mr. Cyril Champkin, for proof corrections and valuable advice.

The dates of Grand's birth and death are not known. According to *Dodwell and Miles* his commission as Ensign was dated 1766, and this would lead us to conjecture that he must have been born about 1749.

WALTER K. FIRMINGER.

SHILLONG, KHASI AND JANTIA HILLS,
23rd January, 1911.

ADVERTISEMENT.

I HAD long determined upon writing a narrative of my life. It was suggested to me by friends who felt for the vicissitudes which I had experienced. I began it therefore in 1801, and continued it, from time to time, till in 1808 I had brought it to a close. The reason of the delay in its publication has been detailed by notifications inserted in the *Cape Gazette.* I thank those who have now afforded me the opportunity of giving it to the world, without subjecting me to a pecuniary loss. I trust in its object removing the animadversions, which men of illiberal dispositions, and perfectly ignorant of what concerned me personally, had endeavoured to impress the Public with, regarding my career of service, and latterly the motives of my actions. Equally do I hope, in behalf of my much esteemed brother servants, that it will conduce to render rulers cautious of infringing and violating rights, which, by covenants executed, and these sanctioned and established by virtue of an Act of Parliament, each civil servant of the East India Company is strongly entrenched with.

Should this have the desired effect, I shall consider myself amply rewarded; and in the pleasure of having been the cause of doing away an evil, and deterring those placed in power from committing in future, acts which are not warrantable, I shall forget the individual wrongs which I have suffered.

CAPE OF GOOD HOPE, *15th April, 1814.* (Sd.) G. F. GRAND.

PREFACE.

I HAVE long promised you, my dear friend, the publication of the narrative of my life. You are well aware that it was written at a period when my prospects of advancement in rank and fortune were, in an instant, blasted. The hasty and unexpected decision of the Court of Directors, on my appeal to their justice, against the arbitrary and illegal act of their servants brought on this misfortune and disappointment.

If befell me, likewise, at such an advanced time of life and after above thirty years of honourable service, both in the Civil and Military lines on the Bengal Establishment, as utterly to incapacitate me, as I then considered my situation, from embracing and following other pursuits, which might have created a hope of retrieving, before Nature closed her end, my fallen fortunes in this world. I, thus, resigned myself to adversity, and contemplated the fortunate career of others of my brother servants, with the philosophic reflection that what they enjoyed in riches and power, they wanted, many of them, in health; for, blessed with a good constitution, and a mind conscious of its unmerited fate, I bade fair to sink in the vale of life, bereft of affluence, but freed from corroding thought and lingering disease.

An incident, suddenly arising, changed this aspect.

A proposition was made to me, which beamed a ray of hope, that fortune again would be favourable.

This revived ambitious views, which scarcely had lain dormant. Sensible that my faculties were unimpaired, I deemed it criminal to give up active scenes, where the strongest expectation of success was grounded. I seized, joyfully, the moment offered, and perfectly free in my election, I repaired, in time of peace, to the Cape of Good Hope, vested with a high station, and the spontaneous assurance that nothing would be left undone, which could tend to raise me again to honours and wealth. Unfortunately, the war broke out, and the wishes of myself, as well as those friends intent on re-establishing me in life, were defeated. You know the sequel. Happy in my second choice of a partner, I upbraided not the worldly opportunity lost. My happiness centered alone in domestic concerns. May you be blessed in the like manner, should it ever be your lot to deplore, as I did, the cruel separation which forced me from the first! I now proceed to my narrative.

NARRATIVE OF THE LIFE OF A GENTLEMAN LONG RESIDENT IN INDIA.

CHAPTER I.

Early Life and First Voyage to India.

Born of a virtuous and noble family (my mother's name being le Clerc de Virly, which Virly was a signorial patrimony in Normandy, long the property and residence of her ancestors, till the despotism of Lewis XIV. by the revocation of the Edict of Nantes, drove the Seigneur de Virly to take refuge with his family in England, leaving his fair possessions and wealth to the spoil of his tyrannical king); educated at Lausanne (in the environs of which delightful city and country, the Lordship of Ecublanc, situated on the banks of the Lake of Geneva, between Lausanne and Morges, had long been the seat of the Grands,)*

* In the history of the "Chapitre de Lausanne" are registered two *nobles Chanoines* of the Catholic Cathedral in the 12th century, *viz.*, Gerard Grand and Eric Grand; and *vice versâ* in the 16th century, by a reference to Moreri's *Historical and Biographical Dictionary*, it will be seen in that century that a descendant, named likewise Girard Grand, Doctor of Laws, and Counsellor of the City of Lausanne, materially assisted with De Watteville, Vinet, and others, in introducing the Reformation in Switzerland.

in the house and under the superintendence of the best Parents, assisted by a private tutor, a clergyman living in the house, and with whom I used to attend the lectures of the first Professors of Science in that celebrated University, I could not otherwise be formed, when I opened my career in the world, but with a disposition inclined to honour, virtue and fraught with every social tie.

Tinctured with a superficial knowledge of almost every science, versed in none, joined with a smattering of Greek and Latin, was I taken at too early an age from my studies to be sent to London. My father, blessed with a numerous family of children, could not, however his partiality for me, resist the offer made to him by an old friend in the mercantile line to receive his son as his apprentice for seven years gratis, and then to succeed to a regular business, which, at the less estimated amount, brought in annually a clear and almost certain income of £5,000 per annum. This person was Mr. Robert Jones of Clement's Lane, Lombard Street, who died in 1774, possessed of a fortune of £150,000, and vacating with his death a seat in Parliament for the Borough of Huntingdon, one in the East India Direction, and an Elder Brothership of the Trinity House. I am thus particular, because it is consistent with the narrative of my life that this person's character should be brought forward to view. From a small beginning, being Captain of a Lisbon Trader, and without any education whatsoever, yet, endowed with a strong genius, and gifted with that talent which the immortal Shakespeare has described, "*Of grasping Fortune when she presents herself*," did he rise to the eminence of rank in life and fortune which is above described.

Accordant with these views, I took leave of the tenderest of parents, and, with a sorrowful heart, I was consigned to the care of a *Voiturier*, to feed and transport me from Lausanne to London. This distance, through the direct road of Franche Comté, Champagne and Picardy, we accomplished by short stages in three weeks. I recollect nothing particular which passed during the journey, excepting having been intoxicated, for the first time in my life, with champagne wine at Rheims, and being exceedingly seasick in the passage across the channel.

Arrived in London, the *Voiturier* took an immediate opportunity to deliver over his charge. On being presented to Mr. Jones, instead of being welcomed as the son of his old friend, to whom he had obligations, I was received by a man of coarse manner and harsh voice, more as a damaged landed Bale of Goods might have been, than with any mark of affection and attachment to the source whence I sprang. He asked me, indeed, how my Father and Mother were, and if I had brought him any Gruyère Cheese, which the *Voiturier* answering for me in the affirmative, seemed to work a happy change. He smiled and bade me approach him; called for the footman, and observing his spare beds were removed into the country, committed me to the care of him, who was diverted to afford me half his bed to sleep on. The next morning after breakfasting with Mr. Jones, I was introduced into the Accounting House, and my first duty prescribed to see it cleaned, the fire well lighted, the desks brushed, the chairs, etc., well placed, and told I should be favoured to run about with Bills for Acceptance, so soon as I became acquainted a little with the streets of London, to be able to find my way in them, until when, I was ordered to accompany the footman, who, on such errands, threw off his livery jacket, to assume an old brown coat cast off by his Master; and he was enjoined to point out to me the principal resorts where this duty called him, after my pigtail had been changed for a cropped head of hair, in order, as Mr. Jones wittily remarked, the people might not take me for a French monkey imported on English grounds.

And now, my friend, view the contrast which so sudden a change created, picture to yourself a youth dressed in embroidered and laced clothes, curled head, *chapeau bras*, solitaire and sword by his side, accompanied and introduced by his Tutor into the first assemblies, both public and private; taught by the attention of those frequenting them, almost to consider himself a man; and behold the transition of the same youth, in a plain English frock, round hat, and hair cut close, trudging after a footman, in all weathers through the streets of London! The disgust which followed was natural. I seized the first moment of well grounded discontent to absent myself. I took refuge at an aunt's of mine, whence my father was apprized with my determination to return to Switzerland, or to avail myself of the friends in the East India direction, which my uncle, recently departed, Mr. John Payne, Chairman in Lord Clive's Government, had left, and to embark for that country in some station to seek my fortune. Unhappily for me, my father did not live to justify his Friend's conduct or to excuse his son's. A putrid fever, with which he was attacked and for which the celebrated Tissot, imprudently, copiously bled him, soon carried him out of this world, and his circumstances not turning out so good as were expected, actuated me to adopt the alternative which I had proposed. In the interim of an opportunity occurring I was sent to the village of Thornhill in Yorkshire, where I boarded at a Mrs. Pollard's, mother of a clerk in Mr. Jones' House, and attended the Clergyman of the Parish, to qualify myself for my destination, by perfecting myself in the English language. I was kindly treated and a Welsh pony being allowed me, I soon joined with the neighbouring Hunts, and was much noticed by some noblemen and gentlemen of the envious, who had experienced, when on their travels on the continent, the civility and the hospitality of my father's cheerful Board. I could not be more happily situated ; however I could not but deeply feel the blow which had, so early in life, befallen me, by the premature deaths of my Father and Uncle, within two months of each other. After passing a few months in this manner, I was removed to Greenwich Academy, where, under the tuitiòn of Doctor Bracken, I was to learn Gunnery, Fortification, and Mathematics, my Friends having determined on a Military life for my career, apprehending, as they expressed, the vivacity and fire which I displayed, were qualifications not suitable to the gravity and sedateness requisite for a Desk, and a regular course of mercantile pursuits.

After a few months' stay at this Academy, which has sent forth several shining Naval Characters, I was called to London, when it was announced to me, that a Cadetship to Ben Coolen awaited my acceptance. In this manner did Mr. Jones acquit himself towards his deceased Friend. Fortunately, my Aunt, Mrs. John Payne, had heard during her Husband's life, amongst those gentlemen from India, whom, as a leading Director, he was in the habit of seeing and entertaining, that no climate in that region, could be compared to this mentioned, for its peculiar insalubrity. Indignant against Mr. Jones, for his unfeeling conduct, the good old Lady ordered her carriage, took me with her to the India House, and had my nomination changed for Bengal. Accordingly, in the month of January 1766, on board of the *Lord Camden*, Captain Nathaniel Smith, did I embark, tolerably equipped at my mother's expence, under the Captain's immediate care, and having his Tables with good Letters of recommendation, to deliver on my arrival in India. I embarked at Gravesend and found myself accommodated, with eleven Writers, each with a standing bed in the great cabin, not one of which gentlemen, excepting Mr. John Makepeace Thackeray of Hadley, is now (1802) living.* Our voyage was

* [Correctly—William Makepeace Thackeray, the grandfather of the novelist.]

pleasant. We touched at Johanna, coming in there the same day with Captain Thomas Bates Rous, commanding the *Britannia* East Indiaman; scarcely had we been at anchor, than, an anxiety to set my foot on land, induced me to avail myself of a canoe, which was alongside, to go on shore, in which were already seated three of my comrades. We pushed off, the people making signs to us not to move, and they would bring us safe, but a panic seizing one of the Bengal Writers, Mr. Mitchell, son of the then Secretary of the India House, he rose up, and the Canoe from the rolling filling, we were in the utmost hazard of our lives, neither of us knowing to swim, and feeling so terrified from being in the water, that those seamen, who plunged instantaneously into the sea, to our assistance, from the Ship, incurred the greatest danger. I recollect grasping by the throat the first who laid hold of me, and would infallibly have been the cause of his death and my own, had not his superior strength enabled him to throw me off. I thus went down a second time, when he, dexeterously swimming around me, bore me up, as I had again arisen, and swam with me to the Ship's boat, which, happily, was very near. I came on board, pretty well soused, and so confused, that I barely heard the reprimand the Captain was pleased to give me and my companions for our rashness. With this I should not have been dissatisfied. Young as I was, I could make allowances for the responsibility which attached to the Captain, from having so many boys committed to his peculiar trust by the parents of each individual, and, consequently,

I could form a judgment. What would have been his feelings, had it pleased Providence, that he should have had to relate the misfortune, which, but for its gracious interposition, might have befallen four of them. But, when I recovered, I felt greatly hurt, by the Captain grudging to let me have ten Spanish Dollars, to present my deliverer with, out of the pocket money which was given to him in charge, and to pay to me, when I came on shore in India. We remained in this pleasant Island three weeks, the Captains of both Ships vying with each other, which should entertain the best. At one of these feasts, a trial of my temper was made. A Gentleman Cadet in our Ship, of the name of Macpherson, who had been a Lieutenant in a disbanded Regiment, after the Seven Years' War, was the person fixed on, and, at once, bringing on the topic of the oversetting of the Canoe, ascribed it to my cowardice. His age and stature had not, however, the effect of affrighting me; I plainly told him, he lied and defied him to a proof of my courage on the following morning. The challenge was accepted, seconds appointed, and the meeting secretly took place; however to keep up the better the farce intended, the Captains of the Ships, who are all looked up to as superior beings, laid their injunctions on us, on pain of their severe displeasure, not to fight. It may be presumed, what the result was, when the parties were, a boy and a huge big man of full thirty. Our pistols, apparently under great form and studied delay, loaded carefully by our seconds, contained only powder. My second contended in my behalf, that I should have the advantage of the first shot, but, after a great deal of parleying discussion, within our hearing, to all appearance reluctantly yielded, upon the plea held out by the other, that my offence had been adequate, the lie direct, being said, to be inexcusable. We fired by signal together, and, naturally, neither of our shots having been murderous, the seconds stepped in, and rejoicing that no blood had been spilled, expressed a hope the matter could be made up, without exposing either of our valuable lives to further risque. I was addressed first, and asked, if I would apologize for the great offence which I had given, to which I directly replied, I would willingly, provided my opponent would retract his charge. This being asserted to, the parties were loudly called to quit their ground, and, supported by each of their seconds, advanced towards one another, uttered what had been agreed upon, and ended the amusement, which, I may say, had been held at my sole expense, the other, of course, being in the secret, by shaking of hands.

When, in process of time, I was made acquainted with the essay which had been practised on my disposition during the passage, I could not but highly blame a person of Macpherson's experience to have joined in it, and particularly one, whose situation in the Military line fully rendered him aware of the delicacy felt by men of his profession on such points ; yet, I regretted him sincerely as a worthy good man, when I learnt, he had fallen a sacrifice to the fatigue of the campaign which he endured, being with Colonel Peach's Bengal Detachment, serving in the Carnatic under

General Joseph Smith, in the war which in 1767 had been undertaken by the Presidency of Madras against Hyder Aly.

On our way from Johanna to Madras, nothing occurred remarkable, excepting the death of one of the Cabin Passengers, Mr. Ray, a Bengal Writer, who was carried off quickly by a violent fever. This young man was one of Lord Sandwich's sons, from his illegitimate connection with the famous Miss Ray ;* and, when I reflect on the accomplishments of Ray's mind, I may say, I never, in my observation, met with one who felt so repugnant to the source from whence he sprang. Instead of glorying, as others, with less strong feelings might have done, in being the son of a noble earl, then a Minister of State, being first Lord of the Admiralty, and whose influence at the India House, had procured for him a writership, he appeared truly debased and chagrined, if the most distant allusion, without even the smallest intention, reminded him of either his connection by birth, or by patronage. Coeval with such sentiments, I am sure he regretted not his premature death, for although in the bloom of life, with the fairest hopes of fortune and advancement, his settled melancholy bespoke his thoughts, and he parted with life, without a sigh. I was much afflicted by this unexpected demise. Mr. Ray had early distinguished me amongst our other companions ; and from our juvenile unreserved communications, of the

* [Martha Ray, a famous singer, was shot dead by her would-be husband, James Hackman, Vicar of Wiveton Norfolk, on leaving Covent Garden Theatre, 1779.]

various relations and expectations of each, seemed to harbour an idea that what he owed to patronage, had been a sacrifice in his favor to a debt of gratitude. In effect Mr. Jones was the Director who had nominated him upon Lord Sandwich's application, and the conditional return was, which existed fully in his conception he being then twenty years old, and well informed, Mr. Jones's admission to a seat for the Borough of Huntingdon, the representation of which City was then divided between His Grace the Duke of Manchester and the Sandwich interest, and besides this, Mr. Jones bargained for a seat in the Trinity House, of which the last mentioned Nobleman was the Governor. To occasion, and ground the above conclusion, I had imparted, that it was through my father's intercession with Mr. John Payne, Mr. Jones had obtained a seat in the East India direction, a fact well known in those days.

CHAPTER II.

CAREER AS A SOLDIER.

WE anchored at Madras on the 2nd of June, [1766] and waiting the 3rd on the Governor, Mr. Palk,* who, from being Chaplain to that establishment, had been selected from his superior abilities, to succeed Lord Pigot in the Government, were invited by him to celebrate His Majesty's Birthday, on the day following. The Dinner, Ball, Illuminations, Fireworks, and the general brilliancy of dress and decorations which reigned, impressed my mind, that what I had read on the passage, relative to the magnificence prevailing in India, was not exaggerated.

We sojourned a fortnight at this Port, whence we shaped our course for Bengal, and taking a Pilot on board in Balasore Roads, proceeded up the river, and from Culpee, where the Honourable Company's ships then usually anchored, embarked in a Budgerow for Calcutta which we came to on the 26th of June. I was here well received by those to whom I had the honor of being recommended. Lord Clive, particularly, spoke of my deceased uncle, Mr. Payne, with affection and respect, but lamented my youth did not permit him, so soon to entrust me with a Commission, adding graciously, that he should send me up to join the 2nd

* [Robert Palk. Returned to England 1767. Member of Parliament for Ashburton. Baronet 1772. Died 1798.]

Brigade, which stood on the roll for Field Service, and enjoin its Commanding Officer, if he saw propriety of conduct, and attention to my duty, to seize the first occasion of putting me in order to act as an Ensign.

This Nobleman, the founder of the English Empire and glory in India, had just returned from the Upper Provinces, where, by uncommon firmness, and the determined spirit which he displayed throughout this trying scene, quelled and corrected that tendency to distress the Government and force it to compliance, which the Officers, by entering into an act of general resignation, hoped therefrom to effect. Some of these gentlemen were brought to trial, and their Commissions forfeited; others were sent to England, without the forms of being arraigned on specific charges before a Military Tribunal; and the most meritorious had their errors pardoned and their Commissions returned, the Governor refusing to accept them, and denouncing such, who hesitated to resume their stations, to be in a mutinous state; His Lordship observing, that this mode which he had adopted, pleasingly gave him the opportunity of weeding the Army of some bad subjects, who had crept in since the period of his first Government in Bengal as Colonel Clive.

When characters are appreciated after the lapse of party prejudice, those of Clive and Dupleix will shine amongst the brightest, whose scene of action was on Indian Territory. They early discerned the field which opened itself for active enterprise, from the dissolution of the Mogul Empire, and the distracted Governments of those Princes, who had shaken off and assumed in their own persons the Imperial authority. Each of these Politicians contended for their respective Nation's Sovereignty ; but Clive was the hero, who effectually established it, with the view of rendering it permanent, knew to prescribe just and prudent limits to its extension.

In the cession of Provinces which he acquired for the English nation, he set their bounds to the River Carumnassah, in the same spirit he re-instated the Nawab Vizier Shujah-ul Dhowlah into the Dominions which his arms had conquered, requiring only from him the transfer of the Fort of Allahabad, with a suitable Jagheer for the maintenance of the sucessor to Timur, and to which he added a certain pension or tribute rather (since it was given in consideration of the cession of the Dewannee of the Company's Provinces, *viz.*, Bengal, Behar, and Orissa*) from the East India Company, of six and twenty lacks of rupees per annum. In carrying these points into execution, his expanded mind had in contemplation the converting of a warlike Prince into a generous and useful ally by the restitution of his territories, and in concert with him, to retain the Mogul, on whom they conjointly had conferred a splendid establishment, within the sphere of their own observation and management.

Nor will it be forgotten his manifest disinterestedness in fixing a certain limit to his fortune. Never was a truer word spoken than, when in his memorable

---

* [The Orissa of the Treaty was the District of Midnapore. Cuttack, etc., did not become British till 1804.]

defence in the House of Commons, standing up in his place as a Member of it, to vindicate his fair fame of a foul impeachment, he boldly avowed what he had received in presents, asserting he might have had more, but that he thought it requisite to reject the liberality of the Indian Princes, when the magnitude of their offers exceeded what he considered would have raised him to a situation too rich for a subject. To evince a proof of this magnanimity, he adduced the Legacy left to him, out of pure friendship and grateful recollection for services rendered, which the Nawab Meer Jaffier assigned to him in his Testament, and this occurring, when His Lordship was in Europe, and his local power had ceased. Lord Clive completely alienated this sum (sixty thousard pounds sterling) out of his, and the reach of his Heirs and Successors for ever, by creating it into a Fund, under the inspection of the East India Company, to serve for the widows of Officers who had gloriously contributed their share to the advancement of his prosperity. And, after exhibiting this testimony, and others, in full refutation of such unjust aspersions, as a Burgoyne (the Hero of Saratoga in the American war) and other envious Detractors had thrown out against him, he concluded, quitting the House, with that truly Ciceronical Peroration, "exhorting the members, that, whilst they judged of his honor, not to lose sight of their own."

In the month of September, 1766, I was in orders to proceed up the Country with a Detachment of Recruits, for the three Brigades, under the command of the late Colonel James Hannay, then Captain Hannay, who, as well as myself, had recently arrived from Europe. Lord Clive was good enough to recommend me to this Gentleman and I experienced from him every attention during his temporary authority.

Arrived at Bankypore, then the Cantonment of the second Brigade, I was introduced by him to the late General Richard Smith, then the Colonel thereof. This Brigade took the Field soon after, repairing to the banks of the Carumnassah, and was there stationed at hand, to assist our Ally the Nawab Vizier Shujah-ul-Dhowlah, had the Afghan Prince Abdallah Khan put his threats into execution, of invading the former's Dominions, and subsequently, in the event of success, conformable to the first design, the Provinces ceded to the Company.

After bearing a soldier's musket on the line of march, constantly attending the mock sieges and battles which took place in our fixed encampment on the borders of the River abovementioned, the Colonel was pleased to accede to the wishes expressed to him in my behalf by Lord Clive, and I suddenly found myself rewarded for the activity and diligence which I had displayed, in unremitting attention to my duty, by being nominated to act as Ensign.

We returned soon after to Cantonments, where I had the gratification of seeing myself confirmed, by a Commission of Ensign, signed by His Lordship on the 4th of September. This early mark of approbation actuated my zeal, and for three years that I served in the European Regiment, under the celebrated Martinet, the late Colonel Gilbert Ironside, I can equally vouch my constant perseverance in the readiest obedience to my superiors, acquired me new Friends, and the esteem of the Commanding Officer of the Brigade, then Colonel Charles Chapman, in whose Family I lived, and acted as Assistant Secretary to his Staff Establishment.

In this period nothing of any importance locally occurred. The Army, at my entrance into the service, was composed of three Brigades, one stationed at the Presidency, another midway at Berhampore, and the farthest station extended only to Bankypore. Each Brigade consisted of one European Regiment, with six Battalions of Sepoys, and a proportion of artillery, with one hundred black Horse, and the highest rank enjoyed for such a command, was that of a Colonel. Besides these there were in different cities of the three Provinces, Militia Sepoys, under the name of Pergannah. These served for the purpose of guarding the Treasuries, where Civilians were fixed to provide the Honorable Company's Investment, and to escort the fleets of boats which conveyed the goods from distant Ports to the Presidency.

In the Carnatic, the war with Hyder Aly was terminated by General Joseph Smith, in 1768, who conducted it with that Military ability, which acquired an increased reputation to the British Troops ; and Colonel Peach, who had commanded the Detachment of Europeans and Sepoys which had been supplied from Bengal, returned this year, with every credit due to him as an Officer, who had won his first laurels in America, under Wolfe, the immortal Conqueror of Quebec.

Our Cantonments, in 1767, took fire, and such was the rapidity with which the thatched Bungalows burnt that scarcely an officer had one moment to save any thing of his equipment. The Government, with that liberality, consistent to men vested with such a trust, required upon honor, a statement from each officer of his loss, and every one was reimbursed, according to the stated amount.

This accident gave rise to the erection of Barracks, both at Dynapore and Burhampore, and the grand scale on which these were formed, entailed such an expence on the Honourable Company, and sunk such a capital, as to have caused them to regret, that the double full Batta had been struck off by Lord Clive, instead of being continued in the field, and the full Batta preserved in the Company's Provinces, conditionally, that each officer found his own Quarters.

In 1768, I was detached to the Presidency with Captain Catlyn, Lieutenants Lumsdaine and Fairfaix, to bring up the recruits arrived from Europe. The latter of these gentlemen was my junior, being a Cadet of 1767, as I had been advanced in the beginning of the year to the rank of Lieutenant.

I mentioned Colonel Ironside's character as a Martinet, but, at this distance of time, although he is no longer alive, I revere his memory as an officer, nor, in my observation, have I ever seen a man so capable to bring up young men, to a sense and knowledge of their duty. His particularities were a matter of just in those days, but reflection has fully confirmed me in the propriety of a Commanding Officer having every Officer in his Regiment, from the major to the youngest Ensign, fitted for command. To the latter was enjoined by him, the having the exercise and evolutions written out, and, after a certain given time, it was expected and often practised, that every officer should, when called out at a moment's warning, evince his capacity in manœuvring the Regiment, so well as the oldest veteran in it, bearing a Commission.

An incident befell him, which is too ludicrous, though characteristic of the National character, not to be related. In one of the mock battles we were performing in the Field, the late Colonel Arthur Ahmuty had assigned to him the command of a wing, and on his corps was the lot fixed, to break and disperse at a certain signal. This order was repeated to him by Colonel Ironside's Aide-de-Camp, whom he gravely requested to bear his respects to the Colonel, desiring some other selection might be made for the execution of such a manœuvre, for his part he must decline it, as Arthur Ahmuty had never, nor would ever, turn his back and fly from the enemy. This disconcerted, of course, the operations and field of action for that day, and occasioned a general laughter; however, I am convinced, the offender was so perfeetly grounded in his principles of a soldier, as never to have felt his ridicule which attached on this singularity of behaviour. In short, he considered it a stigma, and no one could have dissuaded him, that, had he complied, the application of it would have been marked as just.

In the latter end of 1769 our Brigade was ordered to exchange with that which had held for three years the station of Berhampore, and there, soon after our arrival, I had the honor of mounting General Smith's guard, when he took the opportunity of praising my conduct, which had been reported to him by Colonel Chapman, and pleasingly announced his intention of removing me to his brother's Battalion of Sepoys, Major John Smith, stationed at Benares, a situation then most desirable for a Subaltern.

I had not long to await the performance of his voluntary promise. I found myself the next day in orders, and within one month I had joined my destination Here commenced my intimacy with Mr. Thomas Motte,* a man whose philanthropy, thorough acquaintance with India, diversity of historical anecdote, general knowledge and information, joined to a cheerful and sociable disposition, with the truest hospitality, rendered him one of the most pleasing companions within my experience. To our society were soon added the present Major-General William Palmer† and Colonel Patrick Hay, characters well known and held in just estimation by those who had the happiness of associating with them. These compensated for the loss we sustained in the removal of the late General Edward Rawstorne, then called from the Battalion, to his promotion of a Captain in the European Regiment. In Mr. Motte's chosen Library, I met a source of

* [For Th. Motte see Sydney Grier's *Letters of Warren Hastings to his Wife*, and *Bengal: Past and Present.* Vol. IV. p. 505.]

† [See Art. in Buckland *Dictionary of Indian Biography*.]

content, and, assisted by his kind remarks in my studies I improved considerably, in continuing by my own application that system of Education which had been planned for me, and from which I felt conscious to have been too soon ejected.

Lieutenant Rawstorne's promotion brought me to be the eldest Lieutenant in the Battalion ; and however much younger than the other Gentlemen doing duty with me, yet I can with self-satisfaction recollect, that no tone of authority was assumed, neither was any improper superiority ever manifested. We lived like brothers of one family, and never had a dissention one with the other.

The station of this Battalion, with the reserve of the two Battalions kept at Allahabad, as a guard for His Imperial Majesty, was the first encroachment beyond the Boundaries fixed by Lord Clive for the Honorable Company's territorial Possessions. The ostensible reason assigned was the necessity of such a Corps to awe the Nawab Shujahul Dhowlah's Mahomedan Cutwal, or Magistrate of the City, against any sordid intentions on the treasures of the rich Hindoo Bankers, established for centuries in that sacred City ; and, in the event of any design, to interfere with the independence of the Zemindar, Rajah Bulwuntsing, declared in Lord Clive's Treaty with the King and Vizier, an independent Prince, under the Guarantee of the East India Company, to assist the latter immediately, in taking possession of the strong Fortress of Chunarghur,* then occupied by

* [Later on in this book written Chunar.]

a few Troops of Shujah al Dhowlah, commanded by a Siddee, or Abyssinian, men, of all others considered by the Mahomedan Princes of India as deserving of the most implicit trust. Nevertheless, those who saw deeper into the real views of this measure, adjudged the real cause to be, for superintending the recoinage in the Nabob's mint, of the twenty-eight Lacks of Sunnat Rupees, being Rupees annually struck in the Honorable Company's Mint of Moorshedabad, which were forwarded from thence to Benares, and ere they reached the Royal residence, were converted and debased into a new coin denominated vizieree, which specie was then, under the protection of a strong guard from the Battalion, conveyed and paid to His Majesty and Nujuff Khan, *viz.*, twenty-six Lacks to the former and two Lacks to the latter. The Sunnats undergoing this sweating and recoinage, produced to the operators a benefit of at least twenty per cent.*

Lord Clive, and General Carnac, quitted India in February, 1767, leaving the Government to Mr. Verelst, and the command of the Army to General Richard Smith. They, after a period of three years, quitted their trusts to Mr. Cartier, and General Sir Robert Barker.

In the character of Mr. Verelst, so long as genuine worth is respected, his fame as a just Governor, will be, so well as his able treatise on revenue and landed property, handed down to posterity. In General Smith

---

* [*Sunnat* or *Sonaut*, properly Sanwāt, plur. of Ar. *Sana*[*t*], a year. See footnote on p. 775 of 1903 Edition of *Hobson Jobson.*]

there existed every virtue and honourable principle, combined with traits, which lessened the sway which his virtues bore, and rendered him an object of ridicule. His origin was low, and the rank and fortune which he rose to in life, may be estimated, in the chapter of accidents, as marvellous. Sensible of the bountiful talents which Nature had bestowed, he considered these, when displayed by a powerful mind, might tend to throw a veil on his extraction, and cause it altogether to be forgotten. With those, whom it did not affect, it certainly met with that distinction, but with others, whom it did, they could not pass over an arrogance of superiority so unwarranted. India was not the scene alone where such follies were manifested, but even, and nevertheless the taunts and correction, which never failed to accompany the instance, there were some reserved, and acted upon in England.

The present Mr. William Lushington, Member of Parliament, was his Persian Interpreter, when, on a visit to the Nawab Vizier Shujah-ul-Dhowlah, one of the most accomplished Princes, and proud of his birth and rank, General Smith desired Mr. Lushington, to apologize that he had brought His Highness no presents of European curiosities of exquisite workmanship, everything of this sort which he had provided having been sunk with his boats in a storm on the River Ganges. The mode and address, "Tell Shujah, Lushington," evidently made their impression on the Prince, who sarcastically observed, the General could not have brought a greater curiosity than himself, and sagaciously complimented his escape from the fury of the waves. This, Mr. Lushington dexterously interpreted, by saying, that the Prince's joy was perfect in the happiness alone of seeing the General; but with the bystanders, this obvious tendency lost not its effect.

In the county of Berkshire, it will long be remembered that, scarcely had General Smith been vested with the office of High Sheriff, than he called a County Meeting, and when the object was made known, it excited the surprise of the Noblemen and Gentlemen convened, that the purpose alone was to obtain their sanction for a road to be cut through their fields and property, calculated for his sole convenience, in order he might arrive at his magnificent Seat of Chilton Lodge without the necessity of passing through the little stinking town of Hungerford. It is needless to add, such a proposition met with its deserved reprobation.

Another anecdote quoted of him in those days is a proof that plebeian insolence, however supported by fortune and abilities, little assimilates with aristocratic rank and pride, even where title is debased by the most unchecked profligacy. The story told in the circles of fashion, was the following. General Smith came in rather late into one of the Gaming Houses in the vicinity of St. James; and finding no Company, went to sleep on one of the sofas, cautioning the waiter not to wake him, unless some follow, or other, came in, who had spirit enough to throw a main at hazard for three thousand Guineas. Lord Littleton, of notorious memory,* entered the house with some drunken companions, singing the hunting song of "Age and youth urged the chase, and taught woodlands and forests to roar." The message being literally delivered, his Lordship accepted the challenge, and directing the General to be awoke, continued his song converting the words into a parody consistent with the General's wishes :

"Seven's the main, seven says Dick,
"Eleven is the Nick,
"And the man is lost in something divine."

"Good night, General," walking out, and pocketing the Rouleaus and Bank Notes, with a full laughter from his Lordship, and his dissipated comrades, at the General's expense and consummate folly.

From the worst side of the Picture, let us now turn to the best. His generosity in throwing in one hundred and fifty thousand pounds of Bank Notes, to support the Banking House of the Drummonds, at a time when an unexpected run was made on it, owing to the failure in 1772, of the Houses of Fordyce and Sir George Colebrooke, and to this, prompted merely from a recollection of the Heads of that House having given him in his youth, occasionally one Half Crown when sent by his Father with Bills of acceptance was so conspicuous a trait of noble minded conduct as to have inspired the successors to that eminent Banking House with everlasting gratitude.

---

* [The persecutor of the beautiful Mrs. Robinson so well known to us by Sir Joshua Reynolds' portrait.]

Nor will it ever be effaced from the sense which every officer bore to the disinterested assertions of the Generals in opposing the Honorable Court of Directors constant promptitude, in obliging the Ministers, by acceding to their frequent recommendations, in appointing King's Officers to supersede the Company's. Various cases could be adduced, when General Smith calling these nominations in question, by summoning them to be canvassed before a General Court of Proprietors, compelled them, by a decision of the latter to annul and rescind their said partialities.

Equally will a just tribute remain of the wisdom which governed him, when determined on devoting his services to Parliamentary duties. Conscious of his education not having afforded him the advantage of the knowledge of the classics, and however advanced in life, he felt the necessity of being acquainted therewith, ere he could adventure as a speaker in the House. He accordingly entered himself for the two following summers a Gentleman Commoner at Oxford, and applied with such success, as in that short time to have attained to such a proficiency, that his speeches and quotations, both from Roman and Grecian Literature, manifestly displayed the Scholar and the Gentleman.

In the confinement of his person was displayed the rigour of the House of Commons, when bent on an exertion of its fullest power. The General had stood for the notorious corrupt Borough of Hendon, and an electioneering Agent had actively, in the character of Punch, scattered amongst the Electors profusely the General's Guineas, in the hope of his Patron's election being secured by dint of money. The Members destined by the Treasury for Representatives of this Borough, were ousted by this manœuvre; they impeached the validity of the election, and supported by the Minister of the day, then Lord North, the General's return to Parliament was declared void, and several actions for bribery having been in consequence instituted, the General was severely bled in his Purse, besides the conviction having been brought home to him of corrupt practices to influence the honest Electors, the House expressed their sense of such conduct, by sentencing him to a fine and imprisonment for six months. This the General submitted to, and in the King's Bench, so far as splendid living went in a Prison, with every liberality to his fellow sufferers, it may be recorded of him, that he manifested the wealth, generosity, and princely spirit of a Nabab.

So conspicuous did he render himself, that, with other celebrated Characters of that period, he could not well have escaped the lash of the modern Aristophanes, the late Samuel Foote. In his Comedy of the Nabob, the General was the Hero, under the name of *Sir Matthew Miles*,* and so well did the General recognize in the representation the follies which he had been guilty of, that he was the first to laugh at the Author bringing him on the Stage; but expressed a slight indignation, that in some passages there were oblique

* [Sir Matthew Mite.]

attacks on his moral character, which objection, those who knew and appreciated his worth, were sensible, that his exception to the piece was founded in truth.

After a stay of above one year at Benares, the Battalion was directed on a sudden to reinforce the Garrison of Allahabad, an alarm having arisen of a designed attack on our Ally the Nabob Shujah-ul-Dhowlah's Dominions. Here Colonel Primrose Galliez commanded the two Battalions of Sepoys, with a proportion of Artillery, as a guard to His Majesty. We remained stationary some months, when our Corps was ordered to protect the new Lines which had been recently erected at Cawnpore; whence I was detached with one hundred Sepoys to oppose five thousand armed Fakeers,* who were reported to intend forcing a Ghaut or Ferry, and crossing the Ganges, effect their usual depredations in the Nabob's Territories. Their intention was frustrated by timely precaution, and however ambitious I felt to distinguish myself, yet, I must own, I was not sorry for their voluntary dispersion, as I left the Lines impressed from the number reported and the known reputation for personal courage in these bodies of men that the odds against the hope of success of my small corps in action with them, would be tremendous to encounter.

The apprehension which had caused our march to Cawnpore having subsided, we were ordered to return

* [See article on "Sunyasee" in *Hobson Jobson* (1903 Edition). The Mofussil records of Bengal bear witness to the wide extent of this once most formidable source of anarchy, but the subject remains almost as obscure as the records are themselves.]

to Allahabad soon after which, I was compelled to leave the pleasing society of this Garrison with regret, however flattered, as I could not help feeling, of having been selected, which as very few years experience yet, for the discharge of an important trust.* This was a detached command of three companies of Sepoys, directed to encamp opposite the Fort of Chunar, and in the event of the Nabob Shujah-ul-Dhowlah meditating any encroachment on the Zemindary of Rajah Bulwuntsing, the independancy of which was guaranteed by our Government and marching any troops to accomplish such purpose, I was in such a case, of which the judgement and sole responsibility laid with me, to cross the River Ganges, and possess myself in the best and speediest manner of this strong Fortress.

These instructions were known, or probably only conjectured, from the position assumed by the troops which I commanded, and the known communication which I had in the Garrison, with an old Invalid Serjeant, who was stationed there with the Nabob's permission, and a small guard under him, for the protection of a Granary and Military stores, placed there as a safe and near Depôt for our troops acting in the upper Provinces. The suggestion, however, was sufficient for designing men to act upon, who wished for nothing better than to involve the Company with another war against Shujah-ul-Dhowlah; the riches of whose Country, with his own accumulated treasures, were in their contemplation. I had in

* *Vide* Appendix A.

consequence, men from all quarters, and in respectable situations volunteering a correspondence with me and all their letters were to the purport of creating suspicions in my mind. These I defeated by allowing none of these evil counsels to operate. I had confided the delicacy and nature of my situation to an intimate friend, and one of my early protectors, the late General Anthony Polier, an honest Swiss and a highly upright and enlightened mind, who was allowed to reside at the Court of the Nabob of Lucknow. I knew his probity, and perfectly sensible he cherished too much the interests of both Governments to involve them in a hazardous and precarious war with each other, I rested secure against every alarm given, and had fully resolved never to put my troops in motion, until I should learn from this much valued friend, that the Dæmon of Ambition, assisted by his wicked imps, had succeeded with the Nabob in determining him to resume the independent Territory ceded in the Peace made by Lord Clive, to Rajah Bulwuntsing.

During my command the Rajah died, and his successor Rajah Cheytsing was invested with the same privileges without any trouble arising; although the Brigade at Dinapore was kept for some time in orders to march upon the idea thought proper to be entertained, and the sanguine wish it should prove grounded, of the Nabob intending to oppose the succession. Affirmative questions were conveyed to me on this occasion, which disappointed those sighing for plunder, when they found them uniformly answered in the negative, and the tidings of the tranquil change which had taken place having surprised the Political and Military Chiefs in Bahar, *viz.*, the Chief of Patna and the Officer Commanding the Brigade stationed at Dinapore, they were, much to their sorrow, obliged at last to countermand the order for the troops to be ready to take the field at a moment's warning.

The Nabob's pacific disposition and firm adherence to the Treaty having been proved by the undisturbed succession which he allowed to take place, the continuation of my command was thought would carry an appearance of suspicion, and I was consequently ordered to join the corps at Allahabad. We continued there only a few months longer, and in the rains of 1772 the Battalion was directed to join the Brigade, of which it formed a part, at Monghyr.

In the summer of this year,* the old King,† tired of the inactive life which he led, and fully persuaded that the English Government had only buoyed him up with idle assurances to move in his behalf to Delhi, threw himself into the arms of the Mahratta Prince Mahadagee Scindiah,‡ who had flattered him with the hope of re-ascending the throne of his ancestors, and reviving the splendour of the Imperial House of Timur. Instead of our Government opposing, as policy dictated,

---

* [*i.e.* 1772, but Grand is inaccurate here. The Marathas escorted Shah Alam to Delhi in December 1771.]

† [The Emperor Shah Alam whom Carnac had taken prisoner in 1765, and who granted the Dewani of Bengal to the English. He became a captive in the hands of the Maharatas in His eyes were put out by order of the Rohilla Chief in 1788. He died in 1806.

‡ [Mahdagi Sindia.]

such a measure, the placid Mr. Cartier, then Governor, with a Council as inefficient as himself, qualified it with approbation,* and, in token thereof, enjoined the Commander-in-Chief, General Sir Robert Barker, with the two Battalions which had long served as a guard to His Imperial Majesty, and the expense of which was defrayed by him, to accompany the latter to the border of the Nabob Vizier's dominions, who had, in vain, exerted every nerve with our Government to deter its sanction, and who, deprecating the change, evidently predicted what would be its result.

His Majesty certainly reassumed his deserted throne, but it was only to serve as a puppet in the hands of the Mahrattas, and of that crafty Prince Scindiah, who carried his views for plunder so far, as to cause His Majesty to sign a Deed, delegating to him the power of calling on the Bengal Government for payment of the arrears of the Chout (or a fourth part of the Territorial Revenue), a tribute which former Nabobs of Bengal had disgracefully submitted to pay, previous to the Company's acquisition of the Dewannee, conditionally that the Rajahs of Berar and Cuttack should refrain from invasion.

Happily, for the security of the Company's Government, Mr. Hastings was transferred from second in Council at Madras to the Chair of Bengal.† His penetrating genius immediately saw the error which his predecessor had committed; but no longer able to remedy it *in toto* he contented himself by giving a

* [See Notes at conclusion.]

† [Hastings commenced his Governorship on April 13th, 1772.]

spirited and positive denial to the demand, and withdrawing for the future the payment of the Pension, which the Government had paid to the Emperor and his Minister Nujeff Khan, and which the weak administration, to which his firm one succeeded, had manifested the complacence of continuing.

Little did this great character then think that for this meritorious act, which every Company's servant viewed to have been founded on maxims of the soundest policy and justice, he would be arraigned at the bar of the House of Peers some years afterwards; the ingenious Committee of the House of Commons, who, to their disgrace, carried on this impeachment, having devised this sum which not only proved an annual saving to the Company but likewise diminished, in so much as its amount, the resource of the enemy, as one of the acts of high crimes and misdemeanors, which the immortal Warren Hastings had committed during his government, constituting in every impartial local mind a brilliant period of thirteen years' duration.

Arrived at Monghyr, after a wearisome March which had severely shaken my constitution, I was earnestly recommended by the faculty to take a trip to Europe, where only a radical cure appeared to them probable to be effected. Compelled, much to my vexation, to follow their prescription, I quitted the Brigade, and resigning the service, as no temporary leave of absence could then agreeably to established regulations be granted, I gave up the military service in March 1773, and embarked on board the *Marquis of Rockingham*, Captain Alexander Hamilton, for England.

CHAPTER III.

THE WRECK OF THE AURORA—CALCUTTA—A JOURNEY HOME.

I SHOULD have noticed that in the period of my residence at Chunar the Company's provinces were visited with a famine, and, I am sorry to add, only in part natural. At this distance of time, if any are alive who aggravated the calamity, what must their compunction be, in the reflection, of thousands having perished from the want of that succour, which sordid gain had caused them to withhold from the famished breast of the old man, the widow, and her child? *

The cries of hunger had, however, reached the ears of Leadenhall Street, and the aggravators, I will not call them the authors, of that misery would have been by the Directors called to a severe account, but fortunately for them if, to exist with wealth so acquired can be estimated a blessing, all enquiry was buried in the deep, by the loss of the three supervisors nominated for India, *viz.*, Governor Vansittart, Mr. Scrafton and Colonel Ford, who perished, according to the most probable conjectures, in the Mosambique Channel, from an obstinacy of character which the commander, Captain Lee, of His Majesty's frigate *The Aurora*, had displayed at the Cape, persisting in the resolution

* [Compare Col. T. D. Pearse's view. Quoted in Notes at end.]

which he had formed, contrary to every experienced man's advice given, and, equally it was reported, against the wishes of those gentlemen who were sensible of the dangers which in that season, *viz.*, from December to March, they would have to encounter of sudden and violent storms in that sea.

In this ship was to be deplored likewise the loss of Mr. Falconer, the author of the immortal poem "The Shipwreck," and of the Rev. Mr. Hirst,* the astronomer, of equal respectable memory, who had from Madras transmitted to the Royal Society such just and important observations on the transit of Venus over the sun, on 6th June 1761, and subsequently when the second transit occurred, *viz.*, on 3rd June 1769, equally displayed his proficiency in this science, as one of the then Assistants to the Astronomer Royal at Greenwich.

On my way from Monghyr to the Presidency I met the mercantile fleet of the Commander-in-Chief, who preferring a mode more honourable for the acquisition of fortune, reserved to himself the supplying and clothing of the Nabob Shujah-ul-Dhowlah's troops, and sparing to His Highness, for the furniture of his palaces, rich Europe hangings, and elegant ornaments with choice paintings.

During the three months which I spent at the Presidency, previous to embarkation, I lived with my much-valued friend, already mentioned by name and

* [For an account of the Rev. Wm. Hirst, see Hyde: *Parochial Annals of Bengal* pp. 132-34. See also Notes at end.]

character, the late General Anthony Polier. Mr. Hastings had then commenced upon his Government, and knowing how to appreciate men of talent and conspicuous merit, he frequently honored my friend with his company in town, requiring of him, in return, to be constantly one of his guests in his garden house, where genuine hospitality, united to the most social and instructive conversation, reigned for those two days in the week, *viz.*, the Saturday and Sunday, which were uniformly dedicated for this recreation.

In the enjoyment of such society, which was graced with the Ladies of the first fashion and beauty of the settlement, I fell a convert to the charms of the celebrated Miss Sanderson,* but in vain, with many others, did I sacrifice at her shrine. This amiable woman became in 1776, the year of my return to India, the wife of Mr. Richard Barwell, who will live long in the remembrance of his numerous friends, who benefited from the means of serving them, which his eminent station so amply afforded him, and which, to do justice to his liberal mind, he never neglected the opportunity to evince where the solicitation had with propriety been applied. To this Lady's credit also may be recorded, that those who had been partial to her, were ever treated with esteem and gratitude. Much to their regret, the splendor of her situation

---

* [See Busteed: *Echoes from Old Calcutta*. (4th Edn.). pp. 158-9. She married Barwell on September 13th, 1776, and died in November 1778. An inscription has been recently placed on her tomb by the Government of Bengal, at the instance of The Historical Society of Bengal.]

lasted not long; the pain of childbearing, with the effects of the climate, brought, on a delicate constitution, a decay, which too soon removed this fair flower out of the world. Of all her sex, I never observed one who possessed more the art of concillating her admirers, equal to herself. As a proof thereof, we met sixteen in her livery one public ball evening, *viz.*, a pea green French frock, trimmed with pink silk and chained lace with spangles, when each of us, to whom the secret of her intended dress had been communicated, buoyed himself up with the hope of being the favored happy individual. The innocent deception which had been practised, soon appeared evident, and the man of most sense, was the first to laugh at the ridicule which attached on him. I recollect the only revenge which we exacted, was for each to have the honor of a dance with her; and as Minuets, Cotillons, Reels, and country dances, were then in vogue, with ease to herself, she obligingly complied to all concerned, and in reward for such kind complaisance, we gravely attended her home, marching by the side of her Palankeen, regularly marshalled, in procession of two and two.

Nothing remarkable occurred in the passage, excepting the necessity which was felt of going into the Mauritius, in order to repair the damage which our ship had sustained by springing her fore topmast, in a violent gale of wind which we encountered in the latitude of this Island. We found here Admiral de Ternay, Knight of Malta, the Governor, and abstracted from the injunctions laid on the Town Major, not to permit Colonel James Morgan and Lieutenant George Francis Grand, to sleep on shore, nor to go into the Interior, or visit the Fortifications, we and the rest of the passengers, were much indebted for the attentions, which the Governor and his Garrison vied with each other to show to us during our stay. The Irish Regiments of Walsh and Clare composed a part of this Garrison, and had been destined, as well as the Governor himself, to have gone to India, had the war been undertaken, which the Duke de Choiseul had projected, and which, not being approved of by Louis the 15th, or rather rejected through the intrigues of the Monarch's Mistress, Madame du Barré,* caused the removal and disgrace of this great Minister. Mr. de Ternay's naval reputation had been established by the conquest of the Island of St. John, at the termination of the seven years' war, and assisted by the Military talents of the Marquis de Bussy, who was fixed upon for the command of the troops on this expedition, the hopes of success which had been excited in every one's mind were truly sanguine. Our ears were in consequence *feasted* every day with the certainty of the destruction of the English Government in India, whenever it was added, the King would, listening to good counsels, recall his Minister, and direct his attention seriously to this object.

I, who knew that the character of the Frenchman was predominant in vanity, bore with such vain boasting without deigning an observation, but my

* [Du Barry.]

friend Colonel Morgan could not readily excuse such a marked want of politeness to officers in the English service and strangers entitled to hospitality and consideration.

We were much captivated with the beauty of the sex, in general, brunettes, and very handsome. As an instance how well they preserve their looks, notwithstanding the fatigue of matrimony, I recollect dancing with a Lady who I had thought unmarried, and wishing to be reminded of her name the next morning, I enquired of our attendant, the Town Major who told me I had been greatly mistaken in my idea, for the said Lady was the wife of the *Capitaine du Port*, (Harbour Master) to whom she had been married at the age of thirteen and had already borne him six children.*

Our Captain, whose name I have noticed was Hamilton, wished to have it understood by the passengers, that they were indebted for the attentions,which they had met with, to the name which he bore. The son of a fisherman in the Orkneys, he had, when his good fortune in life had risen him to the station of Captain of an Indiaman, assumed the arms of the Hamilton family. These being largely engraved on pieces of plate, and pompously displayed in one or two entertainments which he gave on board, induced him to consider, that he had impressed the French in the Island, with the certainty, of his being a near relation of the noble Duke's. Piqued, with

* [See Notes at conclusion of this volume.]

such inference, I mortified him by observing, that however they had certainly not omitted to remark his armorial bearings were the same as those of the illustrious Peer alluded to, yet, they could not bring themselves to reflect, there was any affinity of blood, since the Captain spoke not one word of French, a language they, in their own conceit, deemed incompatible for a man of birth and education not to have been instructed in, and acquired.

Our next Port homewards was St. Helena, in which I saw nothing remarkable, but the avidity of the inhabitants to make a harvest of the passengers, and the folly displayed by one of the Council, who, being summoned, on the day the Purser and I met him, to deliberate, whether another bullock than the complement, which had early been allotted for the use of our ship should be granted gravely observed, in reply to the Purser's impatience to know the result, that the decisions of Council were secret, until officially made known and regularly transmitted by the Secretary to the person who had solicited and actually been the cause of the meeting.

CHAPTER IV.

"NABOBS"—APPOINTED A FACTOR—FRANCE—ENGLAND.

ARRIVED in London, I was well received by Mr. Jones, to whom my ever valued and much lamneted friends Messrs. Edward and René Payne had intimated that I brought money, rank and character with me, and which kind hearted friends welcomed my return to England with open arms.* We landed at Dover on the 15th of September, and in a Post Chaise and four, Colonel Morgan and myself were soon in the Capital each of us expressing our wonder at the beauteous scenery which diverted the eye, while traversing the whole of that fine County Kent, and concurring most happily in opinion, that nothing we had seen abroad approached in point of soil and richness to what old England afforded. Mr. Jones was on the eve of his departure for Bath, which expence he did not submit to with pleasure, however, his Physicians had assured him, the Bath waters would alone abate the disease, under which he labored. He expressed an expectation of seeing me there, observing jocosely, that purification was requisite to one who had been so many years suffering under a burning sun and evidently, from the yellow tinge which my looks bore, been tanned by the heat.

Having sojourned a couple of months in London, and renewed old acquaintances of my family, I

* *Vide* Appendix B.

proceeded to Bath. In my way I stopped to pay my respects to my old Commander-in-Chief, General Richard Smith, where I found a Triumvirate of East Indian Nabobs, *viz.*, himself, the late Sir Francis Sykes* and Sir Thomas Rumbold,* all of them scheming where they could carry the weight of their purse, with certain effect, to triumph against old established families in getting returned for Members of Parliament. I before remarked where the General's attempt had failed and the punishment which ensued. Sir Francis, whose character was ever disposed to be so pliant as the Vicar of Bray's, contented himself with a quiet return for a Cornish Borough. Not so with Sir Thomas, whose contested election in that Parliament for Shaftesbury, entailed a heavy expense on him. Sir Francis had just purchased the magnificent seat of the Fares at Basilden in the same County, *viz.*, Berkshire, in which General Smith's possession, Chilton Lodge, was situated, and the junction of these men created a powerful weight of interest. Fewer men could have risen from such obscurity to such wealth. He was recognized as having been a menial servant of the Lascelles' in Yorkshire, where his reception, on his return from India, had contributed essentially to disgust him against assuming a figure in any part of the county, much less in the vicinity of his birthplace, the village of Thornhill near Wakefield, where his father, a respectable old man, still take kept a pot ale house and could not be persuaded to

* [See Notes at conclusion.]

down the sign and change his mode of life, by forsaking old habits and connections notwithstanding the independence and comfort which the riches of the son enabled him to proffer. Unhappily, for the latter, he forgot old school companions and rejected their compliments with such ostentation and hauteur, as to have caused them to assemble in a body, and to have stoned him and servants out of the place. This scene, though acted at a distant spot from the Capital, yet became so public as to have reached the ears of Samuel Foote, who, glad of every opportunity of lashing the vices and follies of the age, introduced it in his comedy the *Nabob*, being the humorous dialogue between the hero of the piece, Sir Matthew Mite, and his old school comrade Phil Putty, the glazier.*

However the pleasures of Bath would have attracted me to remain some time longer, yet I could not refuse myself to the inviting offer, which Mr. Jones made to me of accompanying him to Town. His object was to secure me as a fourth person, in order that he might have the Bath Fly to himself and company, which consisted of us two, the late Admiral Young and Captain Palgrave, an old Commander of a ship, and one for whom the interest of Mr. Jones had procured the rank of an elder Brother of the Trinity House. I mention these circumstances, because he was particular in detailing the quality of these Gentlemen, observing that, though independent in fortune and station, yet were they not so imprudent

* See Notes at conclusion.

as East Indians, to sacrifice much money for travelling when they could, by joining for a Coach, travel much cheaper, and equally as comfortable, as in postchaises and four. We set off accordingly, and on this first day's journey, there was full room given for his remark. Sir Thomas Rumbold, whose figure and splendid living excelled every other family of that season at Bath, was a candidate for the Government of Madras, and knowing the powerful interest which Mr. Jones commanded he did not neglect one day, paying his court to him whilst there, and leaving it for town on the same day. Their manner of travelling was different. Mr. Jones with his made up company in a stage coach, and servants as outside passengers ; Sir Thomas' family in a coach and six drawn by his set of horses ; Miss Rumbold and the French Governante in one of his postchaises and four beautiful bays besides the Steward and Butler out of livery on horseback, and full half a dozen servants handsomely mounted in rich liveries. These equippages outstripped us on the road, and arriving first at the celebrated Castle Inn at Marlborough, commanded all the notice. This was sensibly felt by Mr. Jones and soured his humor, until Sir Thomas having sent in a message, if he could have the honor of seeing Mr. Jones, caused a complete change in the waiters' countenance, and, from that moment the passengers in the stage coach were a little more attended to. After a customary refreshment, we proceeded on our journey, and I cannot forget how these three misers, indulged themselves in calculating the Nabob's expences to town and contemplating with self-satisfaction the difference between theirs and his expense. In the same spirit, did Mr. Jones value himself, on the prudent caution which he had used, of not bringing his own horses to Bath, forage being there very dear, without an idea coming across his pleasing thoughts of economy, how often, at his advanced time of life, and weakly state of body, he had exposed his neck to danger by riding hired horses, and when not able to mount a horse, equally by trusting to hired carriages.

No sooner had we reached London, then Mr. Jones pressed my departure to the continent, where my mother and family still resided, entreating I would take charge of his grandson and heir, and leave him under my mother's charge, with directions to select for him such a Tutor as I had in my youth, to attend him privately, and likewise to accompany him to all the public lectures, which the Professors in the different branches of learning were in the habit of giving at Lausanne.

Mr. Jones' commands were law to me. I had communicated to him that the Faculty dissuaded me from following a military career, particularly in a hot climate, and he had assured me in consequence, that so sōon as I returned from the Continent, he would take and introduce me to Lord Sandwich, and with his Lordship's interest and his own united, press on the Directors their request for my appointment as a Factor, on the Civil Establishment of Bengal. I acquiesced therefore in his immediate wish, and the boy being sent for from school, I was introduced to the parents, with whom, I observed, it bore hard, parting with their darling child. Mr. Jones was fully aware of its necessity. Resolved in himself, that the parents should hereafter be dependent on their son, for any ease of comfort, they might hope to derive, from the fortune which he intended to bequeath him, he foresaw the youth would be completly spoiled, if he did not provide for his obtaining an education, far from their reach or superintendence.

It is necessary to remark, that with the bounty of fortune, Mr. Jones had sucked in progressively with the former, the seeds of ambition, and these were so deeply rooted, as to cause him to sacrifice an only daughter's happiness to the splendor of a title and coronet. Lord Sandwich, his friend, was, at that juncture, one of the neediest Peers of Britain, whose pecuniary wants were occasionally supplied from Mr. Jones' Accompting House, and it was devised, between them, that his Lordship's eldest son, Lord Hinchinbrook, should repair the injuries of fortune, by giving his hand to Miss Jones and receiving a handsome sum on his marriage, live with her upon the expectation of the whole of Mr. Jones' possession, or the latter's demise. The young lady, averse to such a barter, took time to consider of it, and being allowed to repair to Wakefield, where dwelt an early companion of her youth, Miss Milnes, soon discovered the blessing of freedom, and availed herself of it, by setting out on a matrimonial excursion, with a Lieutenant of a marching regiment there quartered, who knew perfectly the road to Gretna Green, where he conveyed his fair prize, and speedily made her his own.

It fell on the worthy Mr. Milnes, the friend and correspondent of Mr. Jones, to impart to him this sad event. The denunciations which followed may be easily surmised. In time, however, as violent anger seldom is lasting, the old gentleman becomes through the mediation and persuasion of friends, more pacified, though not thoroughly reconciled. His son-in-law therefore was purchased up to a Lieutenant-Colonelcy, and at the period I formed his acquaintance, I found him vested with this rank in the first regiment of Horse Guards, and through his connection with the Chandos family, a Groom of the Bedchamber to His Majesty. We soon commenced an intimacy, and this brought on confidential details of the old gentleman's cruelty and obduracy towards them. One instance in particular was too curious not to have commanded my recollection. It proved the eccentricity of Mr. Jones' disposition. Being at his seat in Cambridgeshire, with his daughter and son-in-law, he suddenly felt that illness would prevent his attendance at the Assizes which were held at Huntingdon. This plea was converted by the son-in-law into a conclusion, that avarice alone dictated the reluctance, to incur the expense of travelling there, and certainly, what followed, grounded but too firmly the latter's suggestion. Mr. Jones, complaining of ill-health, desired Colonel Adeane to go and represent him, and make his excuse to Lord Sandwich, adding, there would be no necessity, for the Colonel as his Representative, to appear with the figure which himself, as one of the Town Members of Parliament, would have done, could he, as upon other occasions, at this, have been present, that such an expectation, if held, would be preposterous for an officer in the Army. That therefore he had only to ride there, a distance of twenty-five miles and return, as soon as possible, without stopping on the road to refresh, nor much less, to afford his mite at the dinner, to the subscription or charity plates, which, in all likelihood, would be handed about. Colonel Adeane went and submitted to all which was requisite in a gentleman to perform. Mr. Jones thanked him for his diligence and attention, and indulging his rancorous and unforgiving disposition with a calculation, of his unavoidable expenses having amounted to fourteen shillings, instead of nearly so many guineas, which they did, he threw him one guinea, remarking, he exacted no change, being rather desirous the Colonel should feel an obligation to him, than *vice versâ*, himself to the Colonel.

In the same temper of mind, was his answer delivered, when I took leave, and asked him what I should say to my mother, regarding the judgment which might have been formed of the character of the boy. "Say, Sir, to the good lady, that my daughter has, by the disobedience of her conduct, forfeited all right to my kindness; that my son-in-law, with all his accomplishments as a soldier, is, in my opinion, void of common sense and my grandson, such as I adjudge him at present, not fit to scour pewter pots. These, Sir, are my sentiments, and nothing but affinity of blood, which compels me to let him inherit, could ever have induced me to allow of such beings, succeeding to the wealth, which honest "industry acquired, and dignified economy improved."

We left London the 23rd December, young Adeane, with Mr. Thomas Bird, the son of a friend of Mr. Jones, and brother to one of my Indian intimates. Mr. Bird readily embraced the permission, which his father gave him, of so favourable an opportunity to see the Continent; and providing ourselves with a good post chaise, from Mr. Dessein, at Calais, we rolled on comfortably to Lisle. Here we met, at Table d'Hôte, with a Leghorn merchant, a Mr. Raguenanu, who proposed to us to travel together, provided we would go with him so far out of our way as Brussels, where his mercantile concerns obliged him to repair. To this proposition we readily agreed, both from the principle of diminishing our expenses and increasing the satisfaction of travelling with the advantage of so well-informed a companion. In this charming city, and envious, we sojourned one week. It was then the residence of many people of the first fashion, and being the capital of Austrian Flanders the Governor for His Imperial Majesty, Prince Charles of Lorrain, displayed a brilliant court and was particularly civil and engaging to strangers.

Quitting Brussels, we traversed Austrian and French Flanders, Picardy and part of Champagne, without anything particular occurring until we came to Chalons. At this place we had the usual post horses harnessed to our carriage, when the Chevalier de Narbonne, Lieutenant-Colonel of the Queen's regiment, which regiment was in garrison at Nancy, came post from Paris, having, as other young men of fashion serving in the Army in those days did, prolonged his stay to the last hour in the capital, and travelling day and night with an *ordonnance* for relays to his destination. This put a stop to our proceeding. The horses were calmly taken out of our carriage, and as all this was done *selon les régles*, it was in vain to complain.

Getting out, the Chevalier accosted us with all that politeness so natural to a man of quality, expressing his regret at our disappointment, which he sincerely hoped would be lessened, by reflecting on the serious situation in which he would be placed, were he not, at a moment his furlough expired, present with his regiment. His anxiety seemed visibly to increase so soon as he was informed that it would at least take five hours to repair the damage done to his chaise; but, having made himself acquainted with our route, and observed that our carriage was in perfect condition, with the happiest imagination he conceived it possible, judging we were travelling for pleasure, to induce us to go a little out of our road, to view that five country Lorrain. No sooner was it suggested to his mind, that he made the proposition, adding how happy such a resolution on our part would make him, and promising on his, every gratifying attention during our stay. We consented, and jogged on three in the carriage, besides young Adeane, one of us men, alternately, every post, riding a bidet, and reached Nancy in time for the Chevalier to report his arrival to the Commanding Officer, with credit to himself.

Never did a young man, for a trifling favour conferred, evince a stronger sense of gratitude. *Ses meilleurs amis* were constantly in his thoughts, and, as such, we were introduced to the Officers of his regiment, to all the fashion of the place, and spent a most delightful fortnight in that beautiful city.

We retraced our way back to Besançon, and entering Switzerland, by crossing the mountains of Jura, over heaps of snow, arrived at Lausanne in January 1774, and whilst the severest winter reigned. The reciprocal joy which was felt after an absence of nine years may be easily judged. I found my worthy mother impatient to return to the circle of her friends and relations in England, and I had the happiness of contributing, before the end of that year, essentially to her removal. The friends and school companions of my youth expressed much satisfaction at our meeting again, and these, with my own family, and the English of distinction, then sojourners along the enchanting lake of Geneva, occasioned the time which I remained to pass most agreeably. Amongst the latter was the last Marquis of Lindsay, of the noble family of Bertie, Dukes of Ancaster, who, after having distinguished himself in his country's cause, during the whole of the campaigns in the American War, soon after the Peace of 1783, paid an early tribute to nature. I never knew a young nobleman so gifted in figure, nor one endowed with more noble sentiments. His heart was expanded to all those who were honoured with his acquaintance, and who truly lamented the severe loss which they suffered in being bereft of so valuable a friend and patron. The tutor who accompanied him was the well-known writer of travels, Brydone,* whom his Lordship left to his compositions, to follow the dictates of his own inclinations and pursuits. In the career of the latter, none appeared to have made a stronger impression than the military turn, which his Lordship, and his greatest intimate, the late Colonel Humberstone Mackenzie, killed in India, imbibed from loyalty to their sovereign, and the warmest attachment to their country. These two young men adopted the resolution of rendering themselves immediately serviceable. The fortune and rank which they possessed were insignificant objects, compared to their eager thirst for glory. I was selected by his Lordship to impart to his father and mother the determination formed, and Brydone, who, through me, presented their Graces with his manuscript of a tour through the Grisons and Vallais, begged of me, likewise, to say to his Grace, that all attempt, to cause a deviaticn, would be in vain. The Duke, dreading the loss of an only son, heir to his titles and distinction, with every visible grief on his mind, yet questioned me, if a commission in the Guards would not satisfy the Marquis? I replied instantly, "Nothing, my Lord Duke, but active employment and service in England's contest with America."

The Dutchess, to whom I was next introduced, seemed fully sensible also of the danger their family would incur. I was equally candid with Her Grace

---

* [See Art. in *Dict. Nat. Biog.*]

and however the disappointment to her wishes, I was honored with her attention during my stay in England.

Mr. Bird and I quitted Lausanne in the month of March, and through Burgundy, took the direct road to Paris, where, at the Hotel of Denmark, we spent six agreeable weeks. We here met again our Nancy friend, the Chevalier de Narbonne, who not only recognized us, but was equally profuse in bestowing on us every kind mark of his attachment and gratitude. His uncle, the Cardinal of Toulouse, was the Minister of France, at that juncture, and as the prevailing fashion in compliment to the Monarch's dissipated career, was, for each man of fashion to entertain a mistress, the Chevalier had an understanding of this nature, with one of the first dancers at the Opera, at whose *maison de plaisance*, we were admitted as his friends, and partook often of the *petits soupers* which closed the amusements of the day, and, during which, the utmost decency and brilliancy of wit reigned.

At a place so expensive, it suited us not to prolong our stay, and on our way to Calais *viâ* Amiens and Abbeville, we visited the beautiful palace of Chantilly, where the Prince of Conde then resided, and the grandeur which he displayed particularly in his stables and the number of beautiful horses which it contained, reminded me of what I had seen in India, forming the household and establishment of an Indian Nabob. Little did I then think I should live to pass through this place thirty years afterwards, and have to contemplate, by its ruins, and the deserted state in which everything appeared, the vanity and instability of the first situations in life.

Stopping at Boulogne, and asking for an English newspaper, the very first paragraph which I read was the death of Mr. Jones, and thus were my hopes frustrated ; for although I knew he had actually secured the promise of his colleagues for my appointment, conformably to the assurance which he gave me before I left England, yet I was too well acquainted with mankind, not to be thoroughly persuaded, that such a promise, on the part of those gentlemen would be considered to have expired with their friend's last breath. I soon found my idea verified, when I waited on them, and to do justice to one character in the Direction, the late Sir William James, better recollected by the name of the Bombay Commodore James (from having raised himself into notice by his distinguished conduct, in conjunction with Admiral Watson, in destroying the nest of pirates, which under a chief, named Angriah, infested the Malabar Coast, in the Seven Years War) he frankly owned to me that such were his sentiments.

With this disappointment I must have resumed my military career, had not my worthy friend, Mr. Edward Payne, felt indignant at such worldly proceedings. His trial however was equally vain. Nothing could impress those gentlemen that, as men of honor, they stood bound to the individual, in whose favor their votes had been obtained, notwithstanding his patron had, in the interim demised. Still, venting loudly his opinion, and as Governor of the Bank, carrying some consequence, a compromise was thought proper to be offered by my nomination to a Writership on the List of 1776, which station was accepted, accompanied with the assurances that I should be so recommended to the Government of India, as to be deemed eligible to such situations, as Factors were placed in.

Pending my second embarkation for that country, I had the satisfaction of seeing my mother, sister, and brothers return to England, and after a renewal of her acquaintance in London, the old lady made her election of Beverley in Yorkshire for her future residence.

Within this period occurred the contest between Sir Thomas Rumbold and Lord Pigot for the Government of Madras. The former had been actually nominated to the station through the power of ministerial influences and well disbursed loans or gifts. The latter immediately appealed to a Court of Proprietors, declaring he had made known his wishes to the Directors, although he had not directly solicited. This question came to be discussed before a general Court. The merits of each candidate were with ability displayed, and the comparison held regarding the pretensions of the competitors severely animadverted upon. In fact, Lord Pigot, a civilian, in his memorable defence of the Seige of Madras by Count Lally, rose far above any merit, which could be adduced in behalf of the other candidate. The point which the latter's friends urged most conspicuously to notice, was Mr. Rumbold volunteering, when in the

Civil Service of Madras, to go round to Bengal, with Admiral Watson and the gallant Clive, to rescue the few of their countrymen left, after the affair of the Black Hole in Serajah-ul-Dhowlah's reign, and serving afterwards as Captain of Grenadiers at the Battle of Plassy. Of all the bitter orators of that day, the late Commodore Johnstone bore the palm. Not content with his commanding eloquence having drawn the torrent in fávor of his friend Lord Pigot, he introduced in his speech, sarcasms and the most unjustifiable. Amongst these was the circumstance of the salt business, while Rumbold held the Chiefship of Patna, with Rajah Seetabroy, on whom, as Dewan of the province, an unheard of quantity had been forced at an exorbitant price, in order to have it branched out, and diversified into various provincial channels, subordinate to his power. In an examination before the House of Commons on this subject, Rumbold was asked by the Commodore "If the purchase on the Rajah's parts had been voluntary?" the answer "Certainly, it was so considered." "But," said the Commodore, "do you think, Sir, with reference to your relative, situations, yours as Chief of Patna, his as Dewan of the province, acting under your immediate orders, he would have thought himself at liberty to have refused any request which you made to him, and perhaps might think proper to press on him for acquiescence?" Rumbold's reply attracted the admiration of the House and conciliated the good natured Members favourably towards him. It was pointed and smart. "Without doubt," observed Rumbold, "the Rajah was a well-bred man, and would have deemed himself bound in compl aisance to say, yes."

Even to attract the preference which he wished to command in behalf of his friend, did the Commodore introduce a personal contrast between the respective families of each candidate, in a distant allusion, though sufficiently comprehensive, of the *Jeu de Mol* which had relation thereto, and which Lord Suffolk, one of His Majesty's Secretaries of State, had permitted himself to play off with regard to Mr. Rumbold. This nobleman had the care of forming the Treasury List of Members, and having returned Mr. Rumbold, conjointly with Mr. Mackreth, for the same Borough, the latter complained of such a colleague. Both, in fact, had been originally waiters in the fashionable gaming houses in St. James' Street; but Mackreth having been early successive, had studied, entered himself in Lincoln's Inn and actually had been admitted a Barrister. Lord Suffolk piqued at the impertinence of the remonstrance, bitterly and quickly answered, he knew no reason for complaint, since he believed, so far as his recollection and information directed him, these gentlemen had both been called to the Bar, nearly at the same time.

The discussion ended by a ballot being demanded. In vain did the Court of Directors urge, that had Lord Pigot solicited to go out, his claim would have been regarded by them as transcendant; that, it's not coming in their province to guess his Lordship's wishes, they had after mature deliberation, fixed on an unexceptionable person for this trust, and nominated him accordingly; that such decisions of the proprietors marked a want of confidence in the executive power, and tended to weaken their authority. The result was that, by a majority of four votes, Lord Pigot's success was proclaimed, and he proceeded to his Government with a full determination of restoring the King of Tanjore to his country, the Revenues of which had been sequestrated, and the administration usurped by the servants of the Company, united with the Nabob of the Carnatic, on the pretext of realizing those assignments which His Majesty had granted on his aumils, for his contingency towards the support of the war.

The issue of this contest detained me longer in England than I had apprehended I should Sir Thomas Rumbold having proposed to me to accompany him, however my friends had unreservedly, thrown the whole of their weight in the scale of his adversary. I enjoyed the pleasure of journeying with my mother and family to their selected retreat, spent some time with them at Beverley, and when the moment of separation came, took a farewell leave, never to meet again, the good old lady ending her days there in May 1783. We sojourned some days in Cambridgeshire, at a cousin of my mother's, Mr. Allix of Swaffham House, the great grandson of the celebrated Minister of Charenton (*vide* Biographa Britannica) who emigrated to England, to avoid Lewis the XIVth's impolitic and base persecution of his Protestant subjects. During our temporary abode, my mother observing the young lady of the house and myself, not averse to each other, planned a match between us, whereby, she hoped to deter me from going again to India, and becoming possessed of a fortune, which, had no will existed, I was the lawful heir to. In order to effect this, the old gentleman, on whom the charge of bequest depended, was, previously, to be consulted. This failed from one of those wise maxims, which certain persons, of limited ideas, seldom omit, being guided by. He professed, having no objection, on the contrary, he avowed his partiality for me ; but added, that, having made his will once in his life, and that forty years before, it did not become him to alter it. My readers, will naturally incline, after this description, to be more acquainted with the eccentricity of the character. It respected the late Mr. Buissiere of Cork Street, Burlington Gardens, who died at an advanced age of above ninety years, leaving his wealth to the eldest son of Mr. Allix.* Mr. Buissiere was the nephew of the surgeon, whom Rapine in his History of England, mentions being the favorite

* This gentleman met with an unexpected death. Having gone out a coursing with his dogs, unattended by any servant, he was suddenly seized with an apoplectic fit, and dropped from his horse. The animal galloped back to the house, a distance of two hours, and would not allow himself to be caught. Mrs. Allix, suspecting her husband had been thrown, directed a servant to mount, and accompany his master's horse, where he might lead him, and procure immediate aid. The mounted and dismounted animals went off with the greatest speed, and having reached the spot, Mr. Allix's horse snorted testified in appearance every regret and fell dead at his master's feet. In the Annual Register of the year in which Mr. Allix died, this extraordinary circumstance is recorded.

of King William III and having been called in to set his collar-bone, but which accident proved to His Majesty, from his great age, mortal. The uncle left a considerable fortune which the nephew early came into possession of, without any talent, or ambitious wish to shine in the world, and improve his patrimony. He found himself on his succession, in the enjoyment of full £4,000 per annum, with a strong portion of good common sense, and he planned for himself, a mode for spending that income in the most agreeable manner, and from which he did not deviate, until infirmity compelled him to give up his sudden transition from place to place. With a good house in London, another in Lincolnshire, where his domains laid, a horse in Paris, and equally one at Chantilly, he divided his time quarterly throughout the year, at each of these situations. He uniformly refused every public station offered to him, repeatedly declined coming into Parliament, and never having raised his rents, his managing farmer went in the county by the name of *Golden John.* On Thursdays and Sundays, whilst he resided in London, his house was open for eleven friends. These received no particular invitation, but once they were admitted by him to that rank, each knew he could trust to a cover for that day. His politeness was the finished one of the old school. If illness confined him to bed, or some unavoidable engagement required, indispensably his absence from home, on either of these given days, every one, who he was in the habit of seeing on this footing, were sure of receiving a card expressive of his disappointment. As *la bonne chere et l'esprit* reigned at his table, the number were generally complete. It never could be exceeded, for once *la douzaine* assembled, the porter lamentably observed you were too late for admission, and concluded with a hope you would be more fortunate on the next occasion. In this manner did life glide on with him. He had married a daughter of Sir Thomas Gooch, of Suffolk, but their tempers not agreeing, they soon entered on a separation, and shortly after, the lady died, without having had any children, from her transient cohabitation. A *chére amie* consoled him, though to her he was no dupe. His charities to the latter end of his life were extensive, and the sole clause which he added to his will, was a legacy to her of £500 Sterling (beside a fixed annuity), a sum coeval with the legacies he left to his three cousins, Mrs. Grand, Mrs. Payne and Mrs. Burton, the latter of whom being much richer than my mother, and indignant at being so coupled remained in some doubt whether they should accept. My mother hesitated not; the old lady wrote to me, she had as she thought, wisely and readily pocketed the Sterling affront.

CHAPTER V.

Return to India—Madras in 1775.

In December, 1775, I embarked on the Greenwich, *East Indiaman*, Captain Robert Carr, having for my fellow passengers, Mr. and Mrs. Floyer and family, who, from having recently filled the functions of a Bengal Counsellor, by direction of Lord Clive, was again translated to his old Establishment of Madras, and nominated expressly to the Chiefship of Masulipatam, Major John Smith, the brother of General Richard Smith, was the only military passenger, and Messrs. Wombwell, Willes, and myself, the three civilians, Writers for Bengal. Of all the kind hearted, friendly, noble minded, and philanthropic beings which have fallen within my observation, I never knew one possessed of those virtues to a greater degree, than my friend Mr. Wombwell. Brought up at l'Ecole Militaire, at Paris, with some of the first men of fashion, he had imbibed a mode of thinking and of action conformable to the old chevalrous spirit, which shone so brightly, with the French and Spanish Nobility, in the days of the renowned Chevalier Bayard: with this temper, it is not to be wondered, his limited fortune could not keep pace, with the unbounded generosity of his mind. He soon found his means reduced, and fortunately, ere appearance would have proclaimed the disastrous change, he accepted of his cousin the late Sir George Wombwell's offer to go to India, with every support which his seat and influence in the

Direction, could possibly bestow on him. Of noble extraction, his family originally Lords of the Seigniory Domain of Ombella in Normandy, and having, till within the last century, been, since the Conquest, Proprietors of Wombwell Manor in Yorkshire, he felt a certain degradation which his father had suffered in following mercantile pursuits ; * and he lamented that necessity equally drove him to officiate as a Writer, the dread of which employment, actually at times, affected his spirits. Equally did his apprehensions extend to a life on board of a ship. He literally considered it a prison, with just a sufficiency of food, allowed to keep body and life together, and having laid down 150 days for the length of the passage, reckoned every day, as it elapsed, a choice blessing. I shall never forget the surprise which was excited in him, when I resolved a question he put to me, and which arose from the injunctions which the Captain laid on his steward, in the presence of his table guests. We had the first day we sailed from Portsmonth severe weather, and no possibility of having any fire on board, to cook hot things, either for the men or ourselves. The table, however, was covered with everything which could be wished for, cold, and the Captain added pleasingly, that whenever

* This gentleman's father, my father, with Mr. Coxon, His Britannic Majesty's Consul at Alicant in Spain, formed in London, and in the former city, the respectable houses of commerce, under the well-known firm, at that juncture, of Wombwells, Grand, and Coxon.

any of us had a wish to dine in our respective cabins, or wanted either Hock, Claret or Madeira, to drink in them, he hoped we would experience from his steward, as ready an obedience to our orders, as he doubted not, he should to his own. I perceived Wombwell's amazement, and concluded he had treated it as a rhodomontade, and forgotten it accordingly. But, scarcely had we risen, and come upon deck, that taking me by the arm apart, "Is it possible, my dear fellow," said he, "that the Captain could have been serious?" I assured him, from the character which I had heard of him of constant noble treatment to his passengers, that I firmly believed it. The result proved the truth, and this conduct, so contrary to Wombwell's expectation, having completely conciliated him, he, everyday, manifested his sense of it to the Captain, by the most marked personal attentions.

The gale increasing, and meeting with a foul wind, just as we were about to leave Channel, our Captain thought it prudent to go into Falmouth, where I was much diverted in Wombwell and myself falling into lodgings, the lower apartments of which were occupied by-a tallow chandler. *Ses habits sentaient toujours le suif*, and lavender and other perfumes were used in abundance. After awaiting ten days in this harbour for a fair wind, we continued our journey to the Cape of Good Hope touching at this Paradise of climates, in the height of the fruit season. We met here with the most pleasing civilities, and at this distance of time, I cannot but contemplate with astonishment the difference in the expense of every article. Major Smith,

Mr. Wombwell, and myself, lodged at a Mr. de Wit's. We staid a full month, and fared sumptuously; each of us, besides, had a half aum of the best Constantia; we gave likewise a handsome ball and supper to those who had claims on our returned attention, and with washing, waggon hire to Constantia, etc., the reckoning of each person came to no more, than four and forty Pounds Sterling.

We landed at Madras in June, 1776, and found that Government in the greatest degree of agitation. The positive orders which Lord Pigot carried out with him, for the restoration of the King of Tanjore to his Kingdom, and freeing the adminsitration of it from those *bloodsuckers* which had fed on it some times was sufficient to raise him a host of enemies. His Lordship's character was not of that mould, to be appalled with the risks, which he personally incurred. Fully sensible of the propriety of the measure, he persevered in it, notwithstanding every opposition, and carried it completely into execution.

Unfortunately the Government was ill-constituted. Instead of a Governor *in* Council, it was a Governor *and* Council, and such was the power which the distribution of wealth created, that his Lordship having only the casting vote, when the numbers on any motion were equal, soon encountered a majority against him, to thwart every measure which he proposed. This naturally irritated a proud mind, and conscious of the rectitude of his pursuits, he adopted methods, which were not strictly legal, in the hope of conducting the machine to a good harbour. These failed. The majority of the Council, obtained the sanction of the Commander in Chief of the Army, Sir Robert Fletcher, his second in command, General James Stuart, and they suspended Lord Pigot from his official functions, and arrested his person, confining it at the Mount, under a guard of artillery, where his Lordship gradually pined away and resigned his breath, before the result of the decision could reach him, from the appeal made to England.

At this place commenced my acquaintance with Sir John M'Pherson,* who was Mr. Hastings' agent, and to whose direction Colonel Macleane with whose official dispatches, for his friend the Governor-General of India, I was entrusted, had ordered me to submit. I had understood this gentleman to have had in readiness a vessel to have conveyed me immediately to Bengal, but this not being the case, I continued my voyage from Madras in the Greenwich, only accompanying the Purser to town in the first boat which was dispatched, after the ship had anchored in Saugur roads. I was received by Mr. Hastings with that affability and benevolence which were so characteristic in that great man, and directly was taught to consider myself an inmate of the family, and one, partaking in a certain degree of his confidence, having the honor of being admitted to his Bureau, to transcribe his official dispatches and secret papers.

---

* [See below p. 118.]

CHAPTER VI.

CALCUTTA IN 1775.

IN this Presidency reigned another instance of the same inefficiency of Government, the late General Sir John Clavering, the Hon'ble Colonel Monson, with the present Mr. Philip Francis, forming a majority against the Governor, and Mr. Barwell, his only support.

Against a Government so constituted, Mr. Hastings had in vain pleaded. The Directors swayed by the Ministry, were compelled to support those whom the latter had nominated. Happily the hand of Providence interfered, and by the death of Colonel Monson, in September of that year, gave a spring to those exertions, which Mr. Hastings' capacious mind had devised for the public good. This pleasing change had nearly suffered an interruption, by Colonel Macleane, Mr. Hastings' agent, having too precipitately given in Mr. Hastings' resignation, whereby Sir John Clavering was elected for his successor, and the late Mr. Edward Wheeler to fill the vacant seat in Council. The Court of Directors, eager to oblige the Ministry, and to sacrifice their invaluable servant to their wishes, neither canvassed nor disputed the legality of Macleane's act, but accepted the tender unconditionally, and even without fixing a precise time for the alteration taking place. Many of Mr. Hastings' friends interposed, and so convinced were not a few of them, that he would not ratify an act which subjected him and his friends to the mercy of his inveterate enemies, nor provided any thing to cause his retirement from the scene of action being comfortable, as to induce the cautions Mr. Wheeler,* on hearing at Portsmouth of the decease of Colonel Monson, to return to town, and to get his commission changed, by being directly appointed to succeed the deceased, and not elected to the vacancy supposed to have been created by the resignation of Mr. Hastings.

Yet the disgust which harboured in Mr. Hastings' proud mind, in seeing the tide of power so adverse to him, was so great, as nearly to have deprived the nation of the services of one, whose eminent talents for Government, shone so transcendantly in the sequel. Had Sir John Clavering conducted himself with common decency in the triumph which he thought he had obtained, not one friend of Mr. Hastings, nor one member of his family, but was fully persuaded, he would readily have abdicated. Instead of sending a conciliatory message to Mr. Hastings, desiring to ascertain his convenience, and, from that moment, trusting all their differences might be buried in oblivion and testifying his wish and inclination to protect those whom Mr. Hastings respected, scarcely had the General finished the perusal of his dispatches, than he peremptorily and bluntly summoned Mr. Hastings to meet him at ten in the morning in Council, and there to deliver over to him the keys of the Treasure and of Fort William. I was then living at a garden house, a short distance from town, with my

---

* [Wheler.]

WARREN HASTINGS, GOVERNOR-GENERAL OF BENGAL.
(By Sir Joshua Reynolds.)

recent acquired consort,* and being in the habit of calling at Mr. Hastings' before I repaired to my office, I met, as I was going up the back stairs, my friend, Major William Palmer, then the Governor's Military and Private Secretary. He seemed agitated, and in haste only whispered to me, that he was going in the Fort, to secure the obedience of the garrison. I continued ascending the steps, and entering the room, found Mr. Hastings busily writing with Mr. Bogle, Mr. Sumner, and Captain Roberts, Sir John Clavering's Aide-de-Camp, who was the bearer of the summons. Palmer soon returned, with the assurance of Colonel James Morgan, then commanding in the Fort, that he neither acknowledged, nor should acknowledge, until Mr. Hastings gave him proper notification, any other authority as Governor than Mr. Hastings. The same injunctions had been immediately transmitted to the late Colonel Granger Mure, who commanded at Barrackpore, five battalions of Native Sepoys, and from whom the same success of implicit submission was equally expected. This was realized, and Mr. Hastings confiding in the justice of his cause, and military support, and indignant at Sir John's harsh proceedings, determined to resist the attempt, to oust him from the chair, and accordingly, directed the Revenue Secretary, Mr. Sumner, to summon the General and Mr. Francis, to meet the Governor and Mr. Barwell, at an ordinary Revenue Council day. With this answer Captain Roberts retired, and at twelve o'clock the

* [The famous conflict for the Governor's chair took place on the 20th June, 1777. Grand's marriage on July 10th.

divided Government were assembled, the latter in Mr. Sumner's office, and the former two gentlemen in Mr. Auriol's, who was then the Chief Secretary of Government.

Parties began to gather. The Governor's body-guard was doubled, and some apprehension arose of a civil commotion. In this temper, and after some messages and conferences from the two Boards, it was at length agreed to call in the assistance and interposition of His Majesty's Judges, and to submit to their reference and decision, the act of resignation, the subsequent nominations, and the proceedings which had occurred in consequence; the respective parties, *viz.*, the Governor and Mr. Barwell, and *vice versâ* Sir John Clavering and Mr. Francis, pledging themselves authentically and solemnly in the presence of the Judges, to abide by the issue.

The Judges were convened to meet in the evening at the Chief Justice's house, Sir Elijah Impey's and gentlemen, were requested to attend on the part of each Member of Government, Sir John D'Oily* and Major Palmer were present for Mr. Hastings, Mr. Addison for Sir John Clavering, Mr. Cator for Mr. Barwell, and the present Sir George Shee for Mr. Francis. During the time the Judges were closetted, intent on conferring, resolving, and having their opinions transcribed, we partook of a gay pleasant supper with Lady Impey, who retired not from table till two in the morning. We had two hours to await,

* [D'Oyly. See notes at conclusion.]

at length the clock struck four, and at that moment, the doors opened, and two packets were given to the respective attendants. I accompanied my friends downstairs, and having had it whispered in my ear, that the Judges had pronounced unanimously in Mr. Hastings' favour, I went home, and resigned myself comfortably, to that rest, which the state of previous anxiety I had endured so necessarily required. In fact, the decisions could not have been otherwise, accordant with strict justice. In the unanimity which prevailed amongst the Judges, it was clearly manifested, that no partial bias had swayed their minds, for Sir Robert Chambers was decidedly a partisan of Sir John Clavering. The Court of Directors had been too hasty in their judgment and determination. An act of this nature demanded a formal deed, notarially signed and executed, with a complete delegated power, made special to this effect, to the person in whom the trust was reposed, and required equally his having been recognized and acknowledged, as a fully empowered Agent, by those to whom he had been deputed. Instead of which, a paragraph of a letter, simply observing, if such and such conditions could not be obtained, so as to render the Governor's situation efficient, an abdication would be preferable to a state of nullity. It was probable, other circumstances might, in the interim, arise, which might cause the Governor to exercise a preponderance, and enjoying this was all he wished, for to enable him to display his talents and services with advantage. This did actually happen, and it could not be supposed, that once in possession of what he ardently solicited, not from any personal consideration but from the consciousness which he felt, that being unfettered, his country would derive the benefit of his operations, he would sacrifice those considerations, himself, and those friends who had supported him, to an uncertain issue. The Judges wisely argued that a resignation must be positive, and not conditional, the time fixed for its taking place specific, and not left to an indefinite period, that an appointment of this magnitude, decreed by the Legislature under the absolute sanction of an Act of Parliament, could not be disposed of, not parted with, in so slovenly and indirect a manner, etc., etc. In short, by their awards the Judges enjoyed the self-pleasing satisfaction of remarking, that the general suffrage of the inhabitants concurred with them most fully in a sense of its propriety.

I am aware it was industriously circulated by the adherents to the Clavering party, that the mock resignation, as it was termed by them, had been no other than a *Ruse de Politique*, equally allowable by those men, slaves to party faction, as a *Ruse de Guerre* practised by Mr. Hastings and his friends to gain time. But those who are acquainted with the work of Mr. Hastings' character, can never subscribe, there entered in that pure and great mind any machiavelian art or system ; nor will those, who well knew the uprightness of Colonel Macleane's principles, amongst which I may be reckoned, readily yield to any idea prevailing, that he could have lent his fair name to become the base instrument of so vile a duplicity. They even went so far, as to assert, that the Chief Justice, Sir Elijah Impey, the Governor's Westminster old school companion, had advised it, and was a party concerned. To such an height will the rage of disappointment often extend! The disappointment to them was certainly severe. It blasted their immediate expectations of fortune and preferment, and it was further augmented by the head of the party, Sir John Clavering, allowing it to prey so much on his spirits, that, with the heat of the climate, brought on an irritation of bile, and which ending in a putrid fever, carried the General off the stage, in less than three months after this event.

I should have noticed in the paragraph preceding, that after the Judges *fiat*, Mr. Hastings was led to consider, that by the assumption the General had vacated his seat in Council, and equally his station as His Majesty's Commander-in-Chief in India. The doors of the Council house were, in conseqnence, refused to the General, when he attempted to enter, and he received a notification, through the Secretary, to this effect. This alarmed Sir John's coadjutor, Mr. Francis, and drew from him a pathetic minute, appealing to the Judges, and to the solemn pledge of the parties to conform implicitly to their opinion, and patiently to await the result of the appeal to England. The Judges deprecated this subsequent measure, and conjured the parties to remain in *status quo* until the event of the reference would be known. This was obeyed, and the intended proscription withdrawn.

Mr. Hastings' intimacy with Sir Elijah Impey could not be doubted. They had been educated together. They were both men of conspicuous talents, equally indefatigable in business, as superior to others in amiability, information, and pointed wit. Souls so gifted could not be otherwise than congenial. Yet in their public walks they were opposed. The Chief Justice, inclined, as most Lawyers are, to stretch their power, beyond the possible limits, it could have been meant with any justice to the country to operate, and ever ready to interpret favourably and to this tendency, whatever appeared rather ambiguous in the Charter of justice, constrained the Governor to the unpleasant necessity of opposing the messengers of justice, which had been deputed into the Districts, to attach, much to the injury of the Revenue, the property of the landholders, *vi et armis.* For this strong act it became indispensable to entreat an act of indemnity, and such was granted, defining for the future, the extension of the jurisdiction of the Supreme Court to the boundary of the Mahrattah Ditch, *viz.*, ten miles around Calcutta; and the great Lord Mansfield was known to say, that, had the institutes of Manu, the Indian Lawgiver, framed and perfected into a Code, fifteen hundred years before the nativity of our Saviour, which laws, Mr. Hastings engaged the celebrated Mr. Halhed to devote his time to the acquisition of the Sanscrit language, with the view of rendering himself able to translate them into English, been known, and been familiar to him, which they were, after the publication took place, his

Lordship would never have given his sanction, for the introduction of English Laws in India.

From a circumstance apparently trifling in its nature, but serious in its consequences, not occurring so soon as it could have been wished, was the welfare of India, and the existence of the British sway in it imminently risked. No man, who surveyed personally the disastrous state of that country, soon after the English laws obtained a footing, but must have felt the danger, to which, by this ill-advised measure, British dominion was subjected I will, as a witness thereof, well acquainted with the general repugnance manifested, and fully confident, many of my contemporaries will concur in opinion with me, not hestitate to declare, that had not Mr. Hastings been at the head of the administration, in whose wisdom the natives held the greatest predilection, a general revolt would have happened His moderation, and the firm reliance which they placed, that his remonstrance to England against the assumed extent of their operation, would have full effect, determined them to await patiently the result, and yet, that patience would have been exhausted, had not Mr. Hastings, as I mentioned above, boldly incurred the hazardous responsibility, of checking the evil, ere it spread beyond a remedy, by force.

SOOKSAGUR HOUSE.

(From Colesworthy Grant's *Rural Life in Bengal.*)

CHAPTER VII.

MARRIAGE—PHILIP FRANCIS INTERVENES.

While I remained in the family of Mr. Hastings, I was in the habitude, with my friends, Majors Palmer and Gall, to make occasional excursions at the end of the week, on the river. Our *rendezvous*, generally, was either at the lamented Mr. Croft's plantation of Sooksagur in which he had introduced the growth of the sugar-cane, or at Ghyretty house, the residence of Mr. Chevalier, the Governor of the French Settlement of Chandernagore. At this gentleman's mansion, there reigned the truest hospitality and gaiety. His admiration and personal friendship for Mr. Hastings, ensured the most welcome reception to those who were patronized by this excellent man. In one of these trips from the Presidency, I formed an attachment to Miss Noël Catharine Werlée, the daughter of Monsieur Werlée, Capitaine du Port, and Chevalier de Saint Louis, a respectable old man, whose services had deservedly merited this mark of distinction from his Sovereign. We were not long in expressing to each other our reciprocal inclinations, and an engagement in matrimonial alliance took place, which we agreed should be solemnized so soon as I could obtain a situation, which might enable me to commence housekeeping.

The considerate Mr. Barwell, becoming acquainted with our mutual wishes, and pleasingly, as he said, desirous to alleviate the sufferings of a young couple, ardent to be united, opened of himself the subject to me, and with that liberality of mind, which he truly possessed, authorized me to impart to Mr. Hastings, that whatever he could devize for my welfare, should meet with his hearty concurrence. The Paymastership to the garrisons was the first office which became vacant, and to this I should have been appointed, had not Mr. Hastings sacredly engaged his promise, for the station, to Mr. Kneller. By the removal, however, of Mr. Coates at the same period, to the commercial residency of Chittagong, these worthy friends obtained from the Board of Trade, for me, the office of Secretary to the Salt Committee, and Head Assistant and Examiner in their Secretary's Office, then, the present Mr. Charles Grant the Director.

These situations producing an income of thirteen hundred rupees per month, I felt at full liberty, to claim from the young lady, and her worthy parent, the performance of their promise. The 10th of July 1777 was accordingly fixed for the auspicious day, and as Miss Werlée was of the Catholic persuasion, it became necessary for us, to be married, both in the Romish and Protestant Church. These ceremonies we conformed. On the morning of that day, at 1 A.M., the Popish priest legalized our union in the Church at Chandernagore, and at 8 the same morning at Hughley House, where my old Benares friend, Thomas Motte, Esq., dwelt, the Rev. Dr. William Johnson, by special licence from the Governor-General, pronounced, I had fondly hoped, our indissoluble tie in this world, so long as our respective career of life lasted.

I might well have entertained a reliance of this nature, for never did an union commence with more brightening prospects. On our parts, it was pure and disinterested, and blessed with the sincerest attachment. This continued, I may aver, to the cruel moment, which separated us never to meet again. Those who frequented my house verified the same. When called upon for their evidence before the Tribunal of Justice, in order to identify the person who had committed the irreparable injury, and who, with the boldest effrontery, had, as will be seen, denied in writing his trespass, it was evident how they sympathized in my unfortunate lot. To the questions repeated by the Bench of Judges to each witness, their answer was uniform. "You were accustomed, sir, to visit at Mr. Grand's house, did you ever observe any mark of disunion between them?" "On the contrary my Lords, the happiest domestic union, and we remarked that the most minute and reciprocal attentions prevailed, until this fatal event."

Here I must pause a little, to call my reader's attention to contemplate the instability of human happiness! On the 8th of December 1778 I went out of my house, about 9 o'clock, the happiest, as I thought myself, of men, and between 11 and 12 o'clock returned the same night to it, as miserable as any being could well feel. I left it, prepossessed with a sense that I was blessed with the most beautiful as well as the most virtuous of wives, ourselves honoured and respected, moving in the first circles, and having every prospect of speedy advancement. Scarcely had I sat down to supper at my benefactor, Mr. Barwell's society, who required of his friends to join him every fortnight at this convivial meeting, than I was suddenly struck with the deepest anguish and pain. A servant who was in the habit of attending Mrs. Grand's came and whispered to me that Mr. Francis was caught in my house and secured by my *jemmadar* (an upper servant exercising a certain authority over other servants). I rose up from table, ran to the terrace, where grief, by a flood of tears, relieved itself for a moment. I then sent for a friend out, who I requested to accompany me, but the rank of the party, and the known attachment which I was well aware, he held to him, however, he execrated his guilty action, pleaded his excuse with me. I collected myself, so much as circumstances would admit, and dispatched the servant to acquaint the *jemmadar* I was coming. In my way I thought proper to call on my friend Major Palmer, and request the use of his sword, and to attend me as a friend, the purpose which I had in view being to have released Mr. Francis, and seeing him out of my premises, compelled him to have measured himself with me, until one of us fell. Palmer approved of my determination, and we repaired to the spot. The porter, hearing my voice, opened the gate, and in my lower apartments my friend and I beheld with astonishment the present Sir George Shee, bound to a chair, and endeavouring to obtain from my servants his release;

La Princesse de Talleyrand.
By Madame Vigée Le Brun.
(By kind permission of Messrs. Thacker, Spink & Co.)

with Mr. Shore, now Lord Teignmouth, and the late Mr. Archdekin, companions to him, joining in the same prayer, and entreaty. He complained of having been cruelly treated by them. My Jammadar on the contrary, told a plain tale. It was, that he had secured Mr. Francis to meet the vengeance of his master, until Mr. Shee, assisted by the other gentlemen, upon a loud whistle, sounded by Mr. Francis, had scaled the walls of my compound, rushed furiously on him, and, in the scuffle, occasioned Mr. Francis to escape. I asked Mr. Shee, and his comrades, in the presence of Mr. Palmer, if they had seen Mr. Francis, and contributed to his rescue; but finding I could only draw from them evasive answers, with a declaration, that, what had actuated their coming, was Mr. Shee's running over to Mr. Ducarel's house, which was opposite, in which they lodged, loudly calling for their aid, to prevent their friend Mr. Francis being murdered, they had, between a state of sleeping and waking, ran forward without considering what they were doing. I ordered in consequence their release, and leaving my house to the care of my faithful Jammadar, and servants, I retired to Major Palmer's.

Seated on a chair, borne down with the deepest grief, I anxiously awaited the morning, to require, from the undoer of my happiness, the satisfaction which the laws of honor prescribe, as a poor relief to the injury committed. I wrote to Mr. Francis, that void of every spark of principle and honor, as I deemed him, still, I trusted, he would not deny me the meeting, which I summoned him to immediately, with any friend whom he might choose to bring. His reply was laconic and easy. It was couched in these terms. "That, conscious of having done me no injury, and that I laboured under a complete mistake, he begged leave to decline the proposed invitation, and that he had the honor to remain my most obedient, etc., etc.

I now returned home, sent for Mrs. Grand's sister and brother-in-law from Chandernagore, occupied the lower apartments of my house, whilst Mrs. Grand remained in the upper, and on the Sunday following everything was arranged for Mrs. Grand's returning with them, to live under their mansion, and protection, myself contributing what was requisite for her support, independent of the monthly allowance, which I chose to allot to her own disposal. An interview was entreated, and could not be denied. It lasted three hours, interrupted with the most poignant lamentations. I heard an unvarnished relation of the baseness of the arts employed for the seduction of a stranger, and attained only to her sixteenth year, I pitied her from my heart, I sincerely forgave her, and with a sorrow, approaching to distraction, we parted.

After the addition of insult to injury, which I had suffered by Mr. Francis' reply, a course of law alone remained open, to identify the person, and punish the crime. This I had recourse to, not without experiencing great difficulty, most of the complainant's Advocates of the Supreme Court having either been retained by him, or intimidated from acting. At length I succeeded with one who brought the process to a successful issue. By the testimony of Mr. Shee, Mr. Archdekin, and others, the trespass was fully proved and the trespasser was condemned by the Bench of Judges in damages of fifty thousand Sicca Rupees, with costs of suit.

Mr. Shee, the principal witness on whose evidence every hope of crimination rested had been induced to abscond, in the reliance which was placed, that he would thereby evade the jurisdiction, and save his *noble* patron, from the disgraceful exposure and consequences which naturally followed, and not until the Bench had pronounced such contumely conduct liable to corporal punishment did he return, when the subpœna was regularly served on him, and most unwillingly, was he compelled to appear before their Tribunal. In the course of his examination, it was extorted from him and others, that he had lent his apartments for Mr. Francis to dress in black clothes to visit Mrs. Grand at ten o'clock at night, accompanied with a ladder, ingeniously constructed under Mr. Shee's superintendence, cut and framed out of a large split bamboo, which they applied to the walls of the compound for Mr. Francis' conveniency to ascend, and as some dread was entertained he might be interrupted in his villainous design, it was preconcerted, that Mr. Shee, and others of his adherents and supporters in iniquity should patrole around the house, in order to be within call of lending their assistance, in the event of their hearing the sound of the whistle, with which their patron had provided himself. To facilitate this means of aid it was settled between them, that the ladder should remain, and from this resolution, unfortunate on their part, issued the discovery. My Hookaburdar coming to the chest which stood in a passage through which Mr. Francis had been obliged to pass, observed the ladder resting on the wall, and frightened, he withdrew, and communicated his apprehensions to the Jammadar, and other servants in the back courtyard, of thieves having got in to rob the house. In this conference, they resolved, as the best means of detecting the offenders, and prevent their carrying away the spoil, to pull the ladder in, and arm and post themselves by the door, ready to seize the first person attempting to come out. In this manner did my Jammadar grasp Mr. Francis, who, in vain offered for his ladder and release plenty of *Gold Mohurs*, which it was established in evidence during the trial, he had furnished himself and carried loose in his pocket for the insidious purpose of bribing a gentleman's servant, if the emergency existed equally, was it adduced, that he had been lavish in his promises of promoting my Jammadar, proclaiming the high rank which he was vested with, and his certainty of succeeding to be Governor-General.

But, all his efforts of gold tendered, and promised favor, could not shake or corrupt the fidelity of the honest Rajeput (a sect next to the Brahmins, and as remarkable for bravery as for attachment to those they serve), who, persisting to detain him, until his master came home, reduced Mr. Francis to the shift of effecting his enlargement, by having recourse to the scene which I have above described.

CHAPTER VIII.

GRAND HEAD-COMMERCIAL-ASSISTANT AT PATNA.

THE difference of state, which I had having experienced, sensibly affected my health, and by the advice of those friends, who deeply felt for me, I was advised to change the air. I made my election for Patna, and luckily at this juncture, Mr. John Taylor, Head Commercial Assistant to the Factory, wished to remove to the Presidency. We exchanged our offices, accordingly, and in April 1779, I repaired to my new destination.

IN March, 1779, arrived Lieutenant-General Sir Eyre Coote, as successor to the employments which Sir John Clavering had held, both as Commander of the Forces in India and second in Council, and however the Francisian party were industrious to spread reports of his having declared previous to leaving England, his approval of the measures which Sir John and his party had adopted, (*viz., systematically thwarting Mr. Hastings*) with his intended opposition to Mr. Hastings, it very soon appeared, Sir Eyre's discernment, whatever might have been his opinions before, which none of his friends believed he had made known inclined him to support Mr. Hastings' just policy. At the same time, advice was received, that Mr. Hastings was confirmed by Act of Parliament in his station of Governor-General.

Lord North, with whom the Regulating Act of 1774 originated and with whom the appointments of Messrs. Clavering, Monson and Francis had rested, began to observe with a more favorable eye, the measures pursued by Mr. Hastings. He saw in that great man a certainty, that whilst himself had unhappily involved the Mother Country in a war with her Colonies, which endangered and caused the separation of the latter, Mr. Hastings was, by the energy of his all-commanding talents, preserving the integrity of the British Empire in India, however, the several European and Native powers which he had to oppose. Shortly after Sir Eyre's landing, came Mr. Elliott, a son of Sir Gilbert Elliott, who had from ill-health, contracted in Bengal, been obliged to visit England for its restoration. This gentleman came over-land, and passing through Paris, Lord Stormont, nephew to Earl Mansfield, and then the English Ambassador to the French Government, made him acquainted with the Treaty of Commerce, which had recently taken place between France and America, and which his Lordship had just attained to the knowledge of Lord Stormont would not communicate the same by any written document, but, conscious as he was, that such a measure, when his Court was apprized of it, would be followed by an immediate declaration of war against France, he imparted it only verbally, and under promise of secrecy, to divulge it to no one, than Mr. Hastings and Sir John Clavering. His Lordship obligingly added, he had been the school companion at Westminster of Mr. Hastings, whose abilities claimed his admiration, that Sir John was personally known to him, and, notwithstanding, he was sensible, these gentlemen were political enemies, yet he fully relied, that in what was requisite immediately to perform for the honor of their nation, in consequence of such an event, both these great men were too hearty lovers of their country, not honestly to concur, burying all personal animosity, and sacrificing every private consideration to public good.

Sir John Clavering had, in the *interim*, paid the debt of nature, and Mr. Hastings alone remained, to whom the secret could be disclosed. His own great mind instantaneously formed the same conclusion as Lord Stormont had done, and without awaiting for official directions, he resolved to assume the responsibility of anticipating their consequence, by an immediate attack on the French possessions. It was also a doubt where Count d'Estaing's fleet had sailed. The Governor combining the circumstances of a French Agent, *viz.*, the Chevalier de St. Lubin, having at that juncture been well received at *Poonah* and intelligence having reached the Bengal Government of his being admitted to frequent conferences with the Ministers with the sudden departure of this squadron, adjudged the destination of the latter was fixed for Bombay, in order to co-operate with the evident hostile designs of the Marattahs. Upon reasons of such weight did Mr. Hastings, with the aid of Sir Eyre Coote and Mr. Barwell, carry his proposition in Council, against the voices of Messrs. Francis and Wheeler,* for the French ships in the river being immediately detained, the

* Wheler.

French factory at Chandernagore to have troops stationed in it, and a British flag erected, and that the Madras Government should be earnestly entreated to commence the siege of Pondichery without delay. In vain did Mr. Francis bellow against the preposterousness of the Company's Government, assuming the responsibility of involving the nation in a war with France, declaring such an act of presumption, nay of complete madness, should never receive his consent. Mr. Hastings felt confident on what grounds he acted, and disdaining all personal consequences, he employed to good use his happy preponderance of one vote in council. Embracing everything at once, he resolved upon supplanting the reigning power at *Poonah*, who had listened so willingly to French influence, by engaging the real heir to Ram Rajah, who had died in 1777, to assert his rights, backed by English support. This person was Moodajee Booslah, the Rajah of Berar, descended lineally from Sevajee, the founder of the Mahratta Empire, and the adopted son of Sahoo Rajah, who preceded in the chief authority Ram Rajah, and who had been placed in this situation, in defiance of the adoption, by the intrigues and art of Ballojee, who was the Peshwah, when Sahoo Rajah demised. For this purpose he made his selection of Mr. Elliot, to conduct this negotiation, and not an idea to the contrary exists with those acquainted with the politics of that era, but that Mr. Hastings would have succeeded in actuating the Rajah to prefer his claim by force of arms, and have entered into an advantageous treaty with the English Government, in compensation for their profferred aid, had it not been for the untimely decease of that able servant, as he was journeying to his destination to Nagpoor, the capital of the Rajah of Berar's dominions. Even, though languishing under sickness, he pursued his object with ardour, and the value of what his services might have been, had it pleased the Almighty to have prolonged his life, was evinced during the short stay he made at Cuttack. Here he fell in with Mr. Chevalier, the French Governor of Chandernagore, who had escaped when Colone Dow had marched in with a battalion of sepoys, and with relays of horses, previously stationed through the Burdwan province, had already reached Cuttack, and was hurrying to the Mahrattah capital Poonah, to execute all the arrangement, which the French Deputy, the Chevalier de St. Lubin, had, in conjunction with the Ministers, preconcerted.

Mr. Chevalier was accompanied by Mr. Louis Monneron, a man equally versed in intrigue, and endowed with ability. Mr. Elliot saw immediately the necessity of arresting their progress, and prevailed upon the Rajah of Cuttack, Moodajee Booslah's Deputy in that province, to allow of his arresting these French gentlemen and sending them prisoners to Calcutta. This endeavour delayed Mr. Elliot, for it was not without difficulty effected. The Rajah, however, at length assented, and Mr. Elliot becoming possessed of their persons, as well as papers, discovered by the perusal of the latter a full confirmation of the hitherto guessed designs of the French. Mr. Elliot released them, accepting of their parole constitute themselves prisoners of war to the Governor-General, a pledge, both these gentlemen much to their honor, executed in full, for Mr. Elliot, travelling without escort, had no force to detach with them, to secure and compel their obedience.

So far, from what Mr. Hastings had seriously enjoined to the Madras Government meeting the success which he had flattered himself with, it might do, *viz.*, "the cultivating a state of friendship and alliance with Hyder Aly," to serve as a counterpoise to the Mahrattah power, that, scarcely two months had elapsed from the former measures having taken place, he received an express from Madras, conveying the melancholy tidings of Hyder Aly's irruption into the Carnatic,* and his defeat of Sir Hector Munro, who with the loss of the flower of his army, some guns, and his baggage, had been necessitated to retreat to the Mount, and as, if this news had not brought a full cup for lamentation, the same express was charged to impart that intelligence had arrived at Madras of the French fleet having sailed for India.

The mind of Mr. Hastings, undismayed and unsubdued by such grievous events, and considering with strict propriety of judgment the Carnatic as the keystone to the British Empire in India, suggested instantaneously the expediency of engaging Sir Eyre Coote, notwithstanding the unfavourableness of the seasons to embark directly for Madras with the European troops and treasure which could be spared,

* [July 1780].

while an army of sepoys was formed to march by land through Cuttack and the Northern Sarcars, assisted in passing the former territory by the friendly disposition of its sovereign the Rajah of Berar, and such vessels prepared to act as armed ships, and equipped in a fleet, to re-inforce Commodore Vernon and contribute to the success of his maritime operations in the siege of Pondicherry. Further, that proposals for reconciliations should be transmitted to the Mahrattah Government, so beneficial as to ensure the acceptance of them.

The latter failed, however, the terms proffered had been previously subscribed to in Calcutta, and conveyed from the Supreme Government, through the medium of the Rajah of Berar, whose known partiality for the Governor-General of Bengal founded on that basis of esteem, which great men not personally acquainted still entertain for each other, had caused him repeatedly to tender his good efforts, towards effecting an amicable settlement between the British Government and the Court of Poonah.

When the position in which the Government was placed when these pacific offers were rejected is adverted to, it will not be considered a matter of any wonder. In fact, the Mahrattahs deemed the existence of the Company's Government to be very precarious; nay, verging to its speedy end. They learnt that a fleet of six men-of-war and four frigates had appeared off the coast of Coromandel, under French colours; equally they knew half the army had been extirpated by Hyder Aly, who proclaimed himself certain of driving the rest from the mount, to take refuge in the fort, and to besiege which he expected three thousand Frenchmen, who would soon render him master of it. He had already succeeded against Arcot, and got himself, in consequence, acknowledged Nabob of the Carnatic.

Mr. Francis likewise had sounded the alarm, and as usual most impolitically impeded the Governor's exertions. His minutes, in constant opposition, were either circulated, or their purpose verbally divulged. In these were displayed the exhausted state of the treasury, with his opinion recorded that the period was approximating when, instead of embarking on distant and uncertain expeditions, it would be more consistent with prudence to concentrate the forces, and the resources of the State, to meet in Fort William the local emergency, and shut up in it, by a protracted siege, trust for a renewal of energy, to proper succours being sent from England. He had before ridiculed the aid of the projected fleet under the command of Captain Price,* denominated them the *musquito* fleet, and boldly assuming they could never arrive in time, stigmatized the measure as a useless and expensive sacrifice. Their junction with Commodore Vernon, two of the ships mounting 40 guns each off Pondicherry, proved of singular service, they cut off the supplies to the garrison, caused its speedier reduction, and warranted thereby the plan to have been formed in consummate wisdom.

* [See Sydney Grier. *Op. Cit.* p. 349 et passim.]

The army of Colonel Pearse met with every facility throughout its route.* Its force consisted of ten battalions of native regiments, with a strong body of Artillery. They added materially to the small army which Sir Eyre Coote had brought into the field, and enabled that heroic Commander to retrieve the injury which the British arms had suffered in the defeat of Munro, by completely routing Hyder Aly in four successive pitched battles. Thus was the Carnatic saved by the transcendant genius of Warren Hastings, supported by his worthy colleagues, Sir Eyre Coote and Mr. Barwell.

It is not the object of this narrative to detail the operations of campaigns, nor to amply delineate the characters, nor describe the particular exploits, in which each hero so materially partook. The exertions were worthy of British soldiers, and, however the gloomy prospect which pervaded every considerate mind, when they commenced the issue was soon of that consequence, as to clear the Carnatic, and compel Hyder Aly to sue for peace. This was granted, and this happy termination effected, the whole British force was bent to reduce the Mahrattahs to a similar compliance. It was Mr. Hastings' most sanguine wish, with whom the sole responsibility of the war rested. Deprived of his able colleague Sir Eyre Coote by death†, and of his friend Mr. Barwell, whose ill-health required a change of climate, he had assumed

* [A memoir of the Colonel is in course of republication in *Bengal: P. & P.*]

† [This is an inaccuracy. Coote did not die till April 28, 1783.]

the entire weight of this measure, conditioning only that his plans in the pursuit of it should not be impeded by any unnecessary opposition. This was assented to by Mr. Francis. The negociators were the late Mr. Ducarel and the present Lord Teignmouth, who pledged themselves on the part of their friend, and, on this reliance, a sort of coalition was surmised to have taken place. It certainly did, so far as this point was concerned, and Mr. Barwell, who would not, otherwise, have deserted his friend, the Governor-General, was permitted to embark for England.* Unhappily scarcely was this gentleman's back turned, but promises and protestations, tantamount to solemn engagements, were forgotten; and had it not been for Mr. Hastings' determined spirit, which soon averted the evil, he must have been again subjected to all the misfortune, disappointment, and disgust which a vexatious opposition creates. The Council was reduced to three members, *viz.*, Mr. Hastings, standing solely, Messrs. Francis and Wheeler, jointly. Their united voices were enough to frustrate and arrest the execution of the best plan projected. With this view Mr. Hastings proposed the formation of a detachment under Colonel Carnac, to act in conjunction with the Rajah of Gohud, against Mehadajee Scindiah's Jogheers in the northern parts of India, the province of Malwah, wisely conjecturing that such an attack on this Chief's possessions would soon detach him to their relief from the confederated

* [October 1, 1781.]

Mahrattah force, with which he was powerfully acting in the Peninsula, against General Goddard's army.

No sooner was it mentioned in Council, than Mr. Francis' objections arose, principally, on the score of economy, and a dislike to consider it, as a diversion operating in any shape against that formidable enemy. Mr. Hastings, stung to the quick, and justly considering in his own mind that other motives influenced Mr. Francis' judgment, than those which were in his minute displayed, adverted personally to the breach of faith which he manifested, and this, in so pointed a manner as to leave to Mr. Francis no alternative but the obvious one, either to submit to the disgraceful odium, and absent himself from Council for ever, or resent the injury and aspersion thrown on his character by the observations which Mr. Hastings had permitted himself to make. Indeed, so marked these were, as to have called up the notice of Mr. Markham, the late Archbishop of York's son, who being Mr. Hastings' Private Secretary, could not but feel the unpleasant dilemma in which he had thrown Mr. Francis. Mr. Hastings thanked him, praised his youthful discernment, and, consistent with his noble mind, frankly avowed it was precisely the point to which he had sought to reduce his adversary.

A challenge was the consequence; the parties met,* assisted for their seconds by the late Colonels Pearse and Watson, the one commanding the Corps of

* [Thursday, August 17, 1780.]

Artillery and the other the Corps of Engineers. They baked the powder for their respective friends, loaded the pistols, and arranged every particular for the field contest. The issue was successful to Mr. Hastings. He wounded his antagonist, who, after a tedious recovery, thought only of resigning his office, and retiring to Europe.

Meanwhile the detachment was formed, marched, invaded Mehadajee Scindiah's territories, and proved subsequently of that singular service which Mr. Hastings had promised himself it would, by necessitating Scindiah to conclude a separate peace.

CHAPTER IX.

Events following Francis' Return Home.—Benares—Chunar.

After the departure of Mr. Francis,* Mr. Hastings was left without any control. Mr. Wheeler,† the only member of Council remaining, might minute, but his opinions could only serve to be recorded. Mr. Hastings' mind, unencumbered, thought alone on the pursuit of strong measures to cause a speedy end to the ruinous war in which the Company was involved. For this purpose he devised a journey‡ to the Nawab Vizier Azoph-ul-Dhowlah's dominions, in order to correct the waste and delapidation which had crept into the management of His Excellency's revenues, and by a good system of regulation secure for the future their payment and just appropriation, and likewise, to punish the Rajah of Benares Cheytsing, by a severe mulct for repeated acts of disobedience which he had committed. Vested with a country, which at least brought him in an annual income of seventy lakhs per annum; honoured through the bounty of our Government, with Sovereign and Princely Rights; rated only to pay the moderate tribute of twenty-four lakhs yearly, as the recognizance for the tenure of

---

* [December 3, 1780.]

† [The name should be written Wheler.]

‡ [The visit was proposed to the Board on May 21, 1781.]

his Zemindary, owing, in short, every protection, independence, and comfort, which he so amply was in the enjoyment of, to the liberality of the Governor-General, who thought to make him an useful auxiliary, should ever a rupture between the Company and the Nawab Vizier arise, was his heart ungrateful enough to stir up rebellion, to try to shake off every dependence, and to this effect, he sternly refused to contribute the small extra contingent of five lakhs, in addition to the fixed stipend, which he had been called upon for, as his proportion, towards the general aid, during the continuation of the war.

At first, measures tending to reclaim him, if possible, from his contumacy, were practised. These were ineffectual. In the true Zemindary spirit, he denied, next promised, and finally tried again to evade the payment of the expected supply. Such conduct required a prompt and decisive example to punish his disobedience. Mr. Hastings was prepared to inflict it, but never dreamt, that a force to support his intentions, would be necessary. The sequel proved it so. Never were the Company's interests unforeseenly plunged into such imminent danger. The British Indian Empire hung as Mr. Hastings justly remarked, by the thread of opinion. In the Governor-General's personal safety was the life of every individual involved. Had that invaluable life been sacrificed on the occasion, among the other atrocious acts committed, every tie would have sunk, and in all probability the world and our Indian commercial rivals, would have been gratified, in seeing an end put to our dominion in the East.

Fortunately, Providence interposed, and put a stop to the commission of such deeds. The Rajah was justly punished in the loss of his country, and becoming a fugitive.

To give a faithful history of the transactious which occurred in this awful and eventful scenes it is out of the power of the writer, to exemplify them, for the reader's attention and perusal, better than referring *verbatim* to the accurate, intelligent, elegant Narrative* which emanated from the pen of Hastings, when the whole of the occurrences were recent to his memory.

But, before I introduce them to the said Narrative, it would be an unjust omission, were I not, with others, to express the general concern, which all felt on hearing the melancholy news of the death of the Indian Hero, the gallant Coote.† He had embarked, for the second time, to persue the war with Hyder Aly, and to drive him out of the Carnatic, when being chased, between Balasore Roads and Madras by a superior force, his anxiety was such to escape from the enemy, combined with the vexatious thought, if made a prisoner, be deprived of bringing the war to the glorious conclusion, which he cherished the sanguine hope, by his prudent and decisive measures, to effect, as to cause him to remain, during a chase of forty-eight hours, all the time on the deck, and from thence when the ship anchored in Madras Roads, to be brought on shore insensible, and in this debilitated

* [Included in Vol. II. of Mr. Forrest's *Selections from the State Papers of the Governor-General of India.*]

† [April 28, 1783.]

state, to give up the last breath of his unconquerable mind.

Mr. Hastings, who appreciated the value of his activity, readiness, and support, at the critical juncture in which the Government was placed, wished to eternize his memory, by having brought to Calcutta, and having fixed in the square, the immense column with the lion's image on the top, which was discovered in one of the provinces (Hajeepore, Sabab Bahar) of the district, which I then superintended. He was pleased to suggest to me, of removing it upon truckles to the borders of the Gunduck, to have it floated down that river, upon rafts of timber, and next the Ganges; but the idea was abandoned, from the consideration of the expence, the trouble, and lastly, the danger attending its being damaged by the removal.

This pillar went by the name of Rajah Beemsing's *Lattee* (*id est* walking stick); and the only tradition, which I could ever obtain, was, that it had been there erected, in commemoration of an Hindoo Prince, of the greatest power of body and command of territory. This information, coupled with the geographical description given by Major Reynell, of the situation of Porus' dominion, left no doubt on my mind, it was for him this monument had been intended. There were marks, like letters, hewn on the stone, but they proved perfect hieroglyphics, as the cleverest Pundits of the district of Tirhoot declared their incapacity to decypher the meaning. By the Narrative it will be clearly seen, whatever rights and

Warren Hastings' Bungalow, Chunar.
(Photo. by A. de Cosson, Esq.)

prerogatives were enjoyed by Cheytsing, beyond those of any other Zemindar or landholder under the Company's dominion, they derived from the bounty and indulgence of our Government. That consequently, his obedience to its decrees was not optional, but positive in him to perform. That his means to relieve the Sovereign state, exceeded far beyond the small extra contribution, required in a moment of exigency. That this he at first decidedly refused, next sought by every pitiful shift to evade, and finally, by such meanness and stubborn conduct, was driven into that rebellion, which ended in depriving him of his territories. Further, that his insolence had risen commensurate with his power and riches, in so much as to have dared to meet the Governor-General of India, in whom the executive sovereignty rested, with an armed force, although, bearing in his recollection, as he must have done, that his former sovereign, the Nawab Vizier Shujah-ul-Dhowlah in the year 1773,* coming from his capital on the same purpose, and learning on his route, that the Governor-General was completely unattended, but by his usual staff and suite, dismissed himself, his attendants, and with as humble a state, joined Mr. Hastings.

Before I conclude the transactions of this eventful period, I must be permitted to bring to notice an anecdote descriptive of Mr. Hastings' sportive mind, even amidst the calamities and dangers which surrounded him. It fell to me to take the deposition of

* [1781.]

Jean Honore Mordelai, the only one of the chasseurs who survived the barbarous massacre committed on them by Cheytsing's special order. The poor man, after describing the thick jungle (thicket) into which they had been conveyed for the perpetration of the atrocious act intended, and relating the several wounds which he received, added he had been left in it all the night, *a la discretion des Tigres*, Mr. Hastings jocosely asked me if I ever heard of these animals possessing this virtue. I felt the pleasantry of his observation, and freed the sentence from its obvious absurdity by supplying, for *discretion*, *mercy*, or *clemency*, the word "exposed to the fury of the Tygers." The poor fellow, incapable, from the severity of his wounds, ever to serve again, was allowed to remain in the garrison of Chunar stationary, upon a pension of four and twenty rupees per month, which benevolent subsistence, he lived several years to enjoy, and express his gratitude to his benefactors.

I must not, however, omit, before I quit the Benares subject, to record another trait of Mr. Hastings' magnanimity of mind displayed ever when the most imminent danger suspended over his precious life and those of his attendants. Late in the afternoon, of that day, the evening of which we precipitately abandoned the city, His Highness the Nawab Saadut Aly, perfectly sensible of the inefficiency of our force and situation to resist any attack, and fully aware from his emissaries of the Rajah's wicked intentions, dispatched a confidential messenger, delicately proposing to Mr. Hastings to join him with the thousand

CHUNAR: NORTH FACE OF FORT FROM THE GANGES.
(Photo. by A. de Cosson, Esq.)

armed men composing his retinues to protect the Governor-General's quarters. Mr. Hastings, averse to see any distinction made between *quarters* and *person*, the thought flashed instantaneously on his noble spirit how improper it would be for the ruler of the British Empire in India to be indebted for his safety to native auxiliary support, and, accordingly, politely declining the acceptance of the offer, directly adopted the resolution of fighting his way against all risks, and try to gain the Fort of Chunar. Possessed with the same greatness, equally calm and unruffled in this trying scene, trudging on foot through the narrow streets of Benares, one of the closest nights in that climate, it occurred to him to convert the Nawab's readiness to be useful to those disabled and others appertaining to us, who, dispersed through the city in different habitations, could not have anticipated the project formed, and might, when apprized thereof, be impeded in effecting a junction. A message, as we were passing near his Highness' palace, was conveyed to him, requesting he would extend the advantage of his protection to the wounded Sepoys of Colonel Popham's corps, and to those followers accidentally prevented from marching with us. With this request His Highness scrupulously complied, visiting in person with his own surgeon every day, the sick and wounded left in the hospital, supplying their wants, and carefully attended to preserve our servants free of molestation.

During our confinement at Chunar the Nawab Vizier, Azoph-ul-Dhowlah, visited Mr. Hastings. The latter had received information from various quarters tending to the prejudice of His Highness' sentiments, regarding the English Government, and conjuring the Governor not to trust himself in his power. Mr. Hastings felt, however, so satisfied with the tenor of His Highness' conduct ever since the troubles arose, into which we had so accidentally been plunged, and justly conceiving the Nawab Vizier would be ready to think designing men had been eager in the opportunity of spreading reports to his disadvantage, that to dispel effectually every idea in His Highness' mind of any such impression existing, the Governor determined on paying him the first visit with his shabby retinue. I may well say shabby, for having lost all our wearing apparel at Benares, where my pinnace, with others, had been scuttled, and rifled of every article in it, we had not a decent coat in which to make our appearance. We crossed the river accordingly, and amongst hosts of his troop passed perfectly unmolested, and were received by His Highness with every visible mark of gratitude and kindness beaming on his dark visage.

The following are the names and stations of the gentlemen who comprised Mr. Hastings' suite, and who would, with their worthy chief, have immediately fallen sacrifices to the murderous intent of those appointed to assail the Governor-General's quarters on the night of the 21st of August,* had not their evil purpose been happily diverted by the spirited and

* [1781.]

wise resolution which Mr. Hastings adopted of gaining the Fort of Chunar.

David Anderson, Esq., Assistant to the Governor-General.—Stephen Sullivan, Esq., Private Secretary to the Governor-General.—Major William Palmer, Military Secretary to the Governor-General.—Edward Hay Esq., Deputy Secretary to Government.—Richard Sumner, Esq., Revenue Secretary to Government.—Charles Chapman, Esq., Collector of Ramgarh.—George Francis Grand, Esq., Head Commercial Assistant at Patna.—William Markham, Esq., Resident at Benares.—Richard Johnson, Esq., Second at Lucknow.—John Willes, Esq., Collector of Sylhet.—Edward James Colebrook, Esq., Persian Interpreter to the Governor-General.—Mr. Peter Bowers, first Clerk under Mr. Sullivan.—Major William Popham, Commanding a detachment at Mirzapore.—Lieutenant John Hamilton,* detached with two companies from the said corps to serve as a bodyguard for the Governor-General.—Lieutenant John Edmund Grand, Commanding under Lieutenant Hamilton, the Artillery (two 6 pounders) attached to the body-guard.

There were other gentlemen, likewise, to the number, both in Civil and Military servants, that Mr. Hastings mentioned; but having kept no memorandum thereof, my memory, at this juncture, does not help me to the recollection of any other.

* Now Major-General Hamilton of the King's army serving in Portugal.

When I came to consider the event of our fortunate escape, and pondered over the reasons, which could be adduced for our miraculous preservation, I could not ascribe it, otherwise, than to the genius of those, not whom we had to contend against, but those at whose mercy we completely laid. In fact, it is in their nature not to expect success when engaged with Europeans. Their immediate object was to effect the release of the Rajah. This they accomplished beyond it, they harbored no secondary motive, however the design of their Chief extended afterwards to the hope of extirpating and annihilating the English Government, in consequence of the unlooked for turn which his revolt had created. Had his rank and family sprung from the princes of Hindustan, he might have been assisted in his wish; but for such an upstart, as he was (the origin of his father being the meanest), to summon men and rulers, of real noble descent, to join his standard, became with them, a mere matter of ridicule and contempt.

I must here digress, to supply an omission which occurred in the course of my Narrative, and did not present itself to my memory at the moment I was detailing the events of that period. It is the following:—In justice to the characters of Sir John Clavering and of the Hon'ble Colonel Monson, they shone conspicuous as soldiers. In private life, likewise, their affability and spotless integrity, rendered them highly respected. Yet these men, always thinking they walked in the line of honor, suffered their minds to be so swayed, as to view with a jaundiced eye, everything which had originated with Mr. Hastings.

Instead of determining, on going into no retrospection of past measures, and preventing for the future every abuse in the system of Government, they involved themselves immediately into a labyrinth of trouble. They became the prey of every designing person who had felt disappointed in his views by the preceding administration. Even Sir John Clavering had avowed, he landed with a partial tendency to Mr. Hastings; nevertheless, at the very first meeting of Council, after the formal one which had been held for the respective members being sworn into the stations assigned them, a marked disgust was obvious. Deficiency of decorum ensued, and provoked a personal meeting. The enemies to good order succeeded in this end. Not content with instituting every poison, and causing to be engendered every malignant prejudice in private, they went so far, as to collect mobs to impede his way to the Council house and thereby to inflame the too credulous General against him who was the object of their pointed shaft. In one of these worked up fits of delirium, Sir John imprudently and hastily charged Mr. Barwell with malversation in the Salt Department. So ill-founded an accusation drew an instantaneous bitter reply. Mr. Barwell conscious of the unmerited imputation, declared, "That the man who dared to come forward with such a charge, destitute of any proof, was a—" The General put his hand to his sword. Mr. Barwell bowed and retired, the Council broke up; and in the fields the next morning*, attended

---

* [In April 1775. See Note.]

by proper seconds, the former had a shot at the latter. Fortunately, no evil consequence resulted, and Mr. Barwell, lamenting a man, otherwise of such amiable virtues, could in this instance, have been so injudiciously biassed, would not return his fire. His antagonist suspecting this, delicacy arose from a growing attachment which he had observed to prevail between Miss Clavering (afterwards Lady Napier), called out loudly to him to take his chance of hitting him for, in whatever manner their contest might terminate, the General added Mr. Barwell could rest impressed, that he had no chance of ever being allied to his family ; and in the same passionate tone, expressed his resolution of firing a second pistol. Mr. Barwell, without explaining, but perfectly confident of the good grounds which dictated his mode. of acting, persisted in his previous intention, and thus compelled the seconds to withdraw the hostile parties, professing their opinion that the *point d'honneur* had been in full satisfied.

Returned to Benares, we amused ourselves with hunting and other recreations, until the moment occurred for quitting it, Mr. Hastings having given up the idea of proceeding to Lucknow, the arrangements which he had in view to propose, when he left the Presidency for a journey to the upper provinces, for the benefit of the Nawab Vizier's dominions, having incurred a change in his mind from the incidents arisen. The 5th of February 1782 was accordingly fixed for returning to the seat of Government, and due notice having issued, every one prepared ; but the day was suddenly deferred to the 6th in order

CHUNAR. RIVER VIEW.

(Photo. by A. de Cosson, Esq.)

to celebrate Mr. Hastings' birthday, which it appeared he had promised Mrs. Hastings to observe, when he attained the age of fifty, and then again to repeat it when one hundred. Mr. Hastings was not aware of the cause of the delay, until with the loudest acclamations, and with every wish he might reach the latter period, his health was drunk with three times three at the festive and hospitable board of Mr. Markham, the Resident of Benares, and the son of the late Archbishop of York.*

On our way from Benares to Patna, I frequently paid my respects to Mr. Hastings at breakfast. One morning very early I found him with the map of Behar on his table, and examining with great minuteness the dimensions of the provinces of Tirhoot and Hajeepoore, the latter territory of which extends the distance of one hundred miles north of the Ganges, and as far as Mongheer. He mentioned there had been symptoms of revolt amongst some of the Zemindars during the disturbances with Cheytsing, and expressed the necessity of an immediate European superintendence. Without awaiting any reply or observation from me he suddenly asked me if I thought myself capable of the administration of Collector. I replied, I trusted I could undertake the management to his satisfaction. Then added he, let us breakfast, and so soon as it is over, I will give you a letter for Mr. Charters, whom the Government have deputed as Commissioner to revoke the settlement, which, upon the abolition of

---

* [*Vide* Sydney Grier: *Warren Hasting's Letters to His Wife.*]

the Provincial Councils, had been made with Rajahs Culleansing and Kyallaram,* and to effect a new one, in whatever mode he should consider most consonant to the Company's interests.

The letter was accordingly written, and I took my leave, proceeding with my credentials as quick as possible in a light boat day and night, the apprehension haunting me, Mr. Charters might, previous to my arrival, have fixed and entered upon some other arrangement regarding them. I arrived, however, in time, and was immediately ensured of my success. Before the month had elapsed I received my nomination, and on the 4th of March went to take possession.

---

† [*Vide* Hand. *Early English Administration.*]

CHAPTER X.

COLLECTOR OF TIRHOOT AND HAZEEPORE.

THIS was an important event in my life. From Head Assistant to a commercial factory, in which the duties consisted of prizing of cloths, seeing saltpetre weighed and loaded, attending to the accounts, etc., I was immediately transferred to the government of two considerable provinces, involving the settlement and collection of the revenues, and the distribution and maintenance of justice.

It may well be imagined that from so satisfactory a transition I could not feel happiness in a greater extent than I did. A wide field opened to flatter my ambitions. I looked forward to further rise, and determined to support my claims to such hopes by commanding the esteem, attention, and approbation of my superiors in the discharge of the weighty trust committed to my management. A few days after, embittered this contentment, I was plunged in the greatest grief. Intelligence arrived that my dear brother Lieutenant Robert Edward Grand, of the 1st regiment of Native Cavalry, on whom Mr. Hastings, previous to quitting Benares, had bestowed the staff appointment of Quarter Master to the regiment in which he served, was killed in action on that very day, *viz.*, the 4th of March, against some rebellious Zemindars in the Jaunpore district. This might have operated as an evil prognostick that my career would be checked, and my fortunes subjected to a sudden vicissitude. Yet, however, I reflected on the sorrow which mingled with joy on this occasion, I could not look from the repeated encomiums conferred to so cruel a blow as the one which befell me. I shall here transcribe, for the reader's judgment, *verbatim*, the account which I wrote of it some years since to the same friend for whose principal information this narrative originally was intended.

I shall pass over cursorily the first years of my life and services in India, with only one observation (to which assertion I challenge the testimony of my much beloved brother servants, who, however, by the caprice of fate, separated from, for life, I shall ever hold in the most pleasing remembrance those happy hours which I passed with such men), that in every Department I served, either Military or Civil, either in a subordinate situation, or as the chief, I merited and met with the repeated thanks of my superiors, the esteem of individuals, and the continued honoured protection of my noble friend and patron Warren Hastings (a name that will live immortal in India, both with the natives of all ranks and those Europeans who from local residence had the fairest opportunity of appreciating his great work and talents), but with whose regretted departure from the seat of Government which he had held, with surprising vigour and success, thirteen successive years, commenced the period of my misfortunes and downfall in life.

Mr. Hastings left India in 1785, at which juncture I was Collector or Governor of the provinces of Tirhoot and Hajeepore. To this station I had been nominated by him and his Council unanimously in February 1782. I mention *unanimously*, because he had then an opposition to contend with, in the persons of Sir John Macpherson, Baronet, and the late John Stables, Esq. In this instance, these gentlemen gave their concurrence. I took possession of a country yielding a revenue of above seven lakhs of rupees, but which had suffered from the depredations committed by those who were compelled to abandon the charge to me, and had, besides, been in a state of revolt, owing to the intrigues of the Rajah of Benares, Cheytsing, whose baneful influence had spread so far, and would have spread further, had he not been checked in time by Mr. Hastings' wise and spirited measures. I recovered a large balance due from the farmers to Government, quieted and appeased without bloodshed every disturbance, brought back the disobedient to a just sense of their errors, augmented the revenue, introduced the manufacturing of indigo after the European manner, encouraged the establishments of indigo works and plantations, erected three at my own expense, and thus possessed at that moment of a fortune of £15,000 sterling, looked forward to a proportionate augmentation by continuing in my station and extending my manufactories, which, with my houses, lands, and furniture, tent equipage, horses, boats, etc., etc., stood then upon a valuation, and to which amount I received an offer, to resign and transfer all as they stood, of £10,000 sterling more.

Sir John Macpherson received temporary charge of the Government, on the 1st of February, 1785. In which station he remained until the arrival of Marquis Cornwallis in September, 1786, when he reverted to his former situation of second in Council.

During this gentleman's administration, I was honored with his countenance, favor, and protection; and such was his sense, and his colleague's, John Stables, of the mode which I discharged the duties of my appointment, that they jointly introduced me to the Marquis, when, in November, 1786, I came down to the Seat of Government, to pay my respects to my new Chief, and to report the state of my district, and suggest what I considered requisite for its improvement, as one of the ablest revenue servants, and one of the most intelligent regarding the customs and usages prevailing in the provinces of Bahar.

In Appendix C will be seen the testimony, which his Lordship, soon after his arrival, bore to my merit; and from the purport of the said letter is visible likewise the approbation, which, such information conveyed, met with, from my immediate superiors the Board of Revenue.

These ties were insufficient to secure my permanence against the influence of patronage; for notwithstanding I was guaranteed even by the Regulations of the Hon. Court of Directors, and the Regulating Act of Parliament in 1774, regarding the continuing in employ those revenue servants, whose conduct was unimpeachable,

I was forced to give way to an individual of greater interest than myself. (Appendix D. E. F.).

It might be presumed, that my letter of the 3rd June, 1787, addressed direct to his Lordship, might have created a pang or an hesitation to commit so flagrant an act of injustice, but alas! every attempt, either by letter or mediation of friends on the spot, (and particularly exerted by the members of the Board of Revenue), proved in vain to shake his Lordship's previous determination. My friends were amused in the interim, with fallacious hopes, and their own ideas, that such serious intention could not, in a mind considered upright, exist, and I was favored with no answer to my written application (Appendix G. H.).

Thus the blow was struck, and from that date I fell, perhaps never more to rise; view the portrait, and feel!!!

CHAPTER XI.

Grand loses his Collectorship and is in trouble.

On the 26th of August, 1787, I was in full possession of my appointment, and my fortune was in that progressive state as described in 1785. I was in the enjoyment of every comfort, elegance and luxury of life. I was beloved and respected by those living with me, my assistants Messrs. David var der Heyden,* and Henry Colebrooke,† together with Mr. Steel, my Surgeons, and Mr. Purves, my private Secretary; and I will say, because I challenge the contrary to be proved, or even asserted, almost venerated by the natives of every description under my Government, whose tears, on hearing of my removal, accompanied me from the place of my residence to the Bank of the Ganges, where the limits of the district ceased, a distance of twenty-five miles.

On the 27th of August, 1787, by one stroke of his Lordship's pen was Mr. Robert Bathurst‡ nominated Collector of Tirhoot and Hajeepore; and thus every hope and fair built prospect existing on the preceding day, completely blasted. My houses, which I had

---

* Since Member of Parliament for Westloe.

† Since Member of the Supreme Council in Bengal.

‡ Since retired to England with a considerable fortune, derived from his Indigo Manufactories.

erected at great expence in my district, my Indigo works, having at that moment three extensive ones of eight vats, each of fifteen by twelve feet, with every appendage of land and houses, seeds, plants, etc., which had sank a vast capital, and was only then promising to yield an indemnification ; my furniture, tent equipage, boats, horses, elephants, and all those requisites, which, to a man acquainted with India, are known to appertain to a person in stations became at once of no value, or rather at the arbitrary estimation, which the usurper of my situation chose to put upon them. In my memorial (Appendix J.) will be seen a part of the loss which occurred; and I will do Mr. Bathurst the justice to say, others might have taken advantage, which himself disdained. In short, he allowed me for my houses ten thousand rupees, when it might have pleased him to settle elsewhere, and thus have rendered my habitations, which had cost me *forty* thousand, nor worth *one*. But, to liberality, this gentleman's disposition was never a stranger.

Thus ejected, I repaired to the Presidency, printed my case, and transmitted it to Europe to my relations Messrs. Edward and Rene Payne, the first one of the most respectable Bank Directors and merchants of city; the second, independent of his partnership in the Hamburgh line with his uncle Mr. Edward Payne an associate likewise in the banking house of Smith, Payne and Smith.* These gentlemen had interest to

* The first, *viz.*, Robert Smith, Member of Parliament for Nottingham, since created a Peer of England by the title of Lord Carrington.

be heard in behalf of the relation who they honored with their patronage. I had completed a plain tale, by annexing the thanks of the Board of Revenue, and the repeated ones of Government, to the pamphlet. Its statement could not therefore have been controverted, and the whole would have stamped such an apparent dereliction of all principle of justice on the noble Marquis Cornwallis, that his friend and supporter at the head of the Board of Controul, the Right Honorable Henry Dundas, used every conciliatory means to stop its circulation. My friends were moderate men, always disposed from true patriotism to yield pretensions for themselves and relations, where they thought, and were taught to believe, great public benefit might be derived. They saw his Lordship's continuance in office in this light, and remained content with assurances I should be recommended, and my wrongs redressed. This they notified to me, with the sense, which such a violation of all rule and precedent had caused, imparting that I stood high in the estimation of the gentlemen in Leadenhall Street, the Court of Directors, and that a public testimony of my administration would be conveyed in the most flattering terms (*vide* Appendix K.)

Alas! these men, ever to be regretted by those who knew their public and private virtues, little knew the insufficiency of such a measure. They were strangers to that maxim, which, however horrid, still is just, and forms amongst courtiers, of which Lord Cornwallis had from his youth graced the train, a part of their political creed. It was laid down by

Rochefancoult, and has ever been assiduously followed by such men, in power. Need I quote it? It stands high as the truest axiom, "The man who injures you, never forgives."

In no case has this cruel tendency been more closely illustrated than in mine; for it scarcely will be credited, that I shall expose its bitter continuances in this noble but ignoble mind, wherever an opportunity was afforded, to gratify his spleen.

I take no shame to myself that I entertained no such idea. I was not, as the event proved, so well versed, as others, in the ways of the world. I felt an approbation of what my friends had done, although it went not to repair in the smallest degree, the heavy loss which had attended my recall, and I rejected, in consequence, the advice of those who pressed me, to resign the service, and follow up to England, the spirit of the contents of my pamphlet, which submitted to the wisdom of the Court of Directors, whether, from the illegality of the act, so informal and unprecedented, I was not *bonâ fide* in their consideration the sole Collector of Tirhoot, and not Mr. Bathurst?

But happy would it have been for me, had I adopted their advice, instead of following and acting upon the too generous and delicate sentiments which I felt. I am bold in thus construing them, because, had such men been out of the question, no persuasion on earth would have induced me to relinquish the pursuit of such claims. They impelled me to incline towards what I deemed more reasonable, and, at a juncture when great decisions stamp the character of men, I sunk into a desire to temporize. I remained inactive in Calcutta, without any employment, but with every hope, *viz.*, of being soon restored to the revenue line, agreeably to Marquis Cornwallis' positive assurance to me to this effect, and which, if he lives ever to see this, I challenge his honor, as a Peer of the Realm, to declare, whether such assertion existed in truth or not?

So far from such promise having been considered binding by him, I had the mortification of seeing in this interval others preferred. This partiality affected me,—I fell ill in consequence, and, from my brother-in-law's house Mr. Robert Ledlie, I removed to my friend Mr. Cockrell's house at Belvedere, where the air of the country, a good constitution, flattering messages from the Government house, and even his Lordship, in his afternoon rides, calling to enquire after my health, occasioned my recovery, more speedily, than a proud mind, deeply wounded, might otherwise have been.

But alas, must I again repeat my sanguine disposition, naturally excited by a confidence in men, and a reliance on the honor of such a chief, was as econd time proved to be at variance with my judgment. I only revived to be once more grossly deceived. In September, 1788, Lord Cornwallis, without any previous intimation, as customary with every appointment in the civil service, unsought and unsolicited by me, nominated me Judge and Magistrate of Patna, transferring Mr. Mercer, who had filled that station for four years, to be Collector or Governor of the province of Burdwan. The latter ought to have been my station conformably to promise. The former could not be my choice. It was a gold chain, honorable but burthensome and totally bereft of every emolument. I objected modestly when I came to town, and waited on his Lordship to ascertain if such a resolution, which rumor circulated, had actually passed in council? I found it verified, and declining it, my mouth was stopped by Lord Cornwallis' pressing on me its acceptation, with the further assurance, that he only placed me there, in order that I might be on the spot to succeed to the first vacant Collectorship, in the said Subah (Bahar) out of which I had been removed. He added likewise, that my connexion, my habits, my interests, all laid there, or near that spot; and graciously instancing the translation of my predecessor to Burdwan, in direct confirmation, that the Judge of a capital city was not deemed by him as a bar to be governor of a province, I could not persist, in my refusal, but signified, with full reliance on his Lordship, my cheerful assent.

The next council day I was summoned to take the oaths, which I did in the customary manner; and when taking leave of the board to proceed on my journey, his Lordship condescended, with one of his seducing smiles, to say I must defer for a day or two my intention, that I might eat venison with him before I embarked.

I had scarcely arrived at my destination, and received charge from Mr. Henry Douglas, who had considered himself entitled to the succession having been three years Register and Assistant to Mr. Mercer, than it was signified to me from his Lordship, that I must give up and dispose of my Indigo works in Tirhoot. I observed in reply, that had such a condition been annexed to the appointment, which without my previous sanction had been conferred on me, I would have rejected the latter; that, the retaining them could not operate to any person's disadvantage, since it was well known they were situated fifty miles asunder from my jurisdiction as Judge and Magistrate of the City of Patna, and no undue influence could of course be exercized in promoting their extension. All arguments were vain. A Mr. Hunter, patronized by his Lordship, made an agreement with my Attorneys for them, having previously obtained a contract with Government to supply them from the said manufactories with the quantity of one thousand maunds (80,000lb. C. weight) annually. The sale was known to be forced, and consequently my Attorneys were glad to accept, on my account, of 34,000 Sicca Rupees for the amount, which six months after, on a resale of only two of said works, produced double the amount, *vide* Memorial J.

This was not sufficient persecution. News had now arrived from Europe that I had heavily arraigned his Lordship's justice, by many, justly thought, from a view of a plain statement, not without reason; and I was, consequently, not to be forgiven, I shall only therefore say, that every proposal of mine tending to ameliorate the state of the police, to simplify the proceedings of the office, in short, everything which I suggested met with a determined and obstinate opposition. I was, instead of meeting with support, to be effectually thwarted, and this system was rendered more manifest, when I openly, through Colonel Ross, his Lordship's confidential secretary, reproached and up-braided the said peer for breach of promise, in having nominated Mr. Archibald Seton and Mr. Thomas Brooke, two *junior servants* to myself, Collectors of the provinces of Shahabad and Gyah, both situated in subah Bahar and vacated by Mr. Thomas Law, being summoned to fill a seat in the Board of Revenue and Mr. William Augustus Brooke, being transferred to Burdwan, on the death of Mr. Mercer, who, as I noticed before had been my predecessor at Patna and from thence was called to the Collectorship of Burdwan.

I had also aggravated the noble peer's resentment and bitter unforgiving disposition. I was called upon to denounce everything, which had till then obtained as precarious and fluctuating, and I was to compliment the happy period, when from his Lordship's government, system was to make place for anarchy, and a complete new order of things was to be established, suitable to the comprehensive mind of the enlightened person at the helm, so transcendant in every quality, both public and private, over his predecessors. Such a prostitution of character was not to be expected from me. I had too grateful a sense to the virtues of a Hastings, too firm a conviction of his eminent talents in the science of Government, too elevated a notion of the wisdom which dictated the measures laid down by Clive, to chime in with such extravagant applications, awaited from the efforts of the idol of the day, to excite sacrifices at his shrine.*

The *affirmative* questions therefore sent to me, were most of them answered completely in the negative. Nay, I could not contain myself. My indignation to think, such men as Clive and Hastings were trampled upon, led me to deride the intended innovation. I cautioned his Lordship to deliberate seriously on introducing new rules to an ancient system, which had for its sanction ages to plead (Appendix K). My endeavours were however fruitless. The resolution was fixed, others had applauded it, and were rewarded accordingly.

Yet the sense entertained of the contents of this letter is sufficiently manifested by the letter from the Board of Revenue, addressed to me after my removal; when I claimed it from the justice of those men, to whose Superintendence I had been subordinate, and however the frowns of a Despot, felt too much like Englishmen, not to accord me such a satisfactory proof of their remembrance, and the regret they experienced for a change which bore hard on the mind of every person, sensible of its injustice, and the ruin which it entailed on the individual (Appendix L. M).

---

* *Vide* his Lordship's minute in corroboration thereof, recorded in Council in 1789, the purport of which cast such a reflection, could it have admitted of proof, on the administration of his predecessors. However, so fallacious a statement, as it was deemed, did not pass unnoticed. His very supporter, the Right Hon'ble Henry Dundas, then at the head of the Board of Control, disavowed completely the positions assumed, by representing, on the contrary, the flourishing state which prevailed in India, in his speech in Parliament in 1793, previous to the legislative act of the Charter's renewal, at that period.

I must here introduce one instance of the reform which I proposed in the office of my judicial capacity, because it has so much relation to what happened subsequently to me, and proves to the impartial reader, that, could I have been influenced in that sacred trust, by corrupt motives, I should not have been the first to have proposed a certain mode of discovery, as simple and just, as was the intention in recommending the regulation.

Adverting to the voluminous proceedings, which a cause in appeal occasioned, from every record being translated from the Persian, and my Registrar, Mr. Henry Douglas, then being incapacitated from a disorder in his eyes, to devote that attention to his duties, which otherwise were performed with scrupulous assiduity, I submitted to Government the propriety of only transmitting translates of the petition or plaint, the answer, the rejoinder, the replication, with the cause for appeal, whether founded on a misconstruction of the Mahometan or Hindoo Law; whether on an improper stress laid on certain evidences which, on the plaintiff's conception, might have been done away in its force by the testimonies of these witnesses, which he had adduced; or whether *grounded* and *arisen from partiality* or *other improper motives in the Judge?* These, in his petition for appeal, which could never be denied him, were to be stated distinctly.

Every one acquainted with India, knows well, that such is the litigious disposition of the natives, such the art of those admitted to plead in behalf of their clients, that it has not been unusual often to observe from fifty to sixty depositions, on the respective side of either plaintiff and defendant; and being equally, however contradictory, in their effects, affirmed on oath, creates the greatest difficulty in coming at the truth, with this view, and to avoid a labyrinth of trouble to Government, by directing their judgment, at once to that part alone, which, in the petitioner's eye and sense, rendered the Judge's awards and decree exceptionable, was this proposition made. Nevertheless, it was rejected, and an intimation conveyed, which, in my answer to his Lordship, I spurned, *viz.*, that it was considered as a design existing to crimp the appellant in his full privilege of appeal. Here all further correspondence ceased ! ! !

From the character given in the foregoing part of the Narrative of the noble Lord and of the maxim which governed him in life, where an individual had been bold enough to arraign his justice, the reader may be prepared for the heavy vicissitude which befel my state, caused by the exercise of his arbitrary power, and which, to my sorrow, I have now to relate.

Yet, I will freely own, that, could I have foreseen the consequences which followed, I might have deported myself in a manner more humble, and probably shewn more pliancy to his almighty will, then a consciousness of the chastising rod being unmerited, led me to do. It was not possible for me to think, that, entrenched as I felt myself, by covenanted rights, sanctioned by an Act of Parliament, I should find myself ejected from a service, to the highest elevation of which, I had fondly looked, and in which my only dependence for bread, and for provision in my older days, rested. Nevertheless, this reverse occurred. It fell to my lot to experience, that, without a specific charge brought forward, without that charge, or charges, regularly examined, tried and decided upon subject to an appeal to my Honorable Masters, I was to be thrust out of a service, in which I had honorably served above thirty years, and finally reduced, at an advanced age, to seek my subsistence in a foreign land.

Some friends, prepossessed with a sense of my innocence, attempted to interpose with his Lordship. They urged in my behalf, that from the situation which I had filled, even not rapacious men but men actuated by moderate views, would have amassed, in such a course of years, such a fortune as would have made them indifferent with regard to the result. That my hospitality, and disregard for money, were as notorious, as the desire, which I had always evinced in winning, by my official conduct, the approbation of my superiors. They recalled to him, I had deserved, and met the annual thanks of Government, his Lordship's own in the latter year of my administration in Tirhoot, and finally, the thanks of the Court of Directors, publicly and formally conveyed to me by the Secretary to the Board of Revenue; *and that these were considerations, which, they hoped, would command

* Now the Chief Judge of Appeal, Mr. John Herbert Harrington, a gentleman whom I am proud to call my friend and whose sentiments coincided completely with mine on the permanent settlement of the lands. *Vide* his letters to Lord Cornwallis on the said subject.

his attention. All effort was vain. I had offended the haughty Peer, who would be thought immaculate, and I must be sacrificed. Nay, he bitterly, and sarcastically added, he had good ground for concluding that however I might appear destitute of a sufficient provision for life, coeval with my length of service, and the lucrative offices I had been vested with, yet, there were sums of magnitude, which I had remitted and which awaited my return to Swizerland. I dared his Lordship to any such proof, and in the meanwhile, offered to purge my conscience of any such accusation by the most solemn oath, affirmed before him, or before any Magistrate he should select. My friends were convinced of the malignancy of the assertion; they entreated his Lordship to produce the accuser; this, he refused, and obstinately resisted every conviction, which ought to have flashed on his mind from such declarations.

In fact, his Lordship was ashamed of the engine whence he had drawn such foul streams. Subsequent events occurring to others, and which forced his Lordship to disown him, pointed him out, to be no other than the *famous* or rather *infamous*, Robert Morris, the Secretary to the assembly which had been held in England, for the support of the Bill of Rights; but better known, by his having eloped, and tricked into a marriage, the ward of Chancery, Miss Harford, and left to his care by his friend the late Lord Baltimore.

From the decision which took place against him, and his matrimonial speculation being rendered void, he justly thought England was not the country for him to remain in, and he smuggled himself out to India. Landed in that country, where his practices as he thought, would remain unknown, or at least unnoticcd, he boldly proposed himself to plead in the Supreme Court, grounding his claim to such admission from his having been regularly entered a Barrister in the Temple. His effrontery did not serve him. Sir William Dunkin, one of the Puisne Judges, who, with the much regretted Sir William Jones, and Sir Robert Chambers, formed the Bench of His Majesty's Supreme Court of Justice, rejected his petition in open Court, and added, he should not hesitate to unfold the reasons, if Mr. Morris thought proper to press him for an explanation. Mr. Morris rather deemed it convenient to bow and retire. This disappointment embittered a mind already irritated, and he resolved to vent his spleen wherever he could find an opportunity to breed mischief. With this view, he determined on leaving the Presidency and having excited suspicion in a mind *prone to imbibe such venom, he was led to believe his information and remarks, as he travelled to the upper provinces, would be considered agreeable. My brother-in-law (Mr. Robert Ledlie), who was likewise an English Barrister, and had been acquainted with him in England, was applied to by him, for letters of introduction to his brother the Judge and Magistrate of Patna, which he prudently declined. This was intimated to me by him, observing, that knowing my disposition to attend to

* Need I state Lord Cornwallis.

his recommendations, he had rejected this, conceiving the person in question, a very improper one to become an inmate of any family, for whom he entertained a regard. This communication influenced my conduct towards him. He left his card, I returned mine, but fully resolved he should not experience the civility of numbering himself as one of my guests at any party which I gave.

In a city like Patna, where many dissatisfied beings could not but exist, he met with such which suited his purpose. Taking advantage of my absence on the Saturday and Sunday at a friend's, in the military cantonment of Dinahpore, a distance of fourteen miles, he suddenly visited my jail, saying he had the Governor, Lord Cornwallis' orders to inspect the prisons, and to report their state. Every one versed with the nature of those natives, who happened to be in confinement, will directly conclude, they, with one voice, told him their detainment was unjust. Provided with paper, pen, and ink, and a Portuguese priest who wrote Persian, he hastily framed petitions, and obtained their signatures. All this was effected before my Nazir, who resided with me at Beeknapahree, five miles from the city, could arrive, agreeably to the summons, which his deputy had sent to him, on the appearance of this European gentleman demanding entrance, by command of such authority as he quoted.

To any stranger expressing such a desire, the request would never have been refused ; but, in this instance, the report from the Nazir, who galloped out to me, with a detail of the transactions which had taken place, left not one moment's doubt on my mind how to act. I immediately issued a warrant to arrest Mr. Morris, and hold him in confinement, till a boat, with suitable accommodation, was made ready to send him to his employer, with the various petitions which he had collected, and under an officer's guard of Sepoys to secure their delivery. His faithful Padree's vigilance saved him from incurring this disgrace. Wisely apprehending what would follow, he advised his companion in iniquity to move off with Pandora's box, and to forward it by some safe opportunity to his lordship. Before the mandate could be served, they had escaped into another jurisdiction, whence, as I understood afterwards, the priest was dispatched with the combustibles which they had prepared.

But, to any one inclined to think well of the character of Lord Cornwallis, can it be thought possible that his lordship with such loose materials, which he could not understand, nor would give to others to explain, should come to Council with his pockets filled, and without allowing any of the members of his Council to look into them, each of whom would immediately have discerned their futility, direct the immediate recall of a covenanted servant of so many years, and one who had acted four years in his then station of Judge and Magistrate of a great city. Nay, in order to ensure my instantaneous removal, and to seize on the papers of my court, were both Mr. Archibald Seton, Collector of Gyah, and Mr. Henry Douglas, formerly my Registrar, ordered to repair to the spot, to assume the official charge of my trust.

VIEW OF BERHAMPORE.

(From Colour-drawing by J. Moffat about 1805.)

I obeyed, but prejudiced as I was against the noble peer's arbitrary acts, and fully aware of his inveteracy towards me, I solemnly declared, I did not harbour an idea, I could have been marked as an object for such persecution. Landing at Berhampore, my eyes were soon opened to view the state in which I was thrown, by so informal, so illegal, and so unprecedented a process. My friend Major Edward Clark* then held the command of the cantonments, and seeing me coming to make a friendly call, half seriously, half jocosely, when accosting each other, put the question to me, whether it was mine, or the officer's wish *who had the guard over me*, to have it relieved? He added, it was the general report throughout the country that I was proceeding, under such distraint, to the seat of Government, an occurrence which had given him, and my other friends at his station, the greatest concern.

It may naturally be judged with what temper I continued my journey. I posted day and night, and the moment I found myself at the house of my brother-in-law in Calcutta, I conveyed by a servant a written intimation thereof to Colonel Ross, his lordship's Private Secretary, entreating, however, it was not a regular levée day, I might yet be honoured with an audience the next morning. Colonel Ross returned his compliments, and mentioned Lord Cornwallis would see me at ten o'clock; I was punctual, and, after the first salutation, I remarked his lordship,

* Now Major-General on the Bengal Staff Establishment.

evidently, felt embarrassed. Probably he had, in the intervening time, satisfied himself with the nature of what he had, so surreptitiously, been furnished with, and was sensible they were too vague to deduce into any specific charges. Indeed his countenance seemed to soften. He even deigned a smile, saying, to break the pause, that it seemed to him, the good fat beef for which Patna stood renowned, had agreed very well with me. I replied directly, that I, thank God, was well in body, but cruelly diseased in mind.

In the same tone I proceeded. I asked his lordship what could have been the cause for my being so suddenly ordered to repair to the Presidency? The answer was, he had received complaints, which, he graciously I added, he hoped I should be able to refute. I observed I was ignorant of any having been preferred, but admitting his lordship had that ground to have occasioned his conduct towards me, yet in cases of this nature there was a regular mode of proceeding laid down, without the necessity of having recourse to such an unusual form as had been adopted. That treated as I had been, and in the world's estimation actually prejudged, I had only to express my sincere wish and anxiety, that his lordship would be good enough to bring forward *his* charges with the least possible delay, when after a due examination of what their contents were, I should be able to re-establish my lost reputation, to his, my friends, and the public's satisfaction. That, however, before I took my leave, I must tell him, it was possible I might, in the discharge of an office of such magnitude be found capable of formal omissions, but as to any point which could involve and attach on me criminally, I defied my worst of enemies to bring forward a charge in this shape. With these impressive words, which I uttered forcibly, I rose, and departed; his lordship, half angry at the boldness of spirit which I displayed, and half confused, muttering something indistinctly, to which I, of course, paid no attention.

I received the dinner invitation, which a non-resident in Calcutta was in the custom of being honoured with when his arrival at the Presidency had been announced at the Government House. I returned it politely to the Aide-de-Camp, remarking I could not think of appearing as a guest at his lordship's table, until I was sure he would survey me, with sentiments different to those his severity towards me denoted, he must have entertained. I resolved, moreover, contrary to the opinions of some friends, more accommodating in their disposition than I unfortunately was, and I readily own, more consummate in their knowledge of the world, to abstain from attending his lordship's regular Levées, but to await pātiently the moment, when it would please him, to relieve my anxiety, by making me formally acquainted with the charges which he could proffer, from the representations which he possessed I might long have looked for this result. Three months had elapsed, and no thought thereof existed. My friends lamented, they could make no change in my determination. I knew I was immaculate on the score of corruption. I felt I was defending the covenanted rights of my brother servants, deeply infringled upon, and injured in my person I stood firm. His lordship, I apprehended, apprized I was unalterable, deemed it necessary, to take some step, either to justify, or, at least, to palliate the measure which he had pursued. Accordingly, he instituted, *three* months after I had been summoned to attend at the seat of Government, professionally to purge myself of heavy charges, a committee to assemble on the spot, and there, after giving notice for what purpose they were met, to *enquire*, *ascertain*, and finally *to decide* "*en dernier ressort*" on what might appear before them, which might attach, and affect the manner in which I had discharged the offices with which I had been entrusted. An intimation, conveyed by the Secretary of Government, was the first notice which I received of this star chamber institution.

In this same letter* it was communicated to me, that I had liberty, either in person or by regular appointed Vakeel,† to attend the committee, and *the charges which might be brought against me*. This permission was issued full two months after this junto had been formed, and had full time to obtain, in every manner which they chose to exercise, whatever could operate against the individual, whose condemnation they must have seen from the nature of their instructions, and natures of their mission, would prove a gratification to the all-ruling power.

---

* *Vide* Appendix N. † *Id est*, a Native Agent.

I read the letter with astonishment! I felt what ground I had to stand upon. I felt how untenable their's was. I am told, *early in November*, by the Governor, that the reason of my recall from the seat of my administration arose from charges preferred against me; and, *in the month of March ensuing*, I am apprised by order of the same authority that a committee had been nominated *in January*, to meet, sit *at Patna*, and to proceed to trial and judgment, to which place I had liberty to repair, and appear personally, or, *by native delegate*, before this strange constituted board, to relate what they (this identical tribunal) *might have collected*, against the Judge and Magistrate of a city, who had in these functions acted for four years over an extended population of above three hundred thousand people, comprehending Hindus, Mahomedans, Sics,* and Europeans, the latter of whom thought themselves out of the reach of any police regulation, until I convinced them to the contrary, by those which I established for the maintenance of good order, and to which they subsequently readily subscribed.

Mark, that during this period of four years, no complaint had been preferred! Mark, that the loose petitions transmitted were found too groundless, too malicious, and too idle, to found any direct accusation upon! Mark, the source whence they sprang, with which I was well acquainted. At this hour, labouring

* [Sikhs.] Manick Shah, the founder of their sect erected in Patna his first religious edifice, and was interred in its bosom. [See notes.]

under the misfortunes and inconveniences of life, which this reverse has occasioned, I cannot but reflect, however inconsistent my determination may have been with the advocate's prudence and that maxim, "*never run your head against a stone wall*," yet, that I must have possessed a poor mind, indignant as its sensations were against such unparalleled treatment, had I not come to the resolution of exposing such unwarrantable persecution as I had experienced.

Without cavilling at the nature of the letter which I had received,* I simply replied I should set off immediately, and attend in person, apprehending, as I did, that no gentleman vested with the high situations which I had been, would think of entrusting the defence and vindication of his fair fame, honour, and reputation to a native agent.

I reached Patna in five (5) days.† Instead of receiving on my arrival compliments of the gentlemen of the station, and those of the principal inhabitants, I found myself already in the light of a criminal actually proscribed and prejudged. Scarcely had I recovered from the fatigue of travelling past to my habitation, in the short space of time mentioned, and in the hottest weather, than I received an official letter from the committee, announcing to me, that they had assembled and met and would resume their proceedings on the next day, when they intended to go into an enquiry of such representations which had been made to them,

---

* *Vide* Appendix N.

† A distance of about 400 miles from the Presidency.

since *they had commenced their sittings;* and summoned me, accordingly, to attend in person or by agent.

I could no longer contain myself. My feelings, however acute, which to this moment I had used every exertion of the mind to suppress, burst into loud indignation. To learn they had constituted themselves a Court, and entered *ex parte* into proceedings *before my arrival*, was, beyond what I thought, men with any sense of propriety, would have allowed themselves to act !!! I conceived, therefore, the instructions which they had received to occasion such a dereliction of all form must be as wonderful, as the whole of the process against a covenanted servant (subject alone to established rules, framed for all such cases, and sanctioned by Act of Parliament), appeared in the eyes of all my brother servants. With these sentiments I set forth the rights which I claimed to have a copy of their instructions; I must see what could justify, or rather palliate such a mode of proceeding, as it appeared, from the purport of their letter, they had thought proper to adopt; I must see likewise the *original charges*, which could have dictated the necessity of such instructions, admitting it was under their force, and not spontaneously, they acted. I should then decide upon the summons which they had been pleased to transmit for my guidance.

Their reply was such as I expected. They had *no original charges* given to them, to found their enquiry, and ergo, *no necessity existed, but that of obvious persecution intended to warrant such an appointment.*

They rejected my request to be furnished with a copy of their instructions; finally, they acquainted me they should on the next day proceed, *whether I attended or not*, to examine into the validity of what had been presented to claim their notice since their arrival.*

My rejoinder was concise. I expressed my satisfaction to find *the ground of my recall had originated in suspicion*, and which avowal confirmed the whole of the illegality of the proceedings which had from the commencement obtained against me. That it would be my business to ascertain how far any executive power was warranted in adopting such a line of conduct towards an individual who felt for the violation of those rights, in which he had, from the tenor of written documents, considered himself, since his entrance into the Civil Service, secured against every possible infringement. That without going into any further detail, or adverting to the informality of their assembling, constituting themselves into a tribunal, and proclaiming the purpose for which they had met ere I was on the spot to refute the complaints, which by such a system, as was visible, had governed them, I could not, but say, *they had invited*; I should leave them to a continuation of their *ex parte* proceedings, particularly, as I found they had, in their letter, declared their fixed resolution to this intent and, consequently, whether I attended or not, must be, in their consideration, perfectly immaterial. I ended

* *Vide* Appendix O.—Instructions.

with protesting against whatever they might think proper to deduce and represent.

I repaired a second time to the Presidency, losing no more time on my journey, than what was requisite, to perform it by water, a period of fifteen days. I recapitulated to the Secretary of Government the objections which had arisen, and which had influenced my determination, not to recognize a tribunal so constituted, and one which had proved itself capable of acting in the highly objectionable manner which they had done; at the same time, professing myself ready, to answer to any specific charges which his Lordship might think expedient to bring against me from the nature of the information which he had received. I took this opportunity of inserting in my official letter, *which must stand or record in the consultations of April 1793*,—what I bad declared *verbatim* to the noble Peer, *viz.* "That, possibly, there might have been errors of form in my administratlon, but that I dared my worst of enemies, to come forward with any accusation, *invoking or bordering on criminality.*"

Lord Cornwallis replied. He acknowledged my sudden recall had been built upon suspicion, and vindicated his measure, from an apprehension that, had I remained on the spot, I might have defeated all enquiry, as it seemed in this instance, I had evaded it, *by absenting myself from the place where the enquiry was pending.*

I brought in proof, to refute this assumed position, the indignities to which I had calmly submitted, from the commencement of this unheard of and unprecedented process; the patience, with which for five months, I had awaited at the Presidency, where my attendance was commanded, the result of his Lordship's assurances given verbally on the first day of audience, *viz.* "That he should produce his charges against me, and call upon me to answer them, without the least possible delay;" the readiness which I displayed, when his Lordship changed his mind, and directed me to return to Patna; the anxiety which I still harbored, and which I conjured him to dispel, by accusing me directly on whatever score *he prejudged me culpable;* entreating, likewise, he would desist to proceed *to any extremity*, until he had listened and seen my vindication, which could alone empower him to act *unprejudiced.*

I ventured on this last remonstrance, from his having, and without assigning any reason, ejected me from my station by the actual appointment of Mr. Henry Douglas, to be the Judge and Magistrate of Patna, *vice* Mr. Grand.

In effect, this *summa injuria* took place on the 4th April,* and on that memorable day, *to give a color* to the arbitrary conduct, which he must have been sensible, he had exercised towards me, it was enacted, that *any Native*, who, *hereafter*, should proffer any accusations against a Judge and Magistrate, was to give security in an amount three times to the extent of what might be adjudged was the enormity of the crime

* *Vide* Memorial, 30th June, Appendix P.

with which the culprit stood charged. I must here transcribe it at length for the reader's information.

Extract from the regulations enacted by Lord Cornwallis in April, 1793, for *the better* administration of justice.—"If any person shall charge the Judge of a city or zillah court, before the Provincial Court of the division, with having been guilty of corruption, in opposition to his oath, the Provincial Court is to receive the charge, and to forward it to the Sudder Dewanny Adawlat; provided the complainant shall previously make oath to the truth of the charges, and give security, in whatever sum the Court may judge proper, to appear and prosecute the charge when required."

But the principles on which these rules have been established, may be best explained, by an extract from the minute of Lord Cornwallis, by whom they were introduced, dated 11th February 1793.

"To prevent the character of the Judges being wantonly aspersed, rules should be laid down, to deter people from making groundless accusations. The Provincial Courts should not be permitted to make enquiries in the first instance, into the charges that may be prepared against the zillah or city Judges, but should be directed to forward them to the Sudder Dewanny Adawlat. This Court shall issue a special commission to the Provincial Court to make such enquiries, and to take such evidences respecting the charges as it may think advisable. The observation of this formality will be essential: it will not obstruct the bringing forward of well founded complaints; at the same time, it will operate to deter people from making groundless charges. To delegate to the Provincial Courts of Appeal a power to enquire into such charges, without a previous reference to the Sudder Dewanny Adawlut, would, in fact, be making the Judges of the City and Zillah Courts personally subject to their authority. This would even deprive the City and Zillah Judges of all weight and consequence in the eyes of the people, and lessen that respect with which it is necessary they should look up to their decisions. The Judges of the Provincial Courts should possess no authority over the Judges of the City and Zillah Courts personally; their controls over them should be only that of a superior Court empowered to revise their decrees, when regularly brought before them in appeal."

When the purport of these is considered, I apprehend, the impartial decision will be, from their application being so evident to my case that they emanated in consequence of what had occurred against me, when accusations were invited, *subsequent* to the disgrace of recall inflicted, and, however well known, the prejudged manner in which they were conveyed for examination, yet could not force nor operate a conviction!!

I repeat, that this regulation issued, from the disappointment which his Lordship had felt in the petitions, which had been so clandestinely transmitted to him, proving entirely groundless. I rely, it will also satisfy those versed in the character of the natives of India, that this very rule tended in its purport to defeat every wish, which might have operated in his mind, in order to lead to condign punishment, any civilian in office, so wanton to his trust, and to his fame as to have been guilty of corruption in its exercise. Why not, on the contrary, admitting this had been the view, and not that which I shrewdly suspect, of gratifying an unjust personal resentment imbided against the individual, have adopted the mode which I had recommended, *viz.*, the *charging directly in the petition for appeal*, against his decrees, the Judge, either for a misconstruction of the Mahomedan or Hindoo law, or his judgment proceeding from a *partial bias*.

I have now related what I personally experienced. I had suffered enough from appeals to England to be completely deterred from urging a second. Sir John Shore had, in the meanwhile, arrived from England to succeed to the Government, and my friends advised me to look to that period, which was approximating, for a certain hope of redress. I acquiesced, lived in hope, humbly preferred my claim, and was literally amused until June 1798, when after having received no replies to the several letters, which I addressed to Government on this point, *viz.*, of preferment, agreeably to my rank, and the situations which I had filled, I came to the resolution of forwarding, through the Governor in Council, the appeal* to the Court of Directors, and eventually to follow it up, which I did, by departing for England in February 1799.

---

* *Vide* Appendix Q.

Charles Cornwallis, K.G., first Marquis and second Earl Cornwallis.

CHAPTER XII.

REVIEW OF HISTORICAL EVENTS, 1788—1799.

THE political occurrences, during the period which comprised my nomination to Patna in September, 1788, and the moment of my departure, involved an important and critical epoch for the permanency of the British interests in India. The first event consisted in the sudden and unexpected irruption of Tippoo Saheb in the Carnatic, and the ineffectual opposition which, in the course of one campaign, General Sir William Meadowes* had carried on against him. Lord Cornwallis thought to be more successful.† His personal bravery, and zeal for his country's welfare, were undoubted. It was enough for him to deem his presence would be useful in subduing the enemy, not to hesitate one moment, with a sacrifice to every personal convenience, to fly to the scene of action. Fortunate would it have been for the interests of his employers, that he had proved so good a General, as he indubitably was, a daring soldier. Had his Lordship possessed the former qualification, he might, by his exertions, sagaciously and prudently dictated, have spared to them the expence of two more campaigns, ere his antagonist was reduced to the necessity of suing for peace. His mistakes, as a General had much endangered the Company's sovereign interest. Instead of proceeding direct to

* [The name is spelt Medows.]

† [He assumed command on January 29th, 1791.]

Seringapatnam, after the capture of Bangalore,* which afforded him a strong post for a depôt, he continued losing the best time of the season, by besieging every fort and fortified position lying between Bangalore and the Sultan's capital. The consequence was obvious to every one who foresaw the operations of the siege intended, would be frustrated by the early setting in of the rains, and the swelling of the river, which would render every approach established, of no effect. It so turned out; the works were destroyed by the violence of the torrents falling from the elements; the Beoparries (men accustomed to come in droves to supply the market) were debarred from the possibility of vending their commodities. Rice, and other grain, became scarce in the market; roads were impracticable for artillery; the camp was obliged to break up; the siege raised; the heavy battering guns spiked; and, finally, a resolution taken, for officers and men to disperse in small bodies, and gain Bangalore, in the best confused manner possible. All this was to be effected on the next ground which they were to occupy; but providence interposed, to obviate this fatal measure. On the morning of that memorable day, which must have caused their misery, if not completed their destruction, as the vanguard was moving on in solemn dejection, Colonel William Scott, the Quartermaster General, fell in with the Mahrattah allied army, which ought, agreeably to treaty, long before to have effected its junction, and co-operated with the besieging army under the

* [March 20th, 1791.]

walls of Seringapatnam. The glad tidings entirely overpowered Lord Cornwallis' feelings, and as completely destroyed his prudence. The two chiefs met. His Lordship, with the candour of an English heart, conceiving he had to do with a generous ally, instead of a freebooter (ever ready, from principles of self interest, the only guide for their actions, to join the strongest, or the power which payeth best), imparted to him the situation to which he had been reduced, and congratulated himself and army, that the Mahrattahs had come, so opportunely, to cover by their cavalry the rear of a retreating army, harassed by sickness, and destitute of provision, which they now, from the happy change which had occurred, would amply be furnished with. Here was the misfortune of a commander not knowing the genius of the people whom he had to deal with, and acting upon *his* judgment, when the advice of others, more experienced and versed with the nature of their disposition, would have operated for the service more favorably. Add to this error, the gross one of being such an economist in the disbursement for intelligences so requisite in India, and so easily obtained where liberality is held out, as not to have known where the Mahrattah allied army was, until falling in with it by accident.

The natural consequence followed to the *unreserved* communication made. *The Mahrattah army were wearied* from the *forced marches* which they had performed *in their anxiety* to join his Lordship. The provisions which accompanied their Bazar (Market) were no more than would serve for their own consumption, and as to marching towards Bangalore, this was totally impossible, as they had mostly come without money, depending upon arriving time enough to share in the capture and plunder of the Sultan's capital. In proof of the pleaded scarcity, every article in their said Bazar, had in one day risen to *four times* the amount, for which it was sold before the appearance of the English army. To end this melancholy tale, Lord Cornwallis' army was obliged to submit to these augmented prices, for the supplies they wanted, and his Lordship was obliged to part with what treasure he had, and give assignments for twelve laacks of rupees, ere he could induce the crafty Mahrattah to more from the ground which had been so productive to his grasping views.

The operations of the next campaign became more certain in their issue. They were begun early in the season, and had, consequently, no difficulty to meet in their prosecution. Tippoo's protecting army was attacked by three different columns, beaten, driven across the Cauvery, and compelled to take refuge within the walls of the Capital, the siege of which being pursued with ardour, and the immediate assault by storm dreaded, brought on proposals for capitulation.

The conclusion is known. The haughty Sultan was obliged to comply with the terms imposed. A mulct of three millions of pagodas, and half his territory, both which land and money were regularly to be divided in three proportions, the English Government one-third, the Nizam one-third and the Mahrattas the remaining third.

In this attack, Lord Cornwallis did not display that penetration, which a General Officer, brought up regularly in the Company's service, would have done, from a full knowledge of the enemy whom he had to oppose. His Lordship directed his army at ten at night,* so soon as the moon rose, to move forward in three columns, pointing out in his orders the road each was to observe, keeping certain distances, one from the other, and to rush on with the bayonet, unmindful of the batteries which impeded the road, to assault without artillery an entrenched camp. He led the centre, and assigned to Sir William Meadowes the right. The moon did not shine with that brightness which he hoped for, to secure against any disappointment. The consequence was, that Sir William, instead of taking the circuitous road which was fixed upon, to avoid one of the principal batteries, which defended the approach of the camp, fell in directly with it, and got so entangled, that to storm it, was the only possible mode of extrication. This early firing alarmed and prepared Tippoo. Having learnt by his spies, the disposition which his Lordship had made of his troops, he hastily collected his *corps d'élite* (chosen corps), and with them bent all his force to penetrate and resist Lord Cornwallis' centre column judging from the nature of the ground, the left could not form a junction in time to support, and fully aware the right had sufficient employment in its endeavours to carry the battery.

* [6th February 1792.]

The unexpected offensive operation of Tippoo had nearly disconcerted every hope of success. His Lordship was in the greatest danger; and had it not been for the gallantry of His Majesty's 52nd Regiment, and a battalion of Bengal Sepoys, commanded by Captain Henry White, would infallibly have been made a prisoner. These corps were sacrificed in security for his person. Tippoo finding the object of his immediate impulse frustrated, fled to the Fort, and his troops, in scattered bodies, followed him.

Sir William's column was twice or three times repulsed, but at length drove the enemy out of the battery, and established themselves in it. The morning broke, and from the dispersion of the several bodies of the English army, afforded a proof of the imprudence of a night attack particularly, where the efficient force, from its separations, was precluded to act with that energy, which might, otherwise, have been expected from them. I have heard the late Major-General Duff, bred up from his infancy a soldier in Bengal, and who commanded the artillery, assert that he did everything to persuade his Lordship to desist from his attempt, instancing how often the superiority manifested in the serving of the English guns, had been the only cause of ensuring success against the disproportion of men, which the English had ever, in Indian, actions to encounter.

Equally was his Lordship's judgment at variance, with every political idea, which men bred in the service, would on such an occasion, have manifested. They would have felt the genius of the men with whom they had to treat. They would not have exercised that ill-advised levity which dictated Lord Cornwallis' requisitions, when the humble offer to negotiate, arose only from the certainty which Tippoo entertained, that both his Capital and Kingdom were on the verge of destruction. Without adverting to the eternal principles of hatred, which Tippoo had sworn on the Koran against the English, it unfortunately struck his Lordship, an opportunity was afforded, of displaying an heroic magnanimity and forbearance. Instead of reducing the haughty Sultan to the impossibility of ever again proving himself a dangerous foe to our Government, to convert, by such generosity, that Prince's innate and inherent prejudice, and bring him to the duties, hereafter, of a good and faithful ally, intending him, from this conversion, to serve as a bar against the increasing power of the Mahrattas and the Nizam's. Such a hope could only have been created, and was consistent alone, with European notions, false, and impracticable, with the least promise of success, in regard to Oriental dispositions. The moment that I heard of it at Patna, I and other civil servants of that station expressed our sense of its absurdity. We predicted what would be the result. Our minds were satisfied, it would only tend to generate fresh seeds of discontent, and that the active mind of that Prince would never be at rest, until he had recovered, by renewed exertions, his lopped off territories.

From the instant his pen had signed and ratified the treaty, these exertions were secretly at work, and were brought to operate in full force in 1799, when by the transcendant genius genius of a Wellesley, they were rendered abortive, and ended with the loss of his possessions and life.

I well recollect, I applied the mistaken part which his Lordship had acted to that anecdote which I knew relative to the Czar Peter the Great and the celebrated Duke of Richelieu. The Czar being at Paris, and a great admirer of the talents for Government which the Duke's great uncle, the Cardinal de Richelieu, had shewn when first Minister of State, paid his Grace the compliment to select him for his companion, when viewing that perfection of architecture, the Cardinal's Mausoleum. In his extasy for the character, he suddenly exclaimed: "Would to God thou wert living, gladly would I give thee one half of my extended empire to teach me, *like thee*, to govern the other half!" Here the monarch seem buried in reflection. Not so the Duke. He turned to the gentlemen of his suite and aptly observed, "Were this division to take place the Cardinal would never be at rest, until he had deprived him of the other half."

Lord Cornwallis resigned his Government in September, 1793, and the pliant Sir John Shore, who when in Council, as Mr. Shore, had opposed the inversion of property proposed by his Lordship, who had revolted at the new doctrine introduced, of the Zemindar being the proprietor of his land, but under certain rights and titles described in the tenure, which if not observed by the occupant, rendered him amenable to a forfeiture of his occupancy, now unblushingly stood forth, when succeeding to the Government, to put into execution these new fangled maxims, and on a sudden, completely changing his principles, conferring on these Zemindars the right of hereditary property, subject alone to an annual fixed rent, as unchangeable as inalienable. Here was a prostitution of character, which not one of his brother servants ever thought would have been displayed by the man who, at the head of the Board of Revenue, firmly contended against this innovation, as not only having an impolitic tendency, but, in its principle, actually bearing no ground to justify the hasty conclusion adopted; and who, besides, when he found the arbitrary *je le veux* determined upon endeavoured at least to mitigate the evil consequences, by representing that a settlement in perpetuity could not well be effected, but under the complete knowledge of a regular assessment having previously been formed and obtained which process would necessarily involve a few years consideration and attention, and wisely, therefore, suggested a decennial settlement being enacted, liable to a confirmation *for ever*; where the assessment was fully ascertained to have been judicious, and proportionate, which proof could easily be derived, during that given period, from the payment of the rents being easily made, and without any deduction being required.

Thus, were new rights established for a description of persons, who never dreamt they should enjoy such, much less would ever have thought to have claimed them. It suited the Author of this nefarious system to persuade his Lordship that its adoption would render his name immortal. It enabled him to serve those *tried friends* in his district, who had so eminently contributed to the raising of the immense fortune which he carried out of the country with him. No matter what ensued. The personal ends were answered. The public ones were sacrificed. The Sovereign lost for ever that right which had been vested in him from time immemorial, *viz.*, being Lord of the Soil, and allowing to the occupant the right of possession, from generation to generation, on occasional renewals of tenure, where *no cause of forfeiture* existed.

The reader will here clearly discern that this created a separation from that dependency to the state, so essential to be preserved in Eastern States. It effectually deprived the Sovereign of the pleasing power of remitting to his tenant, oppressed in his stipulated payments, by the unexpected misfortune arisen to him for the rigour of the elements. It debarred him equally from a prospect of increase of rent to the state, by stimulating honest industry, in a distribution of suitable pecuniary advances, tending to promote cultivation. These were ties of long standing and which had uniformly obtained. They were every year scrupulously adhered to in that ceremony of the *Pooneah*, where the subject met the representative of his Lord with due obedience, and in the constant hope of a remission to his fixed rent, in alleviation of real known loss incurred, or receiving from Government a certain advance "Tuccavey," reimbursable in fixed proportions, and stated periods, where the intention was manifested of bringing lands into product, which long lain fallow, or such arable ones, as were deemed fit for tillage.

Further, to exemplify how averse they were to such a change, in no instance did they consider a greater grievance having befallen them. They contemplated, with a melancholy reflection, their consequence as Zemindars, entirely done away, by rendering their occupancies, which for generations had regularly descended to them from their ancestors, liable to be transferred to others, by a sale of a part of the whole for arrears of a rent, hardly, incorrectly, and ignorantly imposed, with the exception of those who received their new possessions on favoured reduced assessments. Distraint by confinement, even stripes, where arrears existed, was deemed preferable by them. It had obtained for ages, and custom in endeavouring to impose on the landlord, by making the best terms for the farm, or procuring from his indulgence unseasonable remissions, had sanctioned such endeavours with no disgrace. Whereas the lopping off of a branch of their Zemindary, was cruelly felt by them, and engendered an inherent discontent, which no future compensation could remove ; and to cause it to operate with greater disgust, this clause was newly introduced and inserted in their cabooleats (agreements) which they were compelled to sign, with every hazard of distress, or to see themselves ejected from these lands, the superintendence and management of which had for ages devolved to their trust.

In my work, written at the desire of a friend, not published for sale, but distributed to friends, and subsequently to every gentleman in the direction, entitled, "Answer to Mr. Law's Rising Resources," will be seen my decided opinion of its fallacy and impolicy. The former could not be doubted by those versed in the nature of India customs, laws and revenue; the latter has been evinced by the evil consequences which have followed.* I will make allowances for the man, who, having the first station within his reach offered him, can sacrifice to obtain that end any doubtful or erroneous opinions which he might till then have entertained; but for one, bred up in the service, and to whom every one looked up for information, not only in the revenue line, where he had long conspicuously shone as the oracle, but, likewise,

* The Rev. Dr. Buchanan, in his Statistical Survey of the Province of Dinagepore, says: "It is evident from the *Ayen Acbarry*, there were *no hereditary proprietors* of land. The natives allege *the office* of Zemindar has always, *under certain conditions*, been hereditary. They then *accounted to Government*, for their receipts; —and they now declare, *they have been injured by the new settlement.*" *Vide*, likewise, James Grant's opinion and Wilks on the same subject, so ably detailed in their celebrated publications. "Even" saith Wilks, to mark his strong disapprobation of the innovation, "after that period, when the pestilent doctrine of the Sovereign being the *actual*, instead of the *figurative* proprietor of the soil, began to be promulgated by the British Government."

And again, comparing what obtains in the Deccan with Bengal "The terms *Meerass* and *Meerassdar* have since been continued, under the British administration, but for the purpose of assimilating everything to the system of Bengal, where a proprietor, *unknown to the history of India*, had for some years been created under the modern name of Zemindar, these *occupants of absolute dominion in landed property* were declared to possess merely the hereditary right of cultivation."

in every point which comprised the laws and ancient usages of India, to at once sacrifice at the shrine of office every idea and knowledge which had rendered his communication an object essential for reference, is such a dereliction of all manly steadiness, as cannot too sufficiently be exposed. I shall abstain from further remark on this point, and only proceed to exhibit the want of energy, arising alone from indolence and supineness which pervaded his Government during a period of five years.

I shall only illustrate to this effect the following points; the first, Sir John Shore suffering calmly the Nizam to be attacked and overwhelmed by the Mahrattahs, contrary to the faith of the guarantee treaty between *the three contracting* powers, in the treaty of Seringapatnam, *viz*, the English, the Nizam, and the Mahrattahs.

The consequence of this (call it by the most moderate terms an impolitic oversight) was the two English battalions, which were stationed with the Nizam, being ignominiously dismissed from his service, and which act conduced to raising the French force under Monsieur Raymond to that formidable and imminent state, which, in a short time after it acquired; and which said force would effectually have been turned against the English, assisted with the whole power of the Nizam, and dictated by his just resentment, after the convention of Kurdlah with the Mahrattahs, had not, most opportunely, the death of the Peshwah Mehadoorow,* and the rebellion of the

* [Mádava Ráo died 12th February 1794.]

Nizam's son Ally Jah occurred, to divert him from his meditated revenge, even, when the Nizam feeling his imprudence in trusting his kingdom to such means of defence, offered *to dismiss the French Corps*, provided the English force, which he required to be stationary in his dominions, was increased. Sir John hesitated, and gave up the proffered alliance, thinking, as his weakness led him to express, such an acquiescence might give umbrage to the Mahrattahs; and thus was so favourable an opportunity lost, both in reducing the expence of the Company's Madras Army, and securing, by an efficient strength, *viz.*, six battalions of Sepoys, with a proportion of artillery, which the Nizam demanded, the certain alliance of this Prince.

The same supineness was manifested by Sir John with regard to the corps which had been raised by De Boigne and was afterwards commanded by General Perron. This corps was kept so independent of the Prince Mehdajee Scindiah's authority, that not a doubt existed, even had Scindiah's own inclination not led to it, but that it would, in the event of the French having landed, have forced this Prince to have taken a decided part against the English Government.

The third may be reckoned in the neglect shown to court Mehadajee Scindiah's alliance. With the political observers of those days it became a point of general conversation and astonishment. It was well known that the uncle, and subsequently the nephew Dhowlah Row Scindiah had manifested a desire of entering into a treaty offensive and defensive; in one instance, when he marched to Poonah, to support the Peshwah

Badjeerow, in another instance, when he apprehended a meditated attack of his territorial possessions in Hindustan by Zemaun Shah. In an acquiescence of either of these propositions the French party would never have risen to that preponderance, as to have caused an imminent danger, when joined, with those whom it was intended they should act, to the British Government.

Finally, what can be said in the omission of selecting a successor to Hyder Beg Khan when his death was announced, and who had been the Minister in whom the Government implicitly trusted for the good management of the Nawab Vizier's affairs? And in his place, allowing to be introduced men whom he knew nay avowed the knowledge of being in their dispositions hostile to the State? In this same spirit did he admit of Vizier Ally succeeding to Asoph-ul-Dhowlah, however, in his elaborate minute, drawn up with the utmost sophistry, he declares his sense of the former's notorious spurious birth, and this, notwithstanding, Saadut Aly, the real and undoubted heir, after the death of his elder brother, to their father Shujah-ul-Dhowlah's dominions had, in order to secure his inheritance, invoked British faith, and appealed to the justice of the administration.

What was the result of these injudicious measures? No other than what almost every man, foreseeing their impolitic tendency, had decried; Sir John was obliged to repair in person to Lucknow, with the known view of deposing the creature whom he had, I may say, ephemerally raised, and the same wretch, when giving a feast to his benefactor, whose lenity he was imploring, meditated the same treachery and revenge against the English, which he, afterwards, too unhappily effected in the person of the much regretted and accomplished Mr. Cherry, the Resident, when his horrid massacre took place at Benares, the city allotted for this traitor to reside in, after his forced abdication, on a munificent pension, far exceeding his deserts. Fortunately, for the safety of Sir John's person, and those gentlemen who composed his retinue, the late Major-General Macgowan, who commanded the troops appointed to escort and protect the Governor-General, suspecting an act of this kind was hatching, directed the Grenadiers of the body-guard, which served as orderlies, to mingle with the servants who were attendants behind the gentlemen's chairs, and thus overawe the intent. In the end it was well ascertained, nothing, but this order could have contributed to their safety; Vizier Aly having harboured the villainous design of having them all stabbed by confidential dependents, on his giving the signal, by plunging his own dagger into Sir John's body.

Sir John Shore gave charge over of his Government in 1798, and Lord Wellesley arrived in May that same year to assume that station, which, in the wisdom of the legislature, had been, but just in time, conferred on this conspicuous nobleman. Discovering at once the faults which his predecessor had committed, he sought to remedy them by a spirit and energy which would impress on the natives, the administration was a far different one

RICHARD COLLEY WELLESLEY—
MARQUIS WELLESLEY.

to that which, from the abdication of Hastings, they had been accustomed to behold. In the short space of one year he had caused the corps under Monsieur Raymond to be disbanded, and the British influence re-established at the Nizam's Court, and this without bloodshed. Above two hundred French officers, who had hoisted the tri-coloured flag, and dictated laws in that Prince's capital, whose bread they eat, and would, with above fourteen thousand troops well appointed, have joined Bonaparte, had he made good his landing on the Malabar Coast, from Egypt, were constituted prisoners of war, and lost those situations which the apathy of Sir John Shore, by not attempting to disturb them, had occasioned them to consider themselves firmly seated in. Equally did his Lordship transport himself to Madras, and bringing the whole weight of Government with him, employed it immediately, and effectually, in completing, by the operations of one campaign, the inveterate enemy to the British, Tippoo Sultan's destruction.

Lord Clive was graced with the appellation of the "Heaven born General." Well might Lord Wellesley have equally had the title of "Heaven born Legislator" bestowed on him. The vigor of mind, which early shone forth in his administration, was the theme of general praise in every one's mouth—even those who had flattered themselves with the hope of acting as mentors to his Lordship, Messrs. Speke and Cowper, both *then* in the Supreme Council, stood petrified with the fund of knowledge and wisdom displayed. The latter, more arrogant and presuming than the other, and confiding so strongly in the indispensable necessity of the Governor having always in his ear such a flapper, met with a severe rebuff in his attempt, which caused him to desist for the future. It happened on a day when Lord Wellesley, being particularly occupied, chose to be closetted with his own mind, and had directed his servants not to permit any person having access to him. This order, Mr. Cowper, who called, unfortunately, at that juncture, could not interpret into a denial of one of his Lordship's *Privy* Counsellors, and men joined with him as members of his Government. He chose to consider himself, and his co-adjutor Speke, as exceptions, and pressing this point on his Lordship's Chubdar, (Usher) prevailed on him to announce to His Excellency that Counseller Cowper was in waiting, and desirous of speaking with him. Lord Wellesley, with that coolness of conduct and prompt decision which marked every action of his, returned his compliments, informing Mr. Cowper, when he should wish to see him in Council that he would receive from the Secretary of Government a regular summons, and when at the Government house, *viz.*, his Lordship's own palace, he should by a special card express his request to his effect. Such was the Chubdar's consternation, who had been in the same office with Lord Wellesley's predecessor and accustomed to contemplate the Governor and Council in that reign, as the trinity in unity, that he could scarcely utter out the message he was charged with. Even the Sepoy sentinel, who had, from the Chubdar's authority, permitted Mr. Cowper to ascend the great staircase, and enter the antichamber to the audience room, described by his looks his amazement at the result. In that pointed manner did every hope cease of having a Governor in leading strings, concluding him, as they did, completely divested of every local knowledge. These gentlemen, who had fed their vanity, with the promise of playing the part of rulers, founding their expectation, from the latter circumstance, *viz.*, *a non-residence in India*, were happy enough, afterwards, to be considered as rays emanating from the same splendid beams, and this, by the indulgence of opinion, admitted, in some measure, to be thought partakers of his radiance and glory.

It is no new observation, but one derived from long experience, that the incidents of fortune often arise from the most unexpected circumstances, and the luck, I may say, of the moment. In no instance could this remark have been more illustrated then regarding Mr. Speke, of whom I have spoken, and myself. Mr. Edward Payne, the Bank Director, who has been mentioned in the preceding part, was our friend and protector. Under his patronage, and from his personal solicitation and interest, we owed our appointments of writers in the Company's services, and the said friend had neglected no opportunity of assisting our views, by constant recommendations to those in India, whose situations afforded them the power of obliging their friend, by attending to his wishes. The said person, when in 1789 the question of nominating a Regency was at issue, and every adherent to Mr. Pitt dreaded his being forced out of the administration, had an opportunity of shewing his, and the sense of the commercial interest in London, for the great services rendered to them by the minister. The disinterestedness of Mr. Pitt was so well known, as to have created a fear, he might be thrown into serious pecuniary difficulties, by the change of party to guide the reins of Government; and apprehending this might work, prejudicially to the nation, on his proud spirit, the respectable mercantile body of the city determined, he should, at least go into opposition independent of monied embarassments. For this purpose a Committee was assembled, and the election to the chair fell on Mr. Payne, who waited on Mr. Pitt, with the request he would accept from his friends the sum of fifty-thousand Pounds which had been subscribed. The minister rejected this munificence, but forgot not his gratitude to the donors. The sequel is well known, by the uncommon address of Mr. Pitt, the firmness of his supporters, with the imprudent discussion of *Right*, brought on by Mr. Fox, to the exercise of the Kingly authority, *inherently devolving* to the Heir Apparent, *subject to no provision* from the Legislature, in the event of the sovereign's incapacity, the question was so spun out, as to have caused the necessity, which had existed, becoming superseded from the Monarch's recovery.

In the subsequent year, the resignation of Sir John Macpherson, as one of the Supreme Council of Bengal,* had occurred, Admiral Affleck, one of the sea companions in glory with Mr. Speke's father, Captain

* [January 17th, 1787.]

Speke,* the Captain of the flagship of Admiral Watson, at the taking of Chandernagore, and equally distinguished before in Hawke's memorable engagement against Conflans, immediately thought this vacation created a hope of serving the son of their old friend. Knowing the kind disposition of Mr. Payne, with whom a good act was always a gratification, he posted to town, and suggested to him the application. This gentleman, without reflecting that the relation to his family, *and to whose interests he had ever bestowed a preference*, was equally eligible to the situation, solicited for Mr. Speke, and obtained readily the minister's consent. By such a caprice of fortune was I ejected, from acting in that sphere, to which, if I had been appointed, I can safely declare, I should have been more tenacious of my brother servants *covenanted rights*, than what Mr. Speke evinced to have been, particularly in my case; I reproached him with his suffering those rights to have been violated, when sitting at the same Council Board with Lord Cornwallis. He could not but acquiesce, that he might have urged them, and resisted the measure of my recall, by a protest to this effect, had his Lordship chosen to persist, in defiance of the objection raised, and which was founded on so solid a ground. Nevertheless, he alleged his conviction of having acted, to the best of his judgment, for his friend. In his opinion, it was prudent to allow of the

* *Vide* Ives' Voyage, and Lord Kaime's Essays, for a character of this respectable officer.

torrent gushing out its foam, and when its force was expended, to bring it to flow more mildly, and consistent with reason,—I could not approve. The mischief had been done. It was irreparable. All that remained, was to regret the effect of Speke's *distempered* sensibility. I would have called his my misled friend, had not his acts of friendship been so much at variance with prudence and justice.

Mr. Charles Purling, an old Bengal Civil Servant, who happened, at this juncture to be in England, had laid in his claims for the succession, and been actually the favored candidate, until Mr. Payne's intercession, in behalf of Mr. Speke, distanced with the Minister all other Competitors. Mr. Payne returned from Downing Street, to Leadenhall, with Mr. Pitt's authorisation to signify to the Chairman and Deputy, Mr. Speke had his best wishes for the nomination. The friends of Mr. Purling then endeavoured to persuade Mr. Payne, he was doing an act of disservice to Mr. Speke, since this gentleman, possessing at that moment the joint appointment of Collector of Radeshy and Resident of the Durbar, would not willingly resign them for an office of less emolument. Mr. Payne did not chime in with such doctrine. He naturally conceived, it would be more flattering for his friend to attain the summit to which his ambition could have looked to reach, rather than have continued in a subordinate office, however more beneficial. In his letter to Speke, announcing the joyful tidings, was this motive detailed, and in the honesty of his worthy heart, he ended by apologizing. *If he had done wrong*, *viz.*, in contributing essentially, nay, being the sole cause of an appointment of Government, with a salary, receivable in Europe, of ten thousand Pounds Sterling per annum, conferred on his friend.

I was too much indebted to Mr. Payne's good office; I respected too much his character, to permit myself, in my next letter to him, any phrase which might be construed into upbraiding him, with having preferred one, estranged from his family, to another so nearly related. I, merely, observed, (after congratulating him on the weight, which this event had displayed so conspicuously, he possessed with the Minister, and which could not be owing, but to the brilliant reputation in which his services stood, when Governor of the Bank in two successive years, *viz.*, 1771 and 1772, the period in which the alarming failures of Sir George Colebrooke and Fordyce's Houses occurred), that I hoped he would recollect me, should a similar occasion present itself, having equal claim, being that of above twelve years actual residence in the Civil Service in India, and besides, having my years of military service to plead. The answer which I received was, that he had not adverted at the moment, to the spirit of the Act of Parliament, regarding those who could be claimants for such distinctions, and, in fact, he had considered the selection of one, was similar to both being nominated, since he judged, we would, reciprocally, be entitled to each other's good offices, knowing, as he did, our mutual esteem and attachment. I am sorry to state, these sentiments were obliterated, and ended completely on the part of Mr. Speke when his unexpected transition elevated him to so superior a sphere.

I have already mentioned, that from Sir John Shore's determination not to restore an old servant, cruelly used by his predecessor, I was compelled before Lord Wellesley's arrival, to address a memorial to the Court of Directors, and having forwarded it, to repair in person for its support.

And, here, from the consequences to which I fell a devoted victim, have I most sincerely to regret, that I did not await the effect of his noble successor's truly liberal disposition. In the preceding administrations, others of my brother-servants has been, from various causes, *suspended from office*, and left on the shelf *without a trial.* His Lordship adverting to the situation of a covenanted servant, precluded from every hope of advancement to independence, but by actual employment, summoned these gentlemen to attend him.

In a discourse truly marking his great mind, he told them, he should not go into any inquiry, that, probably, the punishment they had endured, had met with a just requital, for the errors which they had committed ; that, however, he approved of strong discountenance, for any deviation of good conduct, yet, he could not give his sanction to a system, which in his enlightened conception, bordered on persecution, and therefore, they might hope of being re-employed, with every trust from Government, that, what had past, would cause them to be more cautious for the future.

CHAPTER XIII.

Final Departure from India.

I, accordingly, embarked on board of a vessel, carrying neutral colours, in February 1799. She belonged to Hamburgh, and had been purchased by her owners, from having before served as a frigate. The Captain gave out that her sailing was superior, and that he was wooded, watered, and provisioned for four months, the time which he calculated, she would, from the Bengal river, without touching at any intermediate port, reach the English channel, where, he engaged to disembark any passengers which might make their election of going with him. Such an offer and promise was too flattering to my views, not to avail myself of it. I feared a delay at St. Helena for convoy and I deemed it an object of being on the spot, to urge the purport of my memorial, so soon, as possibly, the voyage could be accomplished. We soon, therefore, came to terms, and on the 4th February, I went on board, my fellow passengers were Captain Williamson, of the Bengal infantry, with Lieutenant Richardson of the same corps, and Lieutenant Raban of the artillery. We had, likewise, a Mahomedan of distinction, Mirza Aboo Taleb Khan. Our Captain had pledged his word to be on board to receive us, instead of which, he loitered some days in Calcutta, and brought to us in Saugur roads, the *joyful Tiding*, that an embargo on the shipping had been directed by Government, from the *La Forte*, a French frigate, being known to cruize in Balasore Roads.

It may be judged how welcome his reception was by us ;—the *sang froid* of the animal made him indifferent to our reproaches. Many a sigh did anxiety rent, whilst this delay existed. In the beginning of March, we heard a tremendous firing, and two days afterwards we saw the ship, which had caused our detention, towed as a wreck up the river by the gallant Cooke, who lost the honors which his victory had commanded by a glorious death from the wounds which had assailed him in his desperate encounter. On the 12th, the embargo was levied, and on the 13th, we sailed in company with other vessels, and our regret was, in some measure, appeased, from the superiority of sailing, which our vessel very soon evinced, she was capable of doing, having outstripped in her race, the rest of the fleet.

Scarcely, however, had our good humour returned, than we had full reason again to mourn. The Captain declared, he must water at the Nicobar Islands. This detained us full eight days, and having supplied ourselves with water and fruit, we pursued our journey. But, alas, with unavailing hope for a speedy relief. We had missed the season for a summer passage round the Cape of Good Hope, and it was not to be regained. The consequence, which arose from our procrastination was, our being baffled by contrary winds for twenty-six days, after we had seen Point Natal, encountering contending gales, and after being exposed to every danger which a ship in raging tempestuous seas could incur, the vessel, likewise, having been struck with lightning, it pleased the Divine Providence to bring us in miraculously into False Bay, where we anchored on the 19th of June.

In such a conflict of distress, anxiety, and disappointment, my fellow-passengers got weary and sick. I was the only one who could keep the deck, and at three in the morning of that propitious day, I announced to each the cheerful intelligence of their unexpected preservation, and deliverance, from such a ship, crew, and Captain.

Never did I come on shore with a heart more grateful to Providence. My friends had lost all hope, and appeared resigned. I confess mine was not very sanguine. Still I trusted. But, when, after having rounded the Cape, accidentally driven by the currents, and prosecuting our voyage to St. Helena, with a fair wind, and with a confidence of there being on board *eighteen* butts of water, the Captain, even without any question of that nature put to him, having, the preceding day, voluntarily declared, possessing that quantity, I saw the Tableland sixty miles on our stern and with the finest breeze, the ship at once changing her course, and proceeding to that land, from the Chief Officer having acknowledged the truth of only *two* butts remaining, I freely avow my thoughts were gloomy. The dread of a want of water bore heavy on my mind, far more than the dangers we had experienced. As we approached, Table Bay, I entreated, in my behalf, and my fellow-passengers, the Captain to put us on shore, with one trunk of linen for each person, pledging our words, we would for this condescension, cry quit with him, and absolve him from every other consequence. No, No, was the brute's constant answer. Providence, as I have said, interposed for us, and against every probability which existed at seven in the morning of the 18th June, brought us the next morning at three to anchor in False Bay.

We landed as early as daylight permitted, and before evening, housed as we were, we had full opportunity to contemplate and appreciate the value of a fine day, in this latitude, and in the midst of winter; for there came on a storm of rain, hail, thunder, etc., which, lasting for three days, confined us to the house we inhabited, and in which we uttered many a thanksgiving for having escaped the effect of this severe gale at sea. So soon as it had subsided, and we had got part of our baggage on land, we set off for Cape Town, and amidst a pleasing society of which the Garrison was composed, soon buried in oblivion the hardship we had suffered.

It may well be supposed, not one of us ever thought of confiding ourselves with such a Captain again. We informed him thereof; and however the flagrant breach of his engagement, we wished not to distress the man, but told him plainly, we should expect half of our passage money to be refunded, not entertaining the most distant idea of continuing our voyage with him. This offer of an amicable settlement he peremptorily refused. The consequence was, we sued him in the Court of Justice, and he was equitably condemned to repay one-half of the sum which he had received, besides incurring his own costs, with the law charges, which we had likewise been debited with.

During my sojournment here, I met in one of the Magazines, the death of my cousin Mr. Réné Payne the only friend of any weight which I had in England and on whose kindness and attachment to me, independent of his strong feelings against oppression, I depended much for the pursuits of my object. His loss startled me for the issue I knew who I attacked, and with whom I had to contend I was aware also, that demands of arrears, justly due, would not meet with a ready ear. Still, hoping for justice, I determined to proceed to England.

No immediate opportunity occurring for a passage to England, and apprehending to meet the winter, after a continued residence of three and twenty years in the warm climate of Bengal, I prolonged my stay at the Cape. In January 1800, after having in vain awaited for a returned home Indiaman I agreed with Captain Robertson of the merchant brig Reguloes for my accommodation, and we sailed on the 14th. The other gentlemen with me were Captain Granger and Lieutenant Tucker of the Royal Navy and Captain Charles Morgan of the 8th Dragoons. Besides these, there was an African born, a Mr. Vermack, who was banished the colony, for having, in an intercepted letter, expressed a wish to his Correspondent in

Holland, that the same revolutionary principles which had taken place in that country, should soon spread their influence in his native soil. This was considered so Jacobinical an act, as to merit the reprobation of Government, and he was, accordingly, embarked on board of this vessel, as a prisoner of State.

I had never seen him, till we met afloat, and having been recommended to my attention and compassion by two families, who had, during my sojournment in Cape Town, bestowed their civilities on me, I was prepared to mitigate the rigor of his situation, by every kindness in my power. His appearance was not prepo ssessing. It did not, however, inspire an idea of his being capable to hatch treason. I listened to his tale, read such papers as he brought forth in palliation, and felt disposed from their perusal, and his relation, to attribute his error, more to absurdity and imprudence, than an intentional criminal act. In the state of the Colony, filled with many a restless being, it was proper in Government to check, in the first instance, this spirit which was breaking forth, and might have weakened its authority. When we arrived at St. Helena the Governor, my old respectable Bengal friend, Colonel Brooke, allowed him, from my mediation, to come on shore and live quietly, and, without wandering over the island, in a house and under a charge appointed to this trust. This I thought was a sufficient indulgence. In the course of the journey from the Cape to the Island, and from thence to England, I had remarked, when he came on deck, a seeming uneasiness prevail. His eyes looked wildly around every direction. He then saluted me, and with a grateful sigh exclaimed, "No ship in sight." I could not but think this constant exclamation bore some particular meaning. I questioned him, and after several fruitless attempts, at length extorted from him, that his sigh proceeded from a relief of fear and which fear was founded on the certainty which he had entertained, and which the opinion of his Jacobin companions in Cape Town had caused him to imbibe, *viz.*, that the Captain had *secret* instructions, to throw him over board in the event of his vessel being chased at sea. I can assure my readers, it was some time, before I could persuade him, no English Government would ever have issued such an order, nor would any English Commander have obeyed one to this purport.

Until within a degree and a half of the Western Islands, we enjoyed at sea the pleasantest weather imaginable; but on the 12th of March, we encountered the Equinoctial gale. The sun burst that morning from the horizon with a most fiery aspect, surrounded by red clouds, reflecting the brightest splendor. I observed its beauty; the Captain said it portended wind and my friend Morgan, who was walking the deck with me, expressed his hope it would be a gale, having never been in one, and wishing to see how our little bark would be tossed about. A look of indignation was bestowed on him from our Commander, and before evening, his desire was amply gratified, for the vessel was obliged to be lain to, the hatches battened, and every preparation made to meet the disasters of the night. It blew with the utmost fury, the sea broke repeatedly over, shivered our bowsprit in pieces, and carried away our foretopmast, throwing the brig on her beam ends, and exposing us to the most imminent danger, until the Chief Mate, a daring seaman, and excellent navigator, relieved us from our immediate fears, by having a cord thrown around his waist, and, springing over board, cleared the wreck from the rigging. About noon on the 13th, the tempest not decreasing, and the vessel laboring much, the Captain came down to the great cabin, expressing his intent to rid himself of his guns, as he thought it would ease her considerably; but, at the same time noticed, if it pleased God to save us, he knew not how he should answer such a measure to his owners, unless he had a certificate denoting its necessity. His Majesty's Naval officers having remained on deck, I took upon myself to be the spokesman. "Go, Sir," said I, "cast every gun into the sea, and be assured of our signature to any paper which it may please you to draw out, for the purpose you have requested it in the event of our surviving." Accordingly, five minutes after we had the pleasure of hearing them pop over the sides, and the effect from the adoption of this measure fully answered.

In the evening the gale came on with redoubled rage; the horrors of that night, I can scarcely describe; the men fatigued; the boat washed over board; everything swept clean off the deck; one of the dead lights in the cabin stove in; all foreboded our speedy end. It pleased the Almighty however to preserve us. Oppressed with want of rest I had sunk into a gentle dose, when the Captain by seven on the morning of the 14th, agreeably disturbed me, by informing me the gale had subsided, and if I would come upon deck, I could convince myself, by seeing a clear horizon driving before it the heavy clouds which had assailed us. In fact, it was worth remarking. The black tremendous clouds ascending, with a bright sky beneath them, looked precisely, and might justly be compared, to light dispelling darkness.

At noon on that day we had an observation, which taught us, that we had driven a degree and a half to the Southward, and consequently, had we been in a latitude parallel to those Islands, *viz.*, in 39 degrees, instead of being in 37½ when the gale commenced, we must inevitably have been wrecked and perished on them. Fortunately, we had sea-room enough for our bark, exposed as she was to the mercies of the seas, to float in the direction we drifted.

The Captain's first care was to repair the damage done, so well as he was able, and the next, was to gain the first port, we steered therefore for Lisbon, destitute of every fresh provision, and the salt beef and rice, even impregnated with salt water.

On the morning of the second day, and within one degree of our destined port, we fell in with the Lisbon and Oporto fleet, convoyed by the *Bellerophon*, Captain Darby, whose ship, by the number of shot holes imprinted on her, bore evident marks of the gallantry which the brave Captain and his crew had displayed in the recent battle of the Nile. He stopped to speak us, and learning that Captain Granger had despatches for the Admiralty Board from Admiral Sir Roger Curtis, the Admiral who commanded the Naval station at the Cape of Good Hope, and Lieutenant Tucker, from Sir George Yonge, the Governor, he took them on board, but, however I mentioned having likewise despatches from the Company's Agent at the Cape of Good Hope, I could not get his ear to listen to my request of being transported to his ship, neither was my friend Captain Morgan more fortunate. Captain Darby was of that species of seamen, who consider military men as land sharks, and deprecated any defence of Old England, than by her wooden batteries. He appealed to the condition in which the ship appeared, with the pumps continually going, to excuse his parting with either mast, spar, or rigging of any kind, but told us to keep in his wake, and if he saw a necessity of doing it, he would veer out a cable, and take the vessel in tow.

This was sad discouragement to men who had lived well to the moment of the recent disaster we had met with; the Captain gave up all idea of steering for Lisbon, and subscribed to joining the convoy under the conditions prescribed. Our only relief consisted in a few oranges, Port wine, and Portugal plums, which at an immoderate price, we got out of one of the Leith traders, and this, with our damaged stores, was to serve us, until we were fortunate enough to reach an English harbor.

Luckily, for our comfort, the Commander observed, that notwithstanding the damaged state of the vessel, we could yet sail in one day, what the fleet, under convoy, would be performing in two. This was improved on by the Mate the next evening, for during his watch, we contrived to separate, and, however, the Captain felt angry with the neglect, yet he yielded at last to persuasion, *viz.*, that it was better to make the best of our way to England, than remain longer in so destitute a situation.

Nevertheless, we had nearly suffered, for quitting the man of war's protection. Entering the English Channel, we espied early in the morning a suspicious vessel on our larboard beam, and as we continued our course, we evidently saw, she was bearing down upon our vessel, with an apparent intention of intercepting our progress. we were to windward, and the Captain, bearing up two points, threw her at a greater distance. She persisted in her course with a press of sail, and succeeded, so far, as to bring up within musket shot of our stern, raking us with two vollies of balls which happily had no effect. This she did in a truly piratical way, for she fired without hoisting any colors. We perceived her deck full of men, and having failed in her object, she put about, and crowded every sail she could hoist, having discerned, sooner than we did, an English frigate in chase of her. This proved to be the *Flora*, Sir Thomas Williams, who, in about half an hour afterwards, hailed us, and receiving an answer in the negative to his enquiry, "whether it was requisite for him to send a prize master on board?" which question was made in the supposition that we had, bereft as he saw us of guns, and any means of defence, struck our colors to the privateer, pursued with ardour his design to cut her off, before she could reach any port on the French coast, crying out, he knew her, having been fitted out at Boulogne, and had committed many depredations in the Channel. We heard, with much satisfaction, subsequently, that his aim had been accomplished ; but though the fellow, who headed her operations, ought to have met his death on the yard arm, yet him and his comrades, when once prisoners, met with that generous treatment inseparable from English seamen.

CHAPTER IV.

IN ENGLAND AGAIN.

WE ran that night up Channel with a very favorable breeze, and about noon next day, having weathered with difficulty Beachy Head the fog having entangled us in the bay which the opposite points form, Morgan and I threw ourselves into the first Deal cutter we fell in with, the master of which bargained to set us on shore at Dover, for the small sum of eighteen guineas. Accordingly, at three in the morning of the 31st March, we found we were in Dover Harbor, after having spent a most tempestuous and rainy night, without any rest, at one moment threatened with our small boat going on shore, at another with being made prisoners, from a French lugger which had discerned us, and *was said* to be fast approaching. It did not require much penetration to conclude, all these different reports were occasionally conveyed into the cabin for the purpose of extorting more money from the Indian passengers which they thought, they had at mercy in their net. Morgan more irritable than I was, and indignant in reflecting the sum we had already been taxed at, put an end to such further tidings by giving them *an English blessing*, accompanied with the remark it was perfectly indifferent to us, whether stranded or becoming prisoners, so that we were rid of their clutches.

This intemperate conduct was soon revenged, for, we were told, that we could not land from the open boat in which we sat until the Collector would give his orders respecting us and servants, the cutter having anchored a small distance from shore, and another guinea from each demanded, for the conveyance afforded. Thus were we, in one of the coldest wet nights which could be experienced, seated from three till seven, most completely soused, and the reason given for it was, that it required a passport from the Alien office, before foreign servants could be admitted to land.

In this inhospitable place we staid no longer than to refresh ourselves and posted to London, when I delivered my dispatches at the India House, and proceeded to Fladong's Hotel in Oxford Street, where good fare, good warming, and good accommodations, concurred to obliterate all recollection of my past miseries.

I had now partly attained the point for which I quitted India fourteen months before. I was in London, where centered those to whose justice I had appealed for a redress of the wrongs which I had so long been afflicted with. I felt light, anticipating the end of my troubles. The reader will sympathise with me in viewing the disappointment of my just expectations.

I waited on the Chairman and each of the Direction respectively, after I had been made acquainted that my memorial, transmitted officially from Bengal, had not then been taken into consideration. I asked the

Secretary why and wherefore such delay had arisen. His answer was brief, "*A pressure of other business more important.*" I could not acquiesce in such a reason, and to refresh the memory of my Judges, and at once to bring the point before them in the most concise manner, so as to ensure their judgment, not wandering from what was submitted to their decision, I drew up the recital of my claims,* and which was founded on the basis of the memorial above alluded to, and thus left them to exercise their award fairly, on the statement of each demand, for the breach of which I solicited remuneration.

My old friends who were in the Direction, the companions of my early days, left their visiting cards in return and were anxious in showing me personal attention. Would to God the examination and sequel had rested with them! Unfortunately, it did not.

The late Mr. David Scott, who, from the most menial situation in life, had risen by accident in Bombay into wealth and power, and who, from such qualifications, ought never to have been entitled to a seat in the Direction, ignorant, absolutely, of covenanted rights, or of any privileges which the civil servants exclusively enjoyed, had by the chance of fate been placed in the deputy Chair, and, devoted to his patron the late Lord Melville, ruled with an absolute sway in Leaden Hall. With such a pliant and servile mind, any animadversion on the administration of a nobleman of such high rank, as the person who I complained

* Vide Appendix J.

against, was vested with could be no otherwise considered than tantamount to a criminal act; and correspondent to these sentiments, instead of fair investigation and subsequent judgment being resolved upon, the individual stood prejudged, guilt was concluded, and punishment denounced.

On the 5th of April 1801, this fatal measure took place. It was in vain I implored a suspension of this arbitrary deed until specific charges were adduced and replied to. Equally did a deaf ear obtain to the covenanted rights which I alleged and pleaded in my behalf, being highly violated by so unprecedented and illegal a resolution. It mattered not. In the Secret Committee it had been carried by Scott's influence. Lord Cornwallis was then Lord Lieutenant of Ireland, His Majesty's representative for that kingdom; and who was the reptile daring enough to arraign the justice of so great a character.

In short, power and wealth were in one scale, poverty and insignificance in the other; the latter could not be considered of weight, with men impregnated with despotic maxims, peculiar to Eastern sovereignty, where the monarch, or his satellites, continually adjudge the balance in favour of the richest. The man of distinction alone, with them, commands attention, whilst the poor one, destitute of friends and means to influence judgment, must ever be in the wrong. Sorry am I to say that these unworthy motives had polluted and pervaded the walls of Leaden Hall, and which actuated those, to whose impartial justice I had appealed, in the decree which they pronounced.

I may be thought too severe, but I am not so without cause and proof. Let the English reader particularly view with reflection, what befell me, and his mind will revolt against such a proceeding. I challenge those who exist to disprove, weaken, or set aside the strength of my assertions. They are grounded; and I feel, at this moment, in my position, an indispensable necessity to have recourse to them, in vindication of my fair fame.

I aver that I stood condemned without the opportunity, in any shape, having been afforded me, either of *answering*, *explaining*, *or even seeing*. Not even did the measure carry with it the palliative of the *summumjus summa injuria*. Its feature was singular.

I was oppressed, without an intention *ever existing* or even excusing such conduct, by adducing any proof in its support; and to sum up the climax, to form the acme, I may justly say, by methods equally irresistible by guilt or innocence.

Lord Chancellor Cowper says "The wisdom and goodness of our Our Law appears in nothing more remarkable, than in the perspicuity, certainty, and clearness of the evidence, which it requires to fix a crime, in which the life, liberty, or property of a man, is concerned; herein, we glory and pride ourselves, and are. justly, the envy of all our neighbours. Our Laws, in such cases, require evidence so clear, that every bystander who hears it, must be instantly satisfied for its truth. It admits of no forced constructions, or of anything, but what is according to the principles of natural justice."

This quotation, so applicable, calls for my remark, England, renowned for the wisdom of her Laws, and for the humane policy of its Criminal Code, the first and ruling principles of which are, that no person shall be held guilty, *till convicted by regular trial;* on the contrary, every person is held and presumed innocent, until the Law, and its operation, *formally* applied, pronounce him guilty.

In my case, the security of three thousand pounds given for me, by my relations and best friends, Edward and Réné Payne, Esqs., of London, warranted me as a *covenanted servant*, against such oppressive conduct. Yet, it took place, however, the Act of Parliament prescribed the terms to be observed, *where accusation was laid.* Even, this did not obtain, and illegally I was dispossessed, prejudged, and ruined *in the very face of that act.*

The most eminent Lawyers of that period, to whom I referred for an opinion in my case, declared I could prosecute and recover my claims from the East India Company, who, they deemed, accountable for the illegal acts of their servants. But where was the means to go to law with a corporate body? Where the number of years which would have been requisite? Where the hope of *substantial justice* against such powerful adversaries in the end?

In the letter notifying *the ex parte decision*, not a shadow of any reason was assigned. The memorable words "*Thought proper*" were *alone* used and adopted on the occasion. I need not, to an English ear, intimate and brand them as the sole expedients which tyrants have resort to, in order to veil or cover their perpetual injustice.

I must here bring in Mr. Barrow's allusion to this act. His misconstruction of it, impels me to elucidate. He is pleased to attach *change of principles*, and *change of name* (the latter, I apprehend, with the view to cover the *apostacy* of the former measure), to my ejection, and, eventually, to my translation to the Cape of Good Hope.

I shall pass over his preamble to these serious charges, with only one observation, *viz.*, that to a writer so flourishing and embellishing as Mr. Barrow, throughout the course of his work, entitled, "Travels in Africa," proves himself to be, that where the *why* and *wherefore* are found wanting to assign in reason of argument and quotation, nothing is so easy as the resource of saying, that I stood ejected from the Honourable Company's service, *for some reason or other.*

I shall equally refrain from that pointed and severe animadversion, which so unfounded an accusation might draw down on the author, from any other person, less inured than I am to the accustomed illiberality of the world when, such a downfall in life, as the one which I have experienced, has marked the individual for notice and unjust reflection. I shall confine myself alone to facts, leaving to the candid reader, to exercise his free judgment on the point submitted for decision ; trusting, with confidence both him, as well as Mr. Barrow, will lament the wrongs accumulated on a hoary head, from so great, to give it the meekest term, an inconsiderate assertion.

I resume.—Mr. Barrow is pleased to assert, that with my translation to the Cape, my principles had undergone a total inversion. In short, that I came swayed and biassed by a decided attachment to the French interest.

So far from any partiality of this nature having been manifested in any instance of my public conduct, I dare appeal to the sense of the British merchants residing in this colony, for my decided interference, when in power, having protected their persons and property, when the authority of Government was attempted, improperly, to be exerted against their interests.

They, like Englishmen, felt grateful for my interposition, and honoured me accordingly with their public thanks.

My family have ever had a powerful interest in Holland, several of the Grands having in remoter years served the Republic. In more recent times, my uncle Sir George Brand* (subsequently Baron

* His eldest daughter, with other officers' wives, proved of singular use to the relief of the wounded, and making up cartridges, during the siege of Savannah, when these ladies were refused by the impolite and inhumane *Invincible conqueror of Grenada* to refire on board of the ships, secured from the dangers of its operations. The journal of the American war details with its particulars their heroic conduct. Under this *Don Quiscotte* title, did Count d' Estaing, with a superior armed force commanded by General Lincoln, summon Lieutenant-General Prevost to surrender. A sister of Mrs. Prevost, and equally accomplished, was married likewise to a Swiss, Lieutenant-General Bouquet, in the service of Holland.

Grand, and grandfather to that distinguished commander in His Britannic Majesty's Service, the present Lieutenant-General Sir George Prevost, Baronet, etc., etc., one of the *two* Colonels for the Militia of Switzerland, habituated to the exercise of the troops, three months in the year, a corps of brave men composed of sixty thousand, and liable to be called out for the defence of their beloved land on the alarm given from signal posts, fixed on the highest mountains, within twenty-four hours, was at the head of the well known house at Amsterdam of Horneca, Hogguer, Grand, and Fizeaux (the latter of whom represented the firm at the head of a considerable House and Manufactory at St. Quentin), had been of signal service to Holland, and which merit, entitled him to a grateful remembrance. My father, at the head of a House in London and in Spain, an intimate friend and correspondent, of the House of Hope; all these were ties sufficient to influence a partiality for a descendant, whose talents and services were considered might be usefully employed in one of their colonies.

But admitting, for argument sake that my appointment had originated from the solicitation of another quarter, doth it follow? Will the impartial reader acknowledge? that such an entire conversion attaches because those of the highest consideration, appertaining to another nation, partook of a lively interest in an individual's welfare? Had such a sacrifice been required, no tie on earth would have caused me to assert; nor would any appointment have been sanctioned by the previous approbation of those revered friends in

England, who I consulted with on the occasion; and to whose opinion, had it been contrary, or affected with such sentiments, I would have bowed with submission.

Finally, to put it out of all doubt, I annex a literal copy of my Commission, together with a translation from the Dutch, for the English reader, relying for conclusion, that in his liberal mind, a sentiment will immediately arise, proceeding from its contents to the effect, that had I been capable of such a dereliction of every tie and principle of attachment which had marked my way through life, my selection would not have been, for the service of a nation, indirectly supposed to be connected with it at that juncture, however the Peace of Amiens had proclaimed and established its independency, but that it would have been directly under the banners and auspices of that same nation, with whom gifts and preferment, of a very superior nature existed to have bestowed on the individual, whose advancement in life formed the grateful solicitude of those who had so essentially in their power, benefits to confer.

To Sir Lionel Darell, Sir Francis Baring, Sir Thomas Theophilus Metcalfe, the Hon'ble Charles Elphinstone, George Smith, Esq., and Colonel Swiney Toone, I bow with gratitude for their endeavours in my behalf. They spoke against the measure, but as most corporate bodies delegate the management and business of their trust, to a few selected for the purpose, in whom the entire confidence rests, so were their interposition of no avail. The latter of these gentlmen, particularly came out of the room, and proposed to me, that, *by quitting my claims for remuneration*, and throwing myself at the mercy of the Direction, I should obtain the pension of a Senior Merchant out of employment, *viz.*, five hundred pounds per annum, a compromise, which I flatly refused, being, in its tendency, as disgraceful to my reputation, as injurious to those interested in my welfare, and eventual success in recovering my just dues.

These now became the immediate object, I quitted the ground of hope of continuance in the service, but maintained that of a servant not liable to be discharged, without a fair reckoning held by his masters, and his arrears of servitude liquidated in full. I exposed this case, as I mentioned before, to the opinion of eminent Lawyers, in particular, to those whose popularity of pleading the liberties and rights of individuals, contending with power, had risen their names to that height of fame, which such conduct and attention in their profession merited. I was satisfied with their opinions on the statement exhibited, but I found, that however the good foundation, which I had to act upon, the Company might spin out the suit which I brought against them, beyond the time. I might reasonably trust to the extension of my career in life; and, independent of this consideration it would require in its pursuit pecuniary means, of which I was totally destitute. I chimed in, therefore, with the advice of a few friends, to content myself with what was conceded, *viz.*, the reimbursement of the postage money claimed during my administration in Tirhoot, *viz.*, the principal alone (*however the principal being allowed to be due, the interest on that principal ought equally to have been adjudged*), and an annuity of one hundred pounds. They urged, that taking these, at that juncture, would not invalidate my reviving the rest of my claims, when an opportunity would be more favorable; and they obligingly added, it might possibly enable them to commute the whole, by a restoration to the service, with a good appointment, so soon, as that interest which governed then so despotically, had in time ceased and been diverted into another channel more promising to my views.

I now come to a conclusion; but previous thereto, I must introduce a contrast between the reward of services to Mr. Hastings and Lord Wellesley, and those honors conferred on Sir John Shore and Sir George Barlow.

Lord Wellesley, who prided himself in having embraced the political system, and having trod, throughout his splendid administration, in the steps of that great Legislator Warren Hastings, paying him the compliment, at the dinner given to Lord Wellesley in Willis' rooms, where, with the officers of state, and the Company's servants of every establishment, a numerous party sat down to table, that he (Mr. Hastings) would have left nothing for him (Lord Wellesley) to enact, had the former been vested with the same power, as the Legislature had thought proper the latter should carry out with him, was recalled, for being too profuse, scarcely allowing him time to consolidate the great empire he had formed, nay, disapproving of those measures, which distanced

THE MARQUESS OF WELLESLEY.
(Painted at Madras, 1799. By R. Home & J. Heath.)

for ever, all native competitors against the English preponderating influence; ejected every hope to the enemy of French local auxiliary aid, in the event of a French expedition to that country; and to crown the absurdity of such proceedings, instructed his successor Lord Cornwailis, whose faculties, whatever they might have been, the disgraceful peace of Amiens witnessed years before, were on the decline, to cede every acquisition of territory, and yield every advantage, which British valor, and the most judicious system, acted upon by men of decided talents, had, so gloriously for the British interest, obtained.

The death of Lord Cornwallis created a hope of a reversion in politics; but such was the pliability of Sir George Barlow's disposition, that, however he had supported Lord Wellesley's plans, he could, for the sake of holding the Government, fall in with the narrow policy, which men, not born to rule an empire, could think the safest system. Both him, and Sir John Shore, were rewarded with titles and honors; the one for endangering the loss of the country, from a want of decision, in not acting, as opportunity, convenience, and prudence dictated; the other, for inviting every concession, which courage and talent had cemented; and, in the midst of the highest pinnacle to which the British power had attained, displaying a shameful apprehension, that it could not be retained, either, from weakness of the local Government, or inability of the Government in England, supporting such an extension of territory, whilst Lord Wellesley was disgracefully recalled, and subjected equally to Hastings, to an accusation or impeachment of his, and their glorious administration.

Posterity will judge impartially, from these connected facts, whether Mr. Hastings and Lord Wellesley, or Sir John Shore and Sir George Barlow, were best deserving of their country's approbation, and honors conferred !!!

I now resume the sequel and end of my Narrative. Viewing, as I had done, with others, the impossibility of such claims for remuneration being passed over with a spunge, however the Junto ruling in Leaden Hall Street, at that period, with such absolute sway, might dispose of me hereafter, I had a good deal lived on the anticipation of their receipt. The disappointment which I incurred, threw me therefore into great difficulties, and equally disappointed those, to whose bounty I had been indebted; and who, concurring in opinion with me, on the perusal of the statement of my case, that these were irresistible, had cheerfully indulged their liberality, in making pecuniary advances to me, adequate to my support. I was consequently obliged to sell every article of value which I had purchased, and was possessed of ; likewise to transfer my annuity for their benefit ; and, after suffering privations and hardships, which fell heavy at my time of life, but which, I thank God, the fortitude, with which he had endowed my mind, enabled me to endure with patience, I was relieved by the generosity of a friend, who had a lively remembrance of attachment and obligation, for the conduct which I had observed during prosperity. With what was left to me, out of this sum, being two-fifths of its amount, I departed for the Continent, my tried friends in England approving of the same, and repeating their assurance, they would not be unmindful, to bring forward my claims, and a reconsideration of my case, when they saw a proper opportunity, to exert themselves in behalf of their injured friend. By this same liberal friend, was I offered a handsome pension to live in ease, and to enjoy for the remainder of my days, where the local was most agreeable, and even I was enjoined by the warmest friends of my youth, and career in life, through whom this bounty was tendered, *viz.*, Sir Elijah Impey and Mr. Wombwell, to accept of it, and quit the paths of ambition, and the future trouble which might again arise and befall me from public situations. I rejected this munificence intended, not from pride, but, from a consideration, I had other ties, which demanded I should not sink into perfect repose, whilst active faculties permitted me to discharge with credit, stations to which I might be elevated. With these sentiments I assented readily to the proposition subsequently made to to me from the Batavian Government, to repair to the Cape of Good Hope in a high station with the promise of a higher, and the eventual assurance of those friends, to whose interest in my behalf, I felt sincerely grateful, that both rank and fortune were once more within my reach and that nothing would be spared to throw me into the state, during my sojournment abroad, of the truly pleasing one *otium cum dignitate.*

With these prospects, and the fullest reliance of performance, did I embark, vested with my new honors, after the Treaty of Amiens*, in a time of profound peace, and with the strongest hope of its continuance, for my destination. The unfortunate war which soon burst out after my arrival, has deprived me of these advantages to which I had looked up with fond delight, not so much for what concerned me personally, but for the gratification of others; and which from the honesty of those, on whose promises I implicitly trusted, I am persuaded I should, otherwise, have reaped.

Accustomed to vicissitudes, nay seemingly born to experience, such, I behold this last, with Philosophic contemplation, *Flecti non Frangi* I feel blessed in my second domestic attachment, and I thank heaven daily, that what I have been denied in consequence say worldly honors and riches, it has pleased the Almighty to compensate to me, in unimpaired faculties, and an uncommon share of health and activity, far surpassing, what might be expected, in my years, God grant to me the continuance of these abundant blessings! and, in the enjoyment of a tranquil mind, not corroded with past events, I shall, when it pleaseth Him to call me, I trust, to a state of immortal happiness, bow with submission, and due veneration, to His divine will.

CAPE OF GOOD HOPE,
1st February 1808. (Sd.) G. F. GRAND.

---

* March 27th, 1802.

Tank Square [now Dalhousie Square] in 1794.
(By W. Baillie.)

APPENDIX A.

Orders from Colonel Primrose Galliez, Commanding the Garrison of Allahabad, and all the troops serving at that juncture out of the Company's Provinces.

To

LIEUTENANT GRAND,

SIR,

You are to proceed with all possible expedition, and take charge of the two companies of Sepoys belonging to the 18th Battalion, that are now encamped opposite the Fort of Chunarghur, at which place you are to remain. You are to pay particular attention to the preservation of the said Fort, for which purpose you are to employ a sufficient number of Harcarahs (spies) to bring you intelligence, should any body of troops move that way, with intention to attack it, or should the Serjeant, now commanding at the Fort, at any time send you information of the Kelladar's having treacherous designs against the English troops in the Garrison, you are, in either of these cases, according to circumstances, the validity and nature of such intelligence, to march your detachment into the Garrison, and assume the command; and should you be attacked, you are immediately to send me information, thereof, in order that a re-inforcement may be sent you, should it be necessary. You are to visit the Garrison twice a week, to see that the Serjeant keeps his people in proper order, as also his Magazine, etc., and should you at any time think proper to send him any orders which you may deem necessary, for the better preservation of the Fort, he is to obey them. I shall also give him directions, to acquaint you with every particular circumstance that may happen in his Garrison.

I have the honor, etc., etc.,

ALLAHABAD, (Sd.) PRIMROSE GAILLIEZ,
19th April 1770. *Colonel Commandant.*

B.

To

LIEUTENANT GRAND.

SIR,

His Excellency the Commander-in-Chief, in consequence of your reference to him, previous to your embarkation for Europe, has ordered me to acquaint you, that throughout the course of your military service, you have deservedly met his approbation, and particularly, for the firm, judicious and prudent conduct, which you displayed, during the important command, with which you were entrusted at Chunarghur.

I have the honor, etc.,
(Sd.) JOHN COCKERELL,
Aid-de-Camp.

CALCUTTA,
February the 27th, 1773.

N. B.—Brigadier-General Sir Robert Barker, Knight, was then the Commander-in-Chief in Bengal, having succeeded Brigadier-General Smith, in February, 1779, in that trust.

C.

Letter from the Board of Revenue to Mr. Grand.

To

G. F. GRAND, Esq.,

Collector of Tirhoot.

Sir,

Having submitted to the Right Hon'ble the Governor in Council, the accuracy with which your collections have been kept up, and the repeated approbation which you have met with from us in the management of your District, His Lordship in Council has enjoined us to convey to you, what we are sensible you will consider as the most pleasing reward his thanks upon the occasion.

We are, Sir, etc.,
(Sd.) Wm. Cowper.
T. Graham.
J. Mackenzie.
J. Evelyn.

Calcutta,
15th December 1786.

D.

Regulations of the Honorable the Court of Directors, upon and expressly denominated, article the 15th of the Regulating Act, sanctioned by Parliament, and passed in 1774, for the better conducting and governing the Hon'ble Company's Territories in India.

" We direct, that in the collection and management of our Revenues, *you continue*, such of our servants whose collections have *been well kept up*, and who have otherwise distinguished themselves in this department of our service."

E.

Regulations of the Honorable the Court of Directors, upon and expressly denominated, article the 20th of the Regulating Act of Parliament of 1774.

"*We direct and enjoin* you that in all cases, and *before the removal* of any *Company's* servant *from any office*, the *party be made acquainted in writing*, with the *accusation* to be preferred that a reasonable time, not less than fourteen days, be allowed him to reply to the said charge; and, if not satisfactorily, *then*, and *then only*, is he to be suspended from his functions, until our pleasure be made known; and that in all such cases you exercise the utmost circumspection and discretion furnishing every document to the party, or parties, in writing, and carefully recording the whole of the proceedings in your regular consultations, in order to serve for our final judgment."

F.

REVENUE BOARD.

To

G. F. GRAND, Esq.,

Collector of Tirhoot.

SIR,

I am directed by the Board of Revenue to acquaint you, that the Right Hon'ble the Governor-General in Council has thought proper to nominate Mr. Robert Bathurst to your station of Collector of Tirhoot.

I have the honor to be,

SIR,

Yours obedient Servant,

(Sd.) J. H. HARINGTON,

Secretary.

CALCUTTA,

27th of August 1787.

To

CHARLES, EARL CORNWALLIS, K. G.,

GOVERNOR-GENERAL, ETC., ETC.

MY LORD,

I learn and, I confess, with astonishment, that a gentleman, Mr. Bathurst, has, from the circumstance of his appointment, being within the limits of those thought proper to be reduced by Government, conceived himself entitled to my Collectorship, and founding his ideas to this injustice, on this ground alone, has commanded your Lordship's attention.

The rules that your Lordship has adopted and is governed by, are marked with such strong impartiality, as to embolden any servant of the Company's whether recommended to your Lordship's particular protection or not, to prefer his claims with confidence, and to trust equally so in your fair decision.

If Mr. Bathurst, therefore, has impressed your Lordship with a sentiment that there is some ground for this claim, I feel myself in the case described, and with cheerfulness, My Lord, humbly will state mine.

On this supposition being warranted, I apprehend, My Lord, Mr. Bathurst must only have pleaded that he is senior in the Civil Service to myself; I know not (and I hope not to be thought presumptuous) any other ground he could have gone upon. It behoves me, in consequence, to do away the strength that may have acquired him, and in this, I trust, I shall succeed. Before, however, the reason of this preference can operate in your Lordship's mind permit me to hope that the point may not be regarded as one of contest between Mr. Bathurst and Mr. Grand. The appointments, My Lord, are not consolidated ; and on that account, Mr. Bathurst, in his plea of seniority, stands on no better footing than any senior to me in the line, and out of employment, making the same claim. I proceed, My Lord, to submit my pretensions to your just consideration ; next December will be two and twenty years, since I became a servant of the Company, I entered into their military line, and, after seven years' service, attaining within the rank of the 8th eldest Lieutenant on the Bengal List, I was obliged from an infirmity, suddenly to resign their service, and return to England, I relied there on a radical cure, but being disappointed, my friends, joined with the faculty, in thinking a military life, and in a hot climate especially, not adapted to the nature of my complaint, and obtained my removal to the civil line, I after two fruitless years spent at home.

I was nominated a writer only, from the Company having come to a resolution of not sending out originally civilians of a higher rank ; but my friends and myself were assured by the Directors, that the rank I had held in the military would be a consideration to their Government abroad, in appointing me to any trusts they might adjudge me worthy to discharge ; and in this predicament, I was considered, by General Clavering, who, on my arrival, held the majority of Government, as he exempted me from being stationed to any particular office at the Presidency. I, from that time, My Lord, served in the Commercial and Revenue lines ; in the first, as Head Assistant to the Commercial Chief at Patna; in the second, as Secretary to the Salt Office, and in my present situation. I believe the character I have held in the course of my service in both lines, Military and Civil, is so established in the world, that I may safely appeal to it to possess your Lordship's favorable opinion. In the military, General Smith, then Commander-in-Chief, upon the testimony of Colonel Chapman, my Commanding Officer, appointed me, on his quitting India, to the eldest Lieutenancy of his brother's batalion of Sepoys, then serving out of the Provinces; and, occasionally, during three years that we remained out of them, I was entrusted with separate commands at Chunar, Allahabad, and the Carumnasseh.

In the civil line, My Lord, Mr. Hastings, in February, 1782, honored me with the appointment of Collector of the Sarcars (provinces) of Tirhoot and Hajeepore, and his Council unanimously concurred in his recommendation. I found a district assessed at near seven lakhs, including a proportion of 130,000 out of five lakhs, that Mr. Hastings two years had put an increase of, on the Revenue of the Subah (*viz.*, Behar) then yielding under forty lakhs; the country had been thrown into confusion; the renters had so mismanaged, as instead of the increased proportion being produced, a large deficiency in the first year had occurred; in the second the system was changed. In the middle of the Hindoostanee year, I was directed to take charge; and notwithstanding a balance of Rs. 70,000 was then due, I realized that, together with the current Revenue, Mr. Hastings was pleased to approve of my conduct, and year after year, My Lord, I have equally, I flatter flatter myself, deserved the same approbation from Government, and I highly esteemed it as an auspicious event, being soon after your Lordship's arrival, *honored with your thanks*. The manufactories founded early by me, the repute they have grown into, and the consequence they will every further year prove to the Company, as well as of a fair advantage to myself, may entitle me likewise to some commendation.

I am aware, that Mr. Bathurst says he has been injured by his appointment having been lessened, and thereby brought into the predicament it now stands. I am willing, My Lord, to own, he may have been so, but that not by myself; no part of his district was lopped off by me, what part was, was attached to other districts, and happened when his appointment probably was considered only a temporary one; being a Superintendent over Meha Rajah Culleansing, who still remained in the management of several Mehals in this Subah, and not a Collector, at all events, My Lord, mine was formed into its present consistency long before Mr. Bathurst's was even judged necessary, and as it certainly has not, My Lord, been an instance of your Government to remove one gentleman, whose appointment is not done away, to put in another, I refer my case, if it is to become one, confidently to your Lordship's sense of justice and propriety.

The only apprehensions I entertained of losing mine, were grounded on the possibility of your Lordship having been guided by the regular seniority of

Collectors, without any reference had to their local knowledge, or to their stations, however not innovated on by these new regulations; had this been the maxim I, certainly, could not have come within the number of those to be employed, and as such, must have yielded, could I not have been in your Lordship's sentiments deserving of some attention and exception, from the several years I have served in the Military, and been in fact a Company's servant twenty-two years.

I have another, point, my Lord, to adduce in my behalf. In this month I am a senior Merchant; and, included in that denomination, have, in the construction of the act, a claim to hold any appointment.

These, my Lord, are the reasons I have to offer for my continuing; and, in the pleasure you have to deal equitably, by all men, I promise myself your Lordship will pardon the intrusion.

I have avoided, my Lord, to touch on want of fortune, however the series of years elapsed since I have been endeavouring to raise a small independency; neither on the irreparable ruin that would attend my removals in the loss of my Manufactories, &c. Such topics, merely calculated to excite pity, I have thought of no weight, compared to arguments in point, submitted to the liberality and candor of an upright tribunal.

I have the honor to be, &c., &c.,

TIRHOOT, *3rd June 1787.* (Sd.) G. F. GRAND, *Collector.*

H.

To

JOHN SHORE, Esq.,

AND PRESIDENT AND MEMBERS OF THE BOARD OF REVENUE.

GENTLEMEN,

As I have not been favored with any reply to my letters of the 20th of May, 15th and 21st of September, one of the latter containing an account, demands, receipts, and disbursements, to the end of the year 1194 Fussily, I beg leave to call your attention again to them, with a view that, before I quit the Presidency, I may receive the self satisfaction of knowing, *whether to the close of the execution of the duties of my station, as Collector of Tirhoot, you deem me deserving of your approbation?*

Should I, in your judgement, be thought entitled to this acknowledgement, it will be an addition to the repeated flattering commendations with which you have honored me; and as such, it cannot escape your discernment, that it concerns my reputation they should not be withheld at this juncture, since their omission would imply an indirect censure on my conduct. I trust, therefore, Gentlemen, you will consider this my solicitation, as a duty I owe to myself, and, in consequence, favor me with your early determination.

I have the honor, &c.,

CALCUTTA, *24th January 1788.* } (Sd.) G. F. GRAND, *Late Collector of Tirhoot.*

I.

Letter from the Board of Revenue to Mr. Grand.

REVENUE BOARD, G. F. GRAND, ESQ.

SIR,

We have received your letter of the 24th instant, on our examination of the annual accounts of your collections for the Fussily year 1194, we have pleasure in observing, that the Revenues lately under your charge have been well kept up. We have also pleasure in acknowledging the essential information communicated in your letter of the 20th of May, respecting the revenues and usages in the District of Tirhoot.*

Adverting, on this occasion, to the recent arrangement of the Province of Bahar, by which another gentleman has been appointed to your late station, we deem it incumbent upon us to express our entire satisfaction with your management and the zeal and ability with which you conducted the functions of that important charge.

CALCUTTA, *29th January 1788.* — We are, Sir, etc., (Sd.) BOARD OF REVENUE.

J.

To

THE HONORABLE THE COURT OF DIRECTORS OF THE HONORABLE THE EAST INDIA COMPANY.

HONORABLE SIRS,

I beg leave to submit to your Honorable Court a summary statement of the claims contained in my

* This letter is wanting to complete the Appendix.

Memorial of the 30th of June 1798; trusting to the liberality of your Honorable Court and the sense of justice which actuates every individual in it, to consider me worthy of some compensation for the hardships I so clearly proved myself to have undergone.

No. 1.

	Sa. Rs.
Dawk or Post charges, by bill sent in 1st September 1787—	
Principal	600 0 0
Interest	......

The established Post for Letters from the Presidency to the Upper Stations extended only to Patna, fifty miles short of the residence at which I was stationed by the Government. This allowance has been claimed and received by others in similar circumstances, *viz*, Mr. Champain, the Judge of Tirhoot, and Mr. Bathurst, as will be found by a reference to the public accounts.

No. 2.

Travelling charges from Calcutta to Patna in March 1793—	
Principal	850 0 0
Interest	......

In the October preceding I was ordered down to the Presidency, where no proceedings were held against me; and, at the time specified, I was referred back to Patna. The customary Travelling Charge was allowed me for coming and this claim is for the expenses of my return, to which I have an equal right.

No. 3.

Salary as Judge and Magistrate of Patna, for six months—

Principal	15,000	......
Deduct the moiety for November, paid me by Mr. Foley, the Civil Paymaster	1,250	......
		Sa. Rs.
Total ...	......	13,750 0 0

I claim the salary as my due, until the date of the appointment of my successor, the office continuing in my name until that period.

No. 4.

A reasonable compensation for the period I was out of

		Sa. Rs.		
employment, when compelled to quit and deliver up my station to Mr. Bathurst, till appointed Judge of Patna.				
Difference between Mr. Bathurst's and Mr. Grand's receipts for one year ...	28,000	......		
Is, for eleven months, *viz.* from the 1st of October, 1787, to the 1st of September, 1788, —...		25,666	10	3
Interest	......	......		
An equitable relief for the damage caused to me by the compulsive sale of my House, and Land, and manufactories.				
Prime cost of the House and Land	30,000	......		
Mr. Bathurst allowed me only	10,000	......		
Difference ...	......	20,000	0	0
Value of the Indigo Manufactories as proved by a subsequent sale ...	84,000	......		
Forced sale by order of Government	35,200	......		
Difference —	......	49,000	0	0

No. 5.

Such a retribution as may be deemed reasonable for my

total privation of office, from the 1st of May, 1793, to the day of quitting India, which ought to calculated at the full difference between 30,000 Sa. Rs. per annum, of which I was deprived, and 4,000 Sa. Rs. yearly, the sum allowed me.

Annual difference, 26,000. Is for five years eight months, *viz.*, from the 1st of May, 1793, to the 1st of February, 1799 ... . Sa. Rs. 1,47,333 4 3

Annual Interest on 26,000 ... .

If your Honors will be pleased to consider the clear and palpable justice of every one of these items, and, at the same time to weigh the incalculable hardships attending a forced residence at the expensive Settlement of Calcutta for so many years, which, of itself, may be deemed a very oppressive fine, ruinous to any private individual, with the loss of the best and most active years of my life, rendered equally useless to my employers and myself; my appeal to your candor and humanity will, certainly, not be offered in vain; and in that perfect confidence, I have the honor to subscribe myself

With due reference and respect,

London, 10th June 1800. G. F. GRAND.

N.B.—This Memorial was delivered in; the former which was transmitted from Bengal, it was intimated to me, had been too prolix to claim *their attentive consideration.*

K.

Copy of a Letter, transmitted to Mr. Grand, by the Board of Revenue in August, 1789.

To

MR. G. F. GRAND,

LATE COLLECTOR OF TIRHOOT.

SIR,—I am directed by the Board of Revenue to acquaint you, that the Honorable the Court of Directors, in their general letter per *Swallow*, have been pleased to express their entire approbation of your services; and the high sense they entertain of the ability manifested in your management of the late Trust committed to your charge.

I am Sir, &c.,

J. H. HARINGTON, *Secretary.*

N.B.—The Revenues were not only kept up annually, but were materially increased during my administration of six years in Tirhoot together with a heavy balance realized, which I found due from the country in the middle of the year when I took charge, and further that not a mowza or village, nor an acre of land, was sold during the whole of that period on account of any arrears or balance of Revenue.

To

THE HONORABLE THE COURT OF DIRECTORS OF THE UNITED EAST INDIA COMPANY.

HONORABLE SIR AND SIRS,

1. With the papers which I have requested Government to forward for your information, and, in appeal

to your justice, I beg leave, Honorable Sirs, to recapitulate what has given rise to your being troubled with such a detail.

2. In February, 1782, after having served in the Commercial line, first, as Secretary to the Salt Committee, and Examiner to the Board of Trade, and secondly, as Head Commercial Assistant at Patna; I was nominated by Governor Hastings, with the concurrence of His Council, Messrs. Wheeler and Macpherson, Collector of the Sarcars Tirhoot and Hajeepore, in Subah Bahar; and, after officiating in that trust five years and a half, with the constant and yearly approbation of Government, and, finally sanctioned with that of your Honorable Court, conveying, and dignifying me with its thanks, for my administration, all which testimonials appear in those exhibits, which the printed case contains, I was most unprecedentedly, and in the face of two Regulations (*vide* 15 and 20 Articles of the Regulating Act of 1774, the tenor of which ensured my permanency in the trust which I held so long, as I acted up to the spirit and letter of them), removed from my office and station, in order to give way, as it will appear in the case, for another servant more highly patronized than I was; and this, I am warranted to say, because not a shew of ground or precedent existed for such an act, and the very reverse had operated on the said occasion in Bengal, when the arrangements were fixed for consolidating the Judicial and Revenue Departments into one nomination, and allotting the several Districts with their respective Chiefs.

3. This case, your Honorable Court knows, however strong my ground of complaint was, and the irreparable ruin that followed it, I forebore to trouble you with, as originally had been the intent; and this, from assurances which I received from the governing power, of every compensation being made me, together with an actual regret expressed that such a removal had taken place.

4. I was thus twelve months out of employment, subsisting on the pension of a senior Merchant, 325 Sa. Rs. per month, when I was appointed, unsolicited, as had been customary with other servants, to the station of Judge and Magistrate of Patna, whilst my predecessor in that trust, Mr. Mercer, was appointed Collector or Chief of the province of Burdwan; and however I immediately begged to be exonerated from the acceptance of the former station, yet the flattering encomiums bestowed on me with a promise it should only be temporary, and Mr. Mercer's promotion cited as an example of the Judicial being no bar to the Revenue line, were reasons and condescensions that made it obligatory on me to assent.

5. After four years spent in this laborious avocation I was ordered, both myself and assistant by separate letters, to repair to the Presidency previously delivering over charge of my offices of Judge and Magistrate to Mr. Henry Douglas, a servant, junior even to my assistant Mr. Cornelius Bird.

6. In compliance with these orders, and ignorant to what other purposes my services might be directed and required, I delivered over charge, and came to the

Presidency. On my arrival, I was told, for the first time, that charges had been given against me. I observed, humbly, if this was the cause of a removal, it did not justify the act, because Government must have known that a positive Regulation, even sanctioned by Parliament, existed to a direct contrary purport, and expressly specifying and prescribing the only form and mode in such cases to be adopted. That, in the present one, my disgrace was proclaimed before trial, nay before examination, and under a perfect ignorance of the grounds. That, nevertheless, if, as I was then informed, there were charges, I entreated, in order that, I might have the opportunity of personally meeting them, that they might be brought forward without delay.

7. To this natural request, I received a direct assent. Nevertheless, on the 28th December 1792, and nearly three months after the first *informal* act was committed, a Committee of three Company's servants, one in high station at Patna, the Commercial Chief, and two other gentlemen out of employ, were nominated to repair to Patna, to enquire into my administration for four years preceding that period, and there *to receive* and *to try to condemnation* or acquittal, any charges which they would think proper *to form* out of the subject of any petitions or complaints which *might be* given in against me, in consequence of *a proclamation* which the Committee, on their arrival, had issued to the said effect. And this tribunal instituted at the Presidency where I was, formed on the spot itself, at Patna, and commencing its proceedings in February

two months afterwards, without *the smallest official notice being communicated to me thereof.*

8. But, on the 11th of the month following, a necessity to this effect existed. For, it appeared, that the Committee meeting and finding that the Instructions of Government went to authorize them to proceed in judgment *endernier ressort,* they rightly judged that their proceedings, so carried on, would be liable in the end to being questioned and impeached as to their validity, and on this head conveying their opinions to Government, they added an humble suggestion of the propriety of the party himself attending or an agent on his part,- legally and sufficiently authorized, and without which, they declared, they could not go into examination, Government, I apprehend, being satisfied with the justice of the suggestion I received from the Secretary, on the 16th of March, *official notification of the Committee's appointment,* on the *preceding December,* with a copy of the Committee's first letter, in consequence of which Government were pleased to signify to me, that with the view of giving effect to the Committee's proceedings, I had it in option, either to attend in person at Patna, or depute a native agent there for the purpose.

9. Without presuming to cavil, however aggrieved I felt, on the whole that had occurred till that day regarding my situation without commenting on the gross impossibility that a servant of any rank, or description, nor indeed a gentleman, could ever entertain the idea of entrusting a *native agent* the defence of

his character, fame, reputation, or property, I briefly replied, by acknowledging the letter and its enclosure and respectfully acquainted Government that I should attend in person.

10. Some days necessarily elapsed before I could travel post, by Dauck bearers being laid at the several stations, etc. I set off, however, on the 21st and on the 26th I reached my destination.

11. Before the occurrences of one week were over I found that the Committee, however well founded their suggestion to Government was, and the result of which they consistently ought to have awaited, had met in Committee, and had actually proceeded *into examination ex parte*. Nevertheless, and however I was denied by them a document, which I conceived in my fullest right to demand, particularly after what had appeared from the Committee's first letter, *viz.*, a copy of their Instructions, I resolved (degraded, as I was, from official function, debarred from every honor and respect due to my station, and likely to be even more degraded, by being confronted with the lowest class of those who had been subjected to my authority as Magistrate), yet, to attend, and to attend even in person; and here, I beg my Honorable Masters will notice that I officially signified in writing to the Committee this resolution. And this impression I wish to convey to their minds, in this place, because they will find in a part of the proceedings, that I was accused, subsequently by Government, of having taken every mode to defeat and frustrate the said enquiry of the Committee.

Yet my degradation was not complete, for I might be ordered to rescue my official functions, from which I felt only virtually suspended and this, not apparently arising from accusation and construed guilt, after the proceedings of the Committee had terminated. But, on the 4th of April, the veil was drawn, notification having arrived that Government had thought proper to appoint, on the 27th of March, six days after I quitted Calcutta, Mr. Henry Douglas to the stations of Judge and Magistrate of Patna, which appointment was to take place and have its full force, with other similar arrangements, for the ensuing 1st of May.

As full time, however, intervened, to enable me by personal application to avert the full effect of this severe stroke, instead of meeting the Committee in person on the next day, as had been fixed, I made all the haste possible to the Presidency; and, on the 16th of April, sent in a letter of respectful remonstrance to the uncommon mode of proceeding, which had in its commencement, and uniformly to that date, operated against me; and submissively entreating, that the resolution of the 27th of March, relative to to Mr. Douglas, appointment to my offices, to take place on the 1st of May, might be revoked, or, at least suspended, until I had undergone trial, and the event of the enquiry and sentence on my conduct been known in the world. That this reasonable boon being granted, and thereby, myself neither prejudged nor punished, I was ready and prepared to met any charge, and eventually appear before the appointed Tribunal, or any other which Government might be pleased to institute as corresponding most with their approbation.

I intimated officially to the Committee my determination of returning to the Seat of Government, and, at the same time, acquainted them, that it would not have the effect of impeding their proceedings, since they already had, however their avowed conviction of its tendency, thought proper to proceed in my case, in an *ex parte* manner, and indeed avowed their intention of continuing the same process whether I attended or not.

My application to Government of the 16th April was negatived, and on the 10th of May I received a letter, assigning reasons for the steps they had been pleased to take, to which I made a becoming reply on the 20th of that month.

I heard no more from the Government till the 27th of August, when I was desired to explain some points regarding an apparent deficiency in the Fund of the deposits of the Court, stated to have been disbursed during my administration, from some individuals, whose oaths were required to that effect, having deposed, that, out of an aggregate of 72,000 rupees, 65,000 rupees of which were acknowledged upon oath to have been *bona fide* received, and without any deduction; and the other 7,000 rupees said not to have been received, however receipts in some cases had been extorted, and in others, comprehended in this sum, the attestations went so far, as to say, that payments had not been made nor receipts had been given.

This, I understood, as the vulnerable point, which Government had deemed proper to extract from the

Committee's proceedings and report, and required, in consequence, a satisfactory explanation. And this, I flattered myself to have afforded by my letter of the 5th of September in answer thereto ; humbly concluding, that I should submit to what Government choose to direct, even, *if the neglect of the Treasurer was to them apparent, to make up the deficiency, if demanded,* although, I trusted, it had not escaped their observation, *the very great disproportion* in the amount of the the payments acknowledged and the amount of those disavowed and, here, I thought had the whole ended ; and I waited, with suitable patience the decision of Government on the above point.

In March 1794, remarking, that many of my juniors in the service had been promoted to stations, whilst my personal applications to Government, for a reinstatement to my station, or an adequate one bestowed lay neglected, I addressed myself in writing publicly to this effect, and I received no answer, though I was led to believe that my letter would meet with a favourable attention.

But the same grievances continuing, *viz.*, of seeing my juniors selected for high stations, whilst I remained out of employ, I humbly, on the 20th of May, 1794, claimed the notice of Government, to the measures which had affected me, and which, situated as I was, I could not, but deem had been harsh, informal, and illegal, and solicited a total revision of my case.

To this entreaty, receiving no answer, I reminded Government of my claim for payment of arrears of salary and travelling charges, both which were denied to me, on a specific reason assigned, *viz.*, that "Government would not take the said claim into consideration, until they came to a decision on the whole of my case." This was sufficient, and trusting it would not be delayed, I forbore to importune. But, falling ill towards the close of the year, and which illness increasing in April, 1795, I then stated to the Board my right to preferment, unless they deemed that in the whole of the proceedings and report of the committee, a bar, rather, to such preferment existed, until some point or points, which, in their opinions, might have militated, against me were not satisfactorily elucidated, and *in this case I required a copy of the whole proceedings and report.*

Again from receiving no answer, I on the 1st September, 1795, assumed the fair deduction that no such bar prevails since no reply to this effect was made nor were a copy of the proceedings, as I required transmitted; and I, therefore, again urged my hope of employment, adducing even the just plea of my distressed situation, both in regard to my feelings as an old servant remaining uncalled upon to act in the service, and my private sensations, from the embarrassed state of my affairs which every day accumulated. But neither did this address, nor the preceding one in April, accelerate in any degree, the decision, which in September 1794, *they had promised*, and I, of course, anxiously expected.

Tired and wearied, having no specific ground for an appeal to the justice of my Superiors in England; on money, nor means at command to resign the service and repair there for redress ; no possibility of extricating myself from the pecuniary embarrassments which fell on me, I bore with every misery that could be endured, in the conscious hope, that by a change of Government, measures would be reversed in my behalf and that system of inattention tantamount to the most cruel injustice, at length, cease.

But, this change being deferred much beyond the time it had generally been conjectured that it would take place, my necessities arose to that pitch of want, which made it no longer possible to bear with such sufferance and I therefore, in September last year, reminded Government that *three years* had *then* elapsed since they had informed me that they would decide on my claim to my arrears of salary and travelling charges, when my case came under their due consideration and that I *implored them* in consequence, to maturely reflect on my situation and issue an order for the said payment.

This letter with the rest that preceded brings to one view the consistency of both applications, however distantly preferred, and as Government were deaf to my distresses and determined, as it appears by their Resolution of the 23rd February, this year, not to relieve them in any shape. This letter written the preceding September, brought forth, at last, the decision of the whole of my conduct as Judge and Magistrate for the city of Patna, during four years ; and this decision (for the delay of which, as affecting an individual, no possible palliation can be liberally admitted) *unheard*, *uncontroverted* and founded as they themselves allege *on presumptive conclusion;* for they declare, without alleging *any specific charge* or *explaining any ground*, "That they nevertheless entertained the fullest conviction of my guilt and plead, as an excuse for not descending into particulars that an alteration in the system of justice having intervened they were precluded therefrom!!!" I trust the freedom with which I have commented on such a plea will be pardoned; and however it may be thought too forcible, yet, that it will draw an inversion of sentiment favorable to what I allege, against so untenable a ground having ever been admitted to stop or retard the course of justice.

Ruined in my fortunes after three and thirty years service; wounded in that fair fame which I sought to acquire in the course of my professional duties, I have verging to the age of fifty, no prospect remaining, but the distant, though brought one of your justice.

Fearful already of this detail being much too prolix, yet submitting it with every confidence, that from its nature so interesting and decisive to my fate, its fatiguing prolixity will not only be generously forgiven, but that its purport will meet with the most earnest commiseration and attention, I shall make no further reference to the tenor of the accompanying letter, but in the eyes of an upright and impartial tribunal, accustomed even to look with remission on the errors of their servants, leave them to rest simply upon their own merits, and unadorned with that flower of language, alone used, and introduced, to throw a gloss, and act, in support to false inferences and tortured constructions, where the desire to convict operates.

(Signed) G. F. GRAND.

Calcutta, 30th June, 1798.

N.

To

G. F. GRAND, Esq.,

JUDGE AND MAGISTRATE OF PATNA.

Sir,—I have it in command from the Right Honorable the Governor-General in Council, to inform you, that a Committee has been appointed in *December* last, to enquire into your conduct as Judge and Magistrate of Patna, to repair to the spot, and receiving what complaints *may be* presented against your administration, to try them, and proceed to judgment.

The said Committee having met and assembled, have thought proper to suggest to his Lordship, how far their proceedings would be validated, in the event of their being prosecuted *ex parte.* You have, consequently, sir, the Governor-General's leave to attend on the said Committee either in person, or *by native agent,* in order to answer and refute whatever charges *are* brought against your official functions.

I have the honour to be, etc.

CALCUTTA: 5th March, 1793

(Signed) G. H. BARLOW,
Secretary to Government.

O.

Instructions for three Company's Civil Servants delegated to proceed to Patna and judge Mr. Grand, or rather to sentence him.

To Samuel Charters, Edward Ephraim Pote, and John Fendal, Esquires, the Committee for enquiring into the conduct of Mr. G. F. Grand, Judge and Magistrate of the City of Patna.

GENTLEMEN,

I am directed by the Governor-General in Council to transmit you the following Instructions.

First. Accompanying you will receive an extract from the proceedings of the Sudder Dewanny Adawlut, respecting a suit instituted in the Dewanny Adawlut of the city of Patna, for the property of the late Lolldass. The Governor-General in Council desires that you will ascertain what measures (*whether entered upon record or not*) were taken by Mr. Grand regarding this suit and property; and report the result of your enquiry to his Lordship in Council, with such remarks upon it, as you may think necessary.

Second. Inclosed is transmitted to you a copy of the correspondence between the Sudder Dewanny Adawlut and Mr. Grand, respecting the property under attachment in the Patna Court and also an account of deposits transmitted by Mr. Douglas the acting Judge. His Lordship in Council desires you will enquire into the manner in which the money deposits, and the proceeds of the property, that has been under attachment in the Patna Court, since Mr. Grand's appointment, have been deposed of: particularly ascertaining whether a fair account of these sums has been rendered to the parties in the suits; and whether they have received the amount to which they were entitled?

Third. You will transmit to the Governor-General in Council for his orders, any complaints that *may be* preferred to you against Mr. Grand or his officers, for acts done in their official capacity.

Fourth. You will enquire into and report upon the following exactions, stated to have been made in the city by the Cutwaal Koarsing.

On all boats, small and large, four pice each on going and coming, and also on moving from one Gaut to another at Patna. From the salt sellers in Sharooff Gunge, some twelve Rupees, some three, some two, *ad arbitrium*, besides a continual exaction of several other Bazar collections.

Mr. Henry Douglas, the acting Judge at Patna, has been ordered to allow you to have access to all the papers and records of the Court, and *to furnish you with such information*, and assistance, as you may require from him.

I am, &c.

(Signed) G. H. Barlow,

Council Chamber, 28th *Dec.* 1792. *Sub-Secretary.*

N.B.—Pray remark that Loldass' business in which Munnowerdass' house was concerned, had been settled *ten* months before and that I had contended with the Board, who had interfered in the behalf of the latter, that my judicial process was perfectly correct, and conformable to every rule of practice of any judge whatsoever ; and here it dropped.

However the time elapsed, Munnowerdass, upon the appointment of this Committee, *was instructed*, to give in a plaint, yet this plaint, fraught with every lie devized on the occasion, was fully investigated by the said Committee, and even by the Committee's proceedings *exparte*, from the time they commenced sitting, to that of my arrival at Patna, I stood amply acquitted.

Pray observe likewise, that these exactions as stated, which I call Heaven to witness, I knew nothing of came to the Board's information, by a Sooruthaal, framed *in November*, signed by a few blackguards of the city, and collected by a Vakeel going about declaring he had Mr. Douglas's directions, and who *acted by the Lora's orders*, to this effect. Ergo, on this ground there was no subject of plaint *prior to my recall in October* ; and I declare to God, if any such complaint had been preferred to me in Court, where I sat daily, against the Cutwal, I would that instant have dismissed him, had it been established !

But it is just in regard to this man to observe, (and he was a man vigilant in his office, active and daring, who had for his capacity, to act in this trust, been promoted thereto by Mr. Ewan Law,* consequently

* A gentleman whose memory will ever be remembered by the natives of every description in Bahar with gratitude and respect, for his equitable administration as Chief of that Province ; and whose amiable character in private life, lives in the esteem of his brother-servants.

no creature of mine,) that I have understood subsequently, he was tried individually on every charge and was fully acquitted on each.

As for the rest of the Instructions, their spirit bespeaks too evidently, not a wish to convert suspicion into proof, (for suspicion *even* appears not to be grounded,) but design into charge; and as such they are too contemptible to excite comment.

But will it be believed? Can it? that in a regular Government, where Regulations, sanctioned by an Act of Parliament, exist, for the governing power, and equally, for the liberty and protection of the individual servant, that in defiance of these, nay, in open vindication of them, a civil servant of so many years standing, (and who had particularly in a former station, wherein he acted as Chief of a district above five years, deserved well and received the thanks of his employers) should, at a minute's warning, have been forced from his station, junior servants running from all points with directions to assume it; and this, from a situation of a Judge and Magistrate of a city!

And the reader will be prepared, from so strong a measure, outstripping every propriety, to see heinous charges, that might palliate so informal an act. Let him read the instructions, prepared for an aweful Tribunal, to sit in judgement on the *proclaimed* culprit, three months after the recall, and candidly judge! It is needless to point out to those acquainted with the term and nature of the document (Sooruthaal,) that in no court of judicature in this country India, it is ever admitted either as evidence or fact. It meets uniformly with a similar contempt, to what the introduction of a Robin Hood statement, would in our law courts, at home, if attempted to be introduced.

S.

Extract vit het Register der Beslaiten van het Staats-Bewind der Bataafsche Republick.

MAANDAGDEN *20th September* 1802.

Op het ter Vergadering geproponeerde, is, ragehoudene deliberatie, besloten tot Raad Consulent van het Gouvernement aan de Kaap de Goede Hoop to benoemen en aan to stellen, zoo alo geschied by deze, den Burger *George Francois Grand*, en zulks op een Tractement van *twee duizend Guldens's* jaarlyks.

En zal Extract dezes aar den Secretaris van Staat voor de Buitenlandsche Zakens en aan der Rand der Asiatische Beizittingen en Etablissementen, worden geryonden, mitsgaders an den Burger G. F. Grand worden uitgereikt, lot informatie en narigt respectivelyk.

Accordeevt met het voorsz Register,

S. DASSEVAEL,

Secretaris.

Aan den Burger G. F. GRAND.

Translation.

Extract from the Consultations of an Assembly of the States governing the Batavian Republic.

Monday, the 20th September, 1802.

In this Assembly it was this day proposed, and after mature deliberation resolved, to nominate Mr. George

Francis Grand to the station of Privy Counsellor of the Government at the Cape of Good Hope; and he is accordingly appointed and established in the above situation, with a salary annexed thereto of two thousand Caroli guilders annually.

And further it was resolved, to transmit copies of this nomination to the Secretary of State for Foreign Affairs, to the Directors of the East India Company, and to Mr. G. F. Grand, in order to serve for their respective guidance.

Conformable to the Extract,
(Signed) S. DASSEVAEL,
Secretary.

TO MR. G. F. GRAND.

T.

The Privy Counsellor G. F. Grand to His Excellency Lieutenant-General Janssens, Governor and Commander-in-Chief, etc., etc., etc.

I have the honor to submit to your Excellency, that several English inhabiting this Colony under the protection of the Laws of the Batavian Republic, and perfectly peaceable and obedient to its Government, consider themselves, notwithstanding the representation which they have made, founded on article the 4th of your Proclamation of the 9th February, endangered in being secluded from its benefit. This apprehension proceeds from some, to whom the option of continuing their residence has already been refused. Many of these have formed local alliances, and blessed with a numerous posterity, have besides an interest in the possessions which they have acquired, to the agriculture of which their attention has been so devoted, that the Natives, by following their example, and improved mode of cultivation, have reaped the most material advantage to their natural soil and its product. Independent of this considerations, Sir, they enjoy a personal respect amongst the first class of people here, who, I am warranted in saying, will readily step forth to become their securities, that, in no respect will they disturb or affect the tranquility and welfare of the Government, under which they are permitted to reside.

Have the goodness therefore to attend to the situation of such who come under this immediate description.

Allow me, likewise, when soliciting in their behalf, by endeavouring to mitigate the rigor of the order against them, in a request, that, at least the time fixed for their departure may be prolonged; an indulgence, if I may so call it, that the state of their concerns imperiously requires, to represent to you, that a measure so enforced without, any distinction, might be the means of causing the most disagreeable consequences, and the severest retaliation, on those Dutch and French, who, in a similar situation, are domiciliated, for the sake of commerce, subjected to the English Government in India. Even in Calcutta, the seat of Government, the respectable house of Messrs. *Vialass et Compagnie*, de Marseille, has there been long known. In that city, a brother, Mr. E. Vialass, directs their concerns, freed from any molestation whatsoever; with the sole exception, in time of war, of being restricted from any armaments by sea; otherwise they pursue, without any restraint, their purchases, sales, and what relates to the internal trade of the country, in the customary manner which prevails amongst merchants, in the most profound time of peace.

Messrs. *Grilliard et Compagnie* form another firm of men, associated for the sole purpose of commercial views, and are each of them Frenchmen born, and consequently subjects of its Government. I could, likewise, with the assistance of memory, bring in point other houses composed of people of that nation, and long established in the seaports of Calcutta and of Madras, &c., as also in principal towns far removed from those harbors, and situated in the interior of India.

Although I entertain no idea, that my declaration, not made without mature deliberation, should be thought wanting by your Excellency of other proof to corroborate its purport, yet as there are many Frenchmen in this town, who have been cccasionally sojourners in India, I would wish, sir, for your satisfaction, that you would call for their depositions on this point, and however, I have not, at this moment, had the honor of any intercourse with the English Commissary for Prisoners, Captain Shaw from Madras, yet, I have no doubt, that in the event of your seeking information from him on this subject, he would, readily, on the sacred word of an officer, give you the same detail, as I have the honor of doing, with every possible hope in favor of men whose demeanour and conduct entitle them to such protection; and who, individually, I may aver, lament and feel unfortunate enough, from their pursuits being disturbed by the war, which has again arisen, without attaching on them consequences, which would, in their tendency, inflict the most irrecoverable and deadly blow to their personal concerns.

I have the honor, &c.

G. F. GRAND.

CAPE TOWN, *Sunday*, *26th February*, *1804*.

V.

BATAVIAN TROOPS IN SOUTH AFRICA.

HEAD QUARTERS, CAPE OF GOOD HOPE,

February 27th, *1804*.

J. W. JANSSENS, GOVERNOR AND COMMANDER-IN-CHIEF OF THE COLONY, THE CAPE OF GOOD HOPE, AND ITS DEPENDENCIES.

To

THE PRIVY COUNSELLOR GRAND.

PRIVY COUNSELLOR,

I yesterday received your esteemed favour. Without having recourse to the testimony of others, I beg to state, that I repose the most unlimited confidence in the facts you have laid before me, and do not therefore doubt but there are foreigners living under the English Government in Bengal, and foreigners too, who belong to nations, at war with Great Britain. I do not, however, conceive, that because in India, where the English are so powerful, some for few persons, subjects of an enemy's country, are permitted to reside, the Dutch in South Africa should, for that reason, be obliged to suffer to remain there, a vast number of English subjects, and especially after certain occurrences which have taken place.

How would the Governor be able to answer for his conduct, if the interest of the tortured but innocent Mother Country were to be sacrified to foreign interests of a power with which we are at war, when, by the adoption of determined and appropriate measures, he might have had it in his power to prevent it?

Why does the English Government refuse Dutch subjects permission to reside in English possessions? Are they not ordered in England to quit it within a very short space of time? and informed that the ships for their conveyence await them. Is it to be supposed, that a few Dutch subject in the Kingdom of Great Britain are more dangerous than so great a number of English subjects in South Africa? There are no personal feelings on my part against individuals; most of the English whom I have seen here, have, in as far as I know, conducted themselves well; but the acts of their Government towards our fellow countrymen, justify, nay, even demand *reprisals*.

With the English it is necessary to be more cautious than with other nations; they are the most unwilling of any peoples to shake off the obligations imposed upon them by their birth; and the laws of their country do not even permit them to break the ties, by which they are bound to the nation.

If the English were required to take oaths, which others take, or would take without hesitation, those who did take them would be perjured, and consequently be unworthy of being trusted afterwards, or they would refuse to take them, and what then? Would not such a demand be more cruel than sending them away?

The measure adopted against the English here, is, without any harshness, general or national; the exceptions must not be numerous and only individual, and strong motives must justify the execution of the Law. It would, in my opinion, be arbitrary on the part of the Governor, and consequently a deviation from his duty, were he to suffer many exceptions to the Law, and, in that case, those, to whom permission to remain was refused, might with justice complain, and, instead of considering the measure as an unfortunate consequence of the war, might look at it as a particular persecution of their persons.

It is, in my opinion, an unreasonable demand, that individuals, previous to addressing themselves, should wish to know, whether their requests will be accorded. I respect national, and even individual, pride, but it must not be at the expense of the dignity of others.

I have commenced by refusing some to continue their residence in this Colony, chiefly, in order that the applications to that end shall not become general; the memorials of those, who have a chance of obtaining favourable decisions, or respecting whom I have not as yet received sufficient information, are at present laying over; and it is my intention in the course of a few days, to signify my ultimate pleasure relative thereto; those who are too late in applying, do not afford an opportunity for the requisite enquiries to be made, and can therefore in no wise expect a favourable result; however, be it as it may, I repeat, that the measure adopted of compelling the English to depart, must remain national, and the exceptions be but few and individual; and even then only in favour of those persons, who, in a most general point of view, can be considered useful to this Settlement among whom, agriculturists ought certainly in the first place to rank; the more numerous foreign connections become, the fewer are those which remain that bind and attach to the Mother Country, and this a Government ought not to countenance and favour.

Altho' I enjoy no pleasure in the Colony, and indeed have none to look forward to during my stay here, still my duty and inclination attaches me to its interests, but in the first place, and *more especially* to those of the Mother Country, which makes such great sacrifices for this possession, and the contributions to the support of which are so heavy a burthen upon the exhausted Republic; under such circumstances, it is painful to perceive so great an attachment to a nation, which, for years past, has contributed so much towards our ruin.

I ascribe the steps you have thought proper to take, Privy Counsellor, to generous principles, and this it is that has induced me to develope to you my sentiments so much at length.

Hail and Esteem !

(Signed) J. W. JANSSENS.

W.

CAPE TOWN, *3rd February* 1806.

SIR,

The British Commander-in-Chief, Sir David Baird, having, upon my application, been pleased to grant, that to such civil Employers, who *ought* to return to Europe, a free passage should be given I have the honor of requesting you to inform me, if you should not be desirous to avail yourself of this favor, and in this case, to state the number which compose your family, and those who you would wish should accompany you, in order that I may have it in my power to arrange the definitive measures to this effect with His Excellency Sir David Baird.

I have the honor to subscribe myself with distinguished considerations.

Your devoted friend and servant,

(Signed) J. W. JANSSENS.

MR. GRAND.

X.

SOUTH AFRICA, CAPE OF GOOD HOPE,
16th February 1806.

SIR,

General Janssens has desired me to inform you, which I have the honor of doing by this address, that

His Excellency has obtained a Passage for you on one of the Cartel ships.

The Adjutant General Rancke will, on account thereof, give you further information.

I have the honor to be, &c.,
Your Friend and Servant,
(Signed) R. DE KLERCK DIBBETZ,
Act. Govt. Secretary.

To MR. GRAND,

No. 37, Pub. Con. 7th April 1794.

To Edward Hay, Esq., Secretary to Government.

SIR,

The Accountant General having signified to me the necessity of obtaining a Certificate from the Treasury that defrayed my salary, of the offices I held to the 1st of May 1793, of Judge and Magistrate of Patna, I have the honor to enclose copy of a letter from the late Collector of Bahar, to this effect.

I have the honor to be, &c.,
(Signed) G. F. GRAND.

Calcutta 31*st March*, 1794.

No. 38, Enclosure from Mr. Grand, 31st March.

To G. F. Grand, Esq., late Judge and Magistrate of Patna.

SIR

In reply to your favor of the 22nd ultimo, I have the pleasure to inform you, that on a reference to the Accounts, you were paid up your salary as Judge and Magistrate of Patna, till October, 1792, only the order for which was issued by me in December of that year ;

and that no other payment appears subsequently to have been made on the said account from the Bahar Treasury

I am, &c.,

GYAH, (Signed) A. SETON,

23rd March 1794. *Collector of Bahar.*

A true copy. (Signed) G. F. GRAND.

No. 38. A. Pub. Cons. 7th April 1794.

THE HONORABLE COMPANY, *Dr.*

To Travelling charges from Calcutta to Patna, in March, 1793, agreeably to the order of the Board, being 400 miles, at 2-2 per mile.

Sicca Rupees 850.

CALCUTTA, *18th February 1794.*

Contents received. (Sd.) G. F. GRAND.

Pub. Cons. 1st September 1794.

Read again Mr. Grand's letter, dated the 31st of March, and recorded on the Proceedings of the 7th of April.

Ordered, "That Mr. Grand be informed, in answer to it, that the Board cannot pass any order relative to the salary he claims from the end of October, 1792, to the 1st May 1793, until they shall have come to a decision upon the complaints against his conduct in the office of Magistrate for the city of Patna."*

---

* Observe this resolution, recorded on the face of their consultations. Observe ts date. Observe that however repeatedly urged to the same purport it is still delayed from year to year, until the 30th June 1798, when I felt compelled, from such manifest injustice, to appeal to

their superiors, and this, without knowing the specifie grounds, as I have in the said Memorial described. Observe in this promise of a decision, the intended verdict points out and rests alone *on charges against the Magistrate*, none against the Judge. The former must have been in allusion to those invited and picked up charges against the cutwal (Lieutenant de Police) *which occurred after my recall*, the harsh and cruel act of which proclaimed my disgrace, and that I stood, contrary to all rule and form of precedent, actually pre-judged and prescribed on these loose and vague accusations, the Instructions to the Committee were founded, and observe my comments thereon, by referring to Appendix O. Never was persecution carried to such an end. In this instance of inviting complaints, contrary to every principle of natural justice, was the majesty of justice invaded, and in the procrastination of deciding on the merits of the case, was the maxim truly verified, that "speedy injustice is preferable to tardy justice." For, in that lapse of time, were uselessly consumed the most active years of my life, and could a good cause have been wanting of eventual interest to be exercised in its support, I should not have solicited, without effect, the powerful interest of my deceased relations and friends. Edward and Réné Payne, Esqs., who, in that interval, had both pai their debt to nature, and whose existence appeared to have been completely forgotten *by some of their contemporaries*, enemies to such virtues, as these valuable men had throughout their career uniformly displayed. The fact was, Sir John Shore and hi Counsellors, could not decide without inculpating *him*, who they venerated, and whose frowns they dreaded. They were sensible that *his* act had been illegal, and was consequently untenable. They drew up, I understood, *after my departure from Bengal*, an elaborate and tortured minute, in excuse of their proceedings; and I pray, my readers, finally to observe, that although I heard it resounded in my ears at the India House by the clerks in office, as an elegant composition in writing, yet, I was by their masters, however, I implored a copy of it, if any forced construction caused a necessity for refutation, *denied access to it*, and to this hour, so help me, God, I have never seen it, nor known its contents?

1st February 1808. (Sd.) G. F. GRAND.

POSTCRIPT TO MY NARRATIVE.

A miserable Author, denominating himself *the Modern Plutarch*, has had the impudence to assert, "That at a dinner given by Monsieur de Talleyrand in 1802, *then* the Minister in France for Foreign Affairs, there sat down to table, the former Mrs. Grand with her former husband, Sir Elijah Impey, who had presided on the bench in the action at law brought by him before his Tribunal, and Sir Philip Francis who had committed the injury." I treated the remark, at the juncture when I saw the publication with the contempt so unfounded an assertion merited; and, it had accordingly escaped my memory, when I was finishing the Narrative of my Life, which I have given.

Having, however, suffered so much under the English Government, which has prevailed where I have resided, as to have been ejected, soon after the Colony had surrendered, from the employment which its brave and humane conqueror, the present Lieutenant-General Sir David Baird, K.B., had bestowed, for the object of its tending to my comfort, in my elder days, *viz.*, Inspector of His Majesty's Woods and Lands, I feel myself compelled to animadvert thereon, and out of justice to both parties implicated in this illiberal and false observation, to refute this calumny in all its points.

I do, therefore, call God to witness, that, to my knowledge, I never saw the first Mrs. Grand, *neither in India nor in Europe*, from that melancholy Sunday, *viz.*, the 13th of December 1778, the sensations of which day I have described, and which fixed our eternal separation. We remained, from that moment, alike those, who having lived for a time in the height of happiness, have witnessed that happiness, suddenly and unexpectedly interrupted by one being cut off, never in this world to meet again. Persons of this stamp can never forget the ties which had existed, we knew the delicacy of each other's sentiments, and never once thought of infringing that line of conduct which such a sense of feeling naturally prescribed, those whose minds are congenial will credit my assertions. They will be reckoned in the number of my English readers, for with most of the French, such an idea would be condemned as preposterous in the extreme. I have known some of this nation, very amiable men, yet assuming the liberty, which an Englishman would, however intimate, refrain from that of entering into your domestic concerns, express themselves to the following effect on this subject. "*Faites divorce aujourddui, mon cher, mais remariez vous demain, cé'st la plus belle femme qui existe.*" Such was the only sacrifice, which the uncommon charms of her beauty had created with such men. They deemed it alone requisite for *l'etiquette, ou l'usage du monde*, to be observed, in the manner which I have related; such is the difference of sentiments existing between two nations, only separated from each other by a branch of the sea; and, nevertheless, each thinking, that honor guides their respective actions.

I certainly went to Paris in June 1802, and with the exception of the friend of my youth, Mr. Wombwell, and my lamented friend Sir Elijah Impey, saw, during my sojournment in that capital, none of the other persons mentioned. I lodged at the *Hotel du Cercle, Ru de Richelieu*, an Hotel, for the accommodation alone of male strangers. Madame de Talleyrand was, as I understood, inhabiting Neuilly, a residence in the environs of Paris, appertaining to Monsieur de Talleyrand. It was in the height of summer, and few people of rank frequented the city. I gratified my curiosity in seeing the public buildings, the Museum, etc., etc., and, after an abode of a very few days, departed for Switzerland, where the reception which I met with from relations and the old friends of my younger days, the agreeable society into which I was immediately admitted, the cheap and delightful furnished lodgings wherein I dwelt, the moderate price required for every article and necessary of life, the salutary air breathed, the beauty of the scene around, all these were considerations, which might have fixed me there for life, had it not been just at an epoch when a civil war was on the point of spreading through its territories. It had broke out in one part, at a little distance from Lausanne, some blood was shed and more would have been spilled, but for the powerful interference of France. General Lapp, the First Council's Aide-de-Camp, repaired to Lausanne, with Bonaparte's mandate to desist from all hostilities, and General Ney marched into Berne with a formidable corps of French troops, in order to enforce obedience and submission, of the differences existing, to his Master's imperious sway. At this moment, the offer was made to me, of the situation which I came rested with subsequently to the Cape of Good Hope; and determined to take no part in the dissentions, which had arisen in the former peacable and tranquil Switzerland, and not forseeing their termination would have been so speedy, I gave my assent to the proposition, and prepared to quit the comforts which I was in the enjoyment of at Lausanne. I had it notified to me, that the ships, on board one of which my passage had been secured were to sail for their destination in all October. My friend, Mr. Wombwell, had engaged when we parted in Paris, to spend his winter with me in Lausanne; but debarred from this intention, by an apprehension of the cold, he resolved to exchange its dreaded severity, for the milder region of Nice. Unwilling, however, we should go such different directions, without once more seeing each other, he wrote, and entreated me to meet him at Lyons, and remain a few days, which he augured would be the last time we should be together. With an equal inclination, as my much esteemed friend had expressed, did I repair to the destination fixed; and to this delay, and the resolution which I had formed, of returning to Switzerland, and pursuing my journey, along the left banks of the Rhine, *viz.*, through Basle, Strasbourg, Mayence, Coblentz, etc., etc., to Holland, with the miraculous interposition of Providence in my behalf, did I owe my escape from shipwreck on the *De Vrede* (the great cabin of which had been assigned to me), an East Indiaman, which went to pieces off Dungeness, and the Captain of which, with the majority of the crew, and all the passengers, perished.

Sir Elijah Impey congratulated me on having been saved from such a disaster, observing, that he trusted, this Almighty miraculous deliverance, portended an omen that I was reserved for happier days, than those which he knew I had recently experienced. I thanked him, and must gratefully repeat, his prediction has been accomplished, in the enjoyment of the blessings of health, of a composed mind, of an amiable partner, and a continued cheerful residence with her worthy family; these having fully compensated for a loss of worldly honors and riches.

(Sd.) G. F. Grand.

Cape of Good Hope,
30th April 1814.

Finis.

APPENDIX No. 2.

I. Documents of the Grand *vs.* Francis Case.

The most important of the Documents connected with the case of Grand *v.* Francis will be found in Dr. Busteed's *Echoes from Old Calcutta*. Students of that book will be interested in the following papers which were published for the first time in *Bengal: Past and Present*. They have been extracted, by kind permission of the Government of India, from the Original Consultations of the Supreme Council at Fort William.

No. 1.

[O. C. 1778, 14th December, No. 1.]

To—Mr. Auriol, Secretary to the Governor-General and Supreme Court.

12th December 1778.

Sir,—As I apprehend no Council is held to-day, I request the accompanying letter and papers enclosed in it may be immediately circulated, that no time may be lost in receiving the Governor-General and Council's permission for copies of these papers to be transmitted to England by either of the three India-men under present orders of sailing or by the Suez Packet, which vessel I judge conveys from hence the next dispatches.

I beg you, Sir, to send round also for the Council's perusal this letter addressed to you, as it will convey to them immediately a plain meaning of my wishes.

I am, etc.,

G. Grand.

No. 2.

[O. C. 14th December 1778.]

TO—THE GOVERNOR-GENERAL AND MEMBERS OF THE SUPREME COUNCIL.

FORT WILLIAM, *11th December 1778.*

HON'BLE SIR AND GENTLEMEN,

Late as this address comes before you, I earnestly entreat that, commiserating my well-known unhappy situation, you will yet indulge me with a compliance to the following request, sending to England by the ships now sailing a copy of it with copies of the other papers enclosed, to be laid before my honorable masters the Court of Directors.

It is, Gentlemen, a justice I owe to myself, to my family and friends in England who possibly might hear of the injury I had sustained without being satisfied of the publicity of the steps I have taken in consequence.

It is besides, Gentlemen, a justice I owe to this Settlement, and to the Servants in general, whom I consider in my case, to have been indirectly attacked in their honour; and therefore however unprecedented this appeal for address may be, yet I trust that the Court of Directors, being a body composed of humane and feeling men, will upon due consideration, attend to my representation.

I must beg to call their attention to the situation of the different parties, and they will then perceive that one of the members of your Hon'ble Board, invested with a legislative part of the administration of this country, instead of making his conduct an example of virtue and decorum, dared to violate the most sacred ties, and by base and insidious acts effected the ruin of a happy family, living partly under this legislative protection; and, after committing the irreparable stain to their dishonour, has been audacious enough to avail himself of the security his person enjoys to refuse the small satisfaction required, and thereby precluding the injured person from almost every species of redress but the one he now solicits.

The accompanying papers will serve in part to corroborate the above assertions. And I mean to bring subsequent proofs, collected from European evidence, which I conceive will effectually establish the identity of his person to have been trespassing in my house at that hour in the night.

I hope my Hon'ble Masters will see, in as forcible a light as I do, the necessity I am reduced to of endeavouring by every (means) I can devise to pursue the just resentment I must entertain against the perpetrators of so base an action and destroyer of my everlasting happiness. In this light I beg them to consider the address of their unhappy servant, and they will then judge whether a member of your Hon'ble Board, governed by no principles of honour or morality, is a fit person to preside as an administrator over a state where the happiness of individuals, and the good order of society is, I apprehend, to be consulted and preserved.

I am, etc.,

G. F. GRAND.

No. 3.

[O. C. 1778, December 14th, No. 3]

IN THE SUPREME COURT OF JUDICATURE AT FORT WILLIAM IN BENGAL.

Between... George Francis Grand ... *Plaintiff.*
and
Philip Francis ... ... *Defendant.*

Rambux Jemmautdar R. Hircarrah, Meerun Kismutgah, Bowanny Hircarrah and Shaic Razeeoolah Durwan, servants of the plaintiff abovenamed severally make oath and say, that these Deponents are respectively acquainted with Philip Francis, Esq., the Defendant abovenamed; And that they (these Deponents) abovenamed on Tuesday the eighth day of December instant, in the evening or night of the same day above of between the hours of ten and eleven o'clock, at a time when the said Plaintiff was absent from home and when the said Defendant Philip Francis had secretly, as these Deponents verily believe, entered the said house by means of a bamboo ladder fixed against the wall of the yard or compound of the said house for the purpose of gaining admission privately into the same, they (these Deponents) having respectively seen the same ladder. And this Deponent Shaic Razeeoolah Durwan positively swearing that he the said Defendant did no enter the said house through the gate thereof, because if he had done so, it must have been known to this Deponent, by reason that this Deponent was not absent from his duty as durwan to the Plaintiff during the whole course of the evening preceding the discovery of the said Defendant in the Plaintiff's house; And this Deponent Meerun for himself further said that about the hour of ten o'clock in the evening of the same day at a time when it was moonlight, this Deponent being in a small straw house within the yard or compound of the Plaintiff and which is built by the Plaintiff for the use of his servants, he (this Deponent) was informed by one Minche Ayah, the servant of the wife of the Plaintiff, that she (the said Ayah) had been sent downstairs by her mistress for a candle, and that having taken the same upstairs she had found all the doors shut and did not know what was the matter, whereupon this Deponent in going from the small straw house, where this Deponent was sitting as aforesaid, towards the house of the Plaintiff his master, this Deponent discovered a ladder fixed against the wall on the inside of the compound; and this Deponent thereupon immediately gave information of the same discovery to the other servants of the Plaintiff who were at that time in the same house with this Deponent; and this Deponent having removed or taken down the ladder from the wall, he (this Deponent) together with the several servants aforesaid, concealed themselves in a place in the same compound to watch for any person coming out of the house; and these Deponents Rambux Jemmautdar Hircarrah, Meerun Kismutgar and Bowanny Hircarrah further say that a short time after the being so concealed as aforesaid and which was a quarter of a Bengal ghurry afterwards, the Defendant came out of the house, dressed in black clothes, and immediately went to the place where the ladder has been fixed and appeared to be searching for the same ladder, when these Deponents Rambux and Meerun went up to him and asked who he was and what he wanted; to which he (the Defendant) replied, in a bad or broken Moors language, that he wanted the ladder and asked if these Deponents did not know him, declaring he was Mr. Francis and that he would make these Deponents great people if these Deponents would assist him using these words: "Hum toom logue burrah admee kurrega," and offered these Deponents many gold Mohurs, which he pulled out of his pockets in both hands, which money these Deponents refused taking; and this Deponent Rambux seized or laid hold of the hands of the said Philip Francis, and said that he (this Deponent) would not let him go, but would keep him till this Deponent's master the Plaintiff, should come home; and this Deponent Rambux then desired this other Deponent Meerun to go and inform the Plaintiff of what had happened, and this Deponent then went and informed the Plaintiff accordingly. And these Deponents, Meerun and Rambux, particularly say that although the said Defendant was dressed in black clothes, as hereinbefore mentioned, which these Deponents understand is not his common dress, yet they these Deponents aforesaid well knew it to be the said Defendant, by reason of having seen him often and often, heard his voice in conversation, and that when he spoke declaring himself to be Mr. Francis and upon the other conversation before mentioned these Deponents would well know his voice as well at the same time remembered his person (for although) it was late at night it was sufficiently moonlight to distinguish the same, besides which conversation these Deponents at such time aforesaid heard the same Defendant speak from the compound or yard below to the Plaintiff's wife then at a window above stairs, when, altough these Deponents did not understand what was said, yet they well knew the said Defendant's voice. And this Deponent Rambux for himself further saith that he (this Deponent) having laid hold of the hand of the said Defendant, as aforeasaid compelled him to sit on a chair in the lower apartment of the Plaintiff's house, and stood close over the same, declaring that he would not let go till this Deponent's master returned, during which time, when the Defendant was so seated as aforesaid, the Plaintiff's wife came down stairs, and, while the said Defendant was sitting in the chair, directed the Deponent to let the Defendant go, which this Deponent refused doing; whereupon the said Defendant whistled loudly and thereupon one Mr. Shee and one Mr. Ducarel came over the wall of the said compound of the Plaintiff's house to the said Defendant's assistance, when a struggle ensued in which the said Defendant made his escape, and this Deponent seized Mr. Shee, and detained him till the Plaintiff's return home, upon which seizure Mr. Shee put three gold mohurs into this Deponent's hands for the purpose of bribing this Deponent, as this Deponent supposes, to let him go, which this Deponent however refued to do; and this Deponent hath now got the same gold mohurs in his custody.

रामबकस जमीदार

The Mark of Meeran ر Kismutgah.
The Mark of Bowanny √ Hircarrah.
The Mark of + Shaic Razeeoolah.

Interpreted by me.
RAM LOCHUN GOSE,
Sworn Interpreter.

Sworn at Calcutta this *11th Day of December 1778.* } Before me. J. HYDE.

No. 4.

[O.C. 1778, December 14, No. 4.]

Wednesday Morning.

PHILIP FRANCIS, ESQ.

SIR,—The steps you took to dishonour me last night bind me to demand that satisfaction which is alone open to me. If notwithstanding your unprincipled behaviour, you have yet one spark of honour left, you will not refuse me a meeting to-morrow morning. The time, place, and weapons I leave to your choice, and will only acquaint you that I shall bring with me a second.

I am, Sir,
Your most humble servant,
G. GRAND.

No. 5.

SIR,—You are certainly under some gross deception, which I am unable to account for. Having never injured you, I know not for what reason I should give you satisfaction. I must, therefore, decline your request, and am.

Sir,
Your most obedient humble servant,
P. FRANCIS.

No. 6.

[O.C.; 1778, December 14, No. 5.]

For Circulation.

A letter from Mr. Grand to the Secretary [words erased] on which I request the orders of the Board.

B. BRUERE,
Asst. Secy.

[Hastings' Minute.]

On a question of so delicate and uncommon a nature the opinions of the members ought to have been taken in their order: but as the papers have been brought to me, as a delay may preclude the effect of the determination of the Board upon it, and as the right of appeal to the Court of Directors has been granted to the servants without any exception or qualification, I shall not hesitate to give my instant consent to the first part of the petition, *viz.*, that a copy of Mr. Grand's letter with copies of the other papers enclosed may be sent to England by the ship under despatch to the Court of Directors, if there be time for it, I think it would be improper to send the papers by the Suez Packet.

W. H.*

I agree R. B.†

[O.C., 1778, 14th December, No. 6.]

[Wheler's Minute.‡]

I agree with the Governor-General in thinking that it would be improper to send the papers by the Suez Packet, but I cannot discover the smallest propriety in sending them by the ships under despatch. Supposing a tresspass to have been committed, or an injury done, of which no proof is or can be established by *ex parte* evidence (especially of black men of the lowest order, and those in the service of the Plaintiff), His Majesty's Supreme Court of Judicature is open to the complaint of the party who may think himself aggrieved.

It is not respectful to that High Court to carry such complaint to any other jurisdiction: but to carry it before the Hon'ble Court of Directors, who have neither civil or criminal jurisdiction over His Majesty's subjects, appears to me equally absurd and disrespectful, since the charge, if proved, no ways concerns their

* Hastings.

† Barwell.

‡ Francis in his Journal, on December 12th, notes "Handsome behaviour of Wheler against the clamour of this cursed place."

service. I am, therefore, against sending the papers to the Court of Directors, and think they should not be recorded, as they have no relation to the Government or to the Company's service.

E. W.*

I agree with Mr. Wheler, F.†

No. 7.

[1779, O.C., 28th January, No. 4.]

CALCUTTA, *25th January 1779.*

[A letter "earnestly entreating" the Supreme Court to call Shee to the Presidency.]

[1779, O.C., 28th January, No. 3.]

No. 8.

TO—THE HON. W. H., ETC.

HONOURABLE SIR AND SIRS,—Having endeavoured without effect for these ten days last past to find Mr. George Shee, a factor in the service of the Honourable Company, in order that he may be served with a *subpœna* to testify in a cause now depending between me and Philip Francis, Esq., in the Supreme Court of Judicature, wherein Mr. Shee is a very material witness for me, and as I have reason to apprehend he secretes himself at Chandernagore to avoid my having

---

* Wheler.

† Francis.

the benefit of his testimony, and as I am creditably informed that Mr. Shee is about to depart soon for Madras or some such place beyond the seas in order effectually to deprive me of his evidence, I am to request the assistance and indulgence of Your Honorable Board in calling Mr. Shee to the Presidency that by means thereof I may have him served with a *subpœna* from the Supreme Court to testify in said cause.

I have the honour to be, etc.,
G. GRAND.

No. 9.

[O. C. 1779, P. C., 28th January, No. 5.]

SUPREME COURT OF JUDICATURE AT FORT WILLIAM IN BENGAL.

Between { George Francis Grand, Esq. ... *Plaintiff.*
and
Philip Francis, Esq. ... *Defendant.* }

Shaik Dooman one of the peons in the service of the Sheriff of Calcutta maketh oath that on the fourteenth day of January instant he this deponent received from the Under Sheriff a paper writing which the said Under Sheriff informed the deponent was a *subpœna* for Mr. George Shee and saith that the said Under Sheriff at the same time informed this deponent that the said George Shee was then at a place called Cowgautchee near Pulta and directed this deponent to go there and serve the said George Shee with this said *subpœna* if this deponent could find him. This deponent further saith that in pursuance of such directions he (this deponnent) on the same day went to Cowgautchee aforesaid but could not find the said George Shee there having been informed by the inhabitants of that place that several gentlemen had been there and was gone to a place a little further up the river called Ballyagaut, he (this deponent) went to Ballyagaut aforesaid in order to serve the said George Shee with said *subpœna*, but the deponent saith that he could not find the said George Shee at Ballyagaut aforesaid, therefore this deponent returned to Calcutta and this deponent saith on his return to Calcutta he (this depnent) made enquiry after the said George Shee at the Garden House of the Defendant in this cause (where this deponent was informed that the said George Shee was) in order to serve the said George Shee with the said *subpœna* ; but this deponent saith, having made enquiry of the servants at that place last aforesaid and which this deponent really did do, he could not find or discover where the said George Shee is or has been for several days last past.

The 20th day of 1779, before me. The marke of } +
J. HYDE. SHAIKE DOOMAN }

A true copy, *Read 21st January 1779.*
RD. LITCHFIELD,* J. DURNFORD,
Prothonotary. *Reading Clerk.*

---

* Married a Miss Fraser—a near relative of Sir E. Impey's.

No. 10.

[1779, P.C., 28th January, No. 6.]

SUPREME COURT OF JUDICATURE AT FORT WILLIAM IN BENGAL.

Between... George Francis Grand ... *Plaintiff.*
and
Philip Francis ... *Defendant.*

Henry Nichols, one of the officers of the Sheriff of Calcutta, maketh oath and saith that, on Tuesday the twelfth day of the instant January, he (this deponent) received from the Under Sheriff of Calcutta a *Subpœna* to testify in this cause directed to Mr. George Shee with directions to serve the same on the said George Shee : other deponent further saith that he (this deponent) on the same day made diligent enquiry after the said George Shee at his apartments in the new buildings near the Court House and at the house of the Defendant in Calcutta in order to serve him the said George with the said *subpœna*, but this deponent saith that he could not find the said George Shee to serve him with the said *subpœna*, this deponent further saith that, having received information from one of the servants of Mr. May who lives in the house of the Defendant, that the said George Shee was gone to Chandernagore, he (this deponent), by the directions of the said Under Sheriff went to Chandernagore aforesaid and on his arrival there made diligent inquiry after the said George Shee, and being in- that the said George Shee resided at the house of Mr. Leonard Collins' at Chandernagore, he (this deponent), on Thursday the fourteenth day of January instant, went twice or thrice to the house of the said Leonard Collins* of Chandernagore in order to serve the said *subpœna*, but this deponent saith that he could not find the said George Shee and this deponent further saith that he was informed by Sergeant at Chandernagore aforesaid that he, the said Sergeant in going to the house of the said Leonard Collins had lately and frequently seen the said George Shee at the house of the said Leonard Collins wherefore this deponent remained at Chandernagore from the fourteenth in the morning until the evening of the sixteenth of the same month of January and during the said time frequently went and sent to and about the house of the said Leonard Collins to enquire after the said George Shee, but to no effect: and this deponent saith that at each time he went to the house of the said Leonard Collins he was met by some of the servants belonging to the said house who enquired their deponent's business, and prevented the deponent going into the said house for some few minutes, until someone of them went in before him and this deponent saith that from the intelligence he received from the said Sergeant and others at Chandernagore and the great precaution taken by the servants at the house of the aforesaid Leonard Collins at Chandernagore aforesaid, he (this deponent) believes the said George Shee

---

* The name should be Collings. Collings was the Commissary stationed to watch over captured Chandernagore.

then was at Chandernagore, and secreted himself to avoid being served with a *subpœna* in this cause.

Sworn this 20th day of January 1779 before me.

J. HYDE. The mark of HENRY NICHOLS. } +

Read 21st January 1779.

A True Copy
RD. LICHFIELD,
Prothonotary.

WILLIAM SMOULT,
Reading Clerk.

II. SOME LETTERS OF MRS. GRAND'S FATHER.

No. 1.

TO—THE HON'BLE WARREN HASTINGS, GOVERNOR-GENERAL AND COUNCIL AT FORT WILLIAM.

BALASORE, *2nd October 1780.*

GENTLEMEN,—Mr. Marriott, your Resident here, has this morning notified to me the orders he received from you last night. I know very well that I am here by permission for my health. I should have departed immediately if I had been in condition to undertake the journey by land, but for four months past I have not the use of my legs, and cannot go from room to room without crutches. If, however, your orders are peremptory that I must absolutely repair to Calcutta, I humbly hope that you will be pleased to defer the execution of them till the month of December, the proper time for proceeding by sea to Bengal. It is not disobedience to your orders, Gentlemen, but the impossibility of going to which I am reduced by my infirmities

(Sd.) VERLEE.

No. 2.

TO—THE HON'BLE WARREN HASTINGS, GOVERNOR-GENERAL AND COUNCIL AT FORT WILLIAM.

3rd March 1781.

HON'BLE SIR AND SIRS,—Your petitioner, prisoner on his parol of honour, received the license of the Hon'ble Board to reside at Balasore for the benefit of his health, had accordingly proceeded to that place, having advanced a small sum of money, his property, to Mr. Marriott, has been afterwards under the necessity of receiving the Ketch *Faquira* of 150 tons in payment of his advances, as that gentleman said he had no other mode of satisfying him. Your petitioner at this crisis, finding that craft was very much in want and having been offered to freight by Mr. Lewis da Costa with rice from Balasore to Madras and back to Calcutta, applied to your Resident at Balasore for a pass, as being now under the protection of the English Government, and having been gratified with it, did not imagine that the Ketch *Faquira* should have been liable to seizure made of her the 12th ultimo.

As your petitioner has shown a strict fealty to your orders ever since he has been made a prisoner, he humbly begs the Hon'ble Board will consider his case and grant the release of his vessel.

VERLEE.

No. 3.

To—The Hon'ble Warren Hastings, Governor-General, etc., at Calcutta.

Calcutta, *the 15th March 1781.*

Sir,—Before I left Balasore I gave my word to Mr. Wodsworth that I, on my arrival here, should present myself to you. I would have done myself that honour had it not been impossible for me to walk by an infirmity which affects me a long while ago, and of which I have informed Mr. Hay by writing. I am now worse than I was on my arrival, and being sixty years old, I take the liberty of intreating you to order a Surgeon in the Company's service to examine me; he will be able to inform you of my unfortunate situation, and his report will, I hope, induce you to grant me the permission to go to my family at Chandernagore and receive the assistance which I am so much in need of.

I am with respect

(Sd.) Verlee.

No. 4.

To—E. Hay, Esq., Secretary to the Hon'ble the Governor and Council.

Calcutta, *22nd March 1781.*

Sir,—In compliance with the order of the Hon'ble the Governor-General and Council I have visited Mr. Verlèe who is an old man, and in a very bad habit of body, his legs being so much enlarged with œdematous swelling that he is scarcely able to walk fifty yards.

I am, Sir, etc.,

Dan. Campbell,

Surgn.-Genl.

NOTES.

Page 9. *Col. Peach.* (Joseph) May or April 1764. Lieut.-Col. May 4, 1765, Col. Feb. 1767. Commanded 1st Brigade in 1767. Having commanded the 2nd European Regiment at Allahabad in 1765. Married in Calcutta Miss Appia Witts on January 30, 1770. Died at Monghyr, July 1770.

Page 13. *Lord Clive, particularly, spoke.* Lord Clive was not in Calcutta at this time, but up-country dealing with the mutiny of European officers.

Page 13. *Budgerow* a species of keeless barge, two-thirds of the aft portion of which was occupied by the cabins.

Page 15. *Jagheer* (Persian *Jágīr*). In the popular sense defined by Foote in the *Nabob:* "the term is Indian, and means an annual income." Technically "a tenure common under the Mohamedan Government, in which the public revenues of a given tract of land were made over to a servant of the State, together with the powers to enable him to collect and appropriate such revenue and administer the general government of the district." Wilson: *Glossary of Judicial and Revenue Terms.*

Page 16. *Burgoyne the hero of Saratoga.* This, of course, is a sarcasm. Burgoyne, who was nothing if not great at censuring, not only his brother officers but his superiors as well, capitulated at Saratoga in October 1777. He was one of the managers of the impeachment of Warren Hastings.

Page 16. *The three Brigades.* See Broome: *History of the Rise and Progress of the Bengal Army.* Page 533. The order for the formation of the three Brigades is dated 5th August 1765. The first at Monghyr was to be commanded by Brigadier-General J. Carnac, the second at Allahabad by Colonel Richard Smith, the third at Bankipore by Colonel Robert Barker. Early in 1766 the third Brigade moved into the Betia country to reduce the refractory zemindars.

Page 17. *Arrived at Bankypore, then the Cantonment of the second Brigade.* The second Brigade was stationed at Bankipore in November 1766. See Broome: *Op. cit.*, p. 622. Grand's dates are confused.

Page 18. *The Army at my entrance into the service.* See Broome: *Op. cit.*, pp. 618-19 for the Pergunnah Battalions. See Long: *Selections from Unpublished Records.* No. 969.

Page 19. *Erection of Barracks both at Dynapore and Berhampore.* For some letters concerning this fire, see *Bengal: Past and Present*, Vol. V, pp. 361-3.

Page 21. *Mr. Thomas Motte.* Motte's account of his visit to the mines of Orissa (1766) will probably follow in due course in this series of reprints. See *Bengal: Past and Present*, Vol. IV, p. 505, for his career. For Mrs. Motte (Miss Mary Touchet), the bosom friend of the second Mrs. Warren Hastings, see Sydney Grier: *Letters of Warren Hastings to his Wife.* "Mott's Lane" in Calcutta commemorates this old Calcutta worthy. It was at Motte's House at Hughli, Grand was married (10th July 1777) by the Rev. W. Johnson to Noel C. Verlee, the marriage having been previously performed by "the popish priest" at Chandernagore. Motte died at Serampore on 29th January 1805, aged 74.

Page 22. *Cutwal.* [Kotwal]. The nocturnal police officer of a town.

Page 22. *Rajah Bulwantsing.* "The family belonged to the clan of Bhuihars, and were intimately connected with the house of Tikari in Gaya. Cheyt Singh's grandfather was an adventurer who started life as a petty landholder." Hand: *Early English Administration of Behar*, p. 3. *Cf.* Grierson: *Notes on the District of Gaya*, p. 20. "Bulwantsing derived the degree of independency which he possessed, during the latter period of his life, from the protection and intervention of our Government." Hastings: *Narrative of the Insurrection.* (Forrest: *Selections from the State Papers of the Governor-General, Warren Hastings*, Vol. II, pp. 134-5.)

Page 28. *First to laugh.* Act III. of the *Nabob* might serve as a useful lesson to Historical Societies.

"*Secretary.* A cork-screw, presented by Sir John Falstaff to Henry V. with a tobacco-stopper of Sir Walter Raleigh's, made of the stern of the ship in which he first compassed the globe;

given to the Society by a Clergyman from the North Riding of Yorkshire.

"*First Antiquarian.* A rare instance of generosity, as they must have both been of use to the reverend donor himself."

"*Sec.* A curious collection, in regular and undoubted succession, of all tickets of the Islington turnpike, from its first institution to the 20th of May."

"*Second Antiquarian.* Preserve them with care, as they may hereafter serve to illustrate that part of English History."

Sir M. Mite's disquisition discussed these points:

1. Did Whittington ever exist?
2. Was Whittington Lord Mayor of London?
3. Was he really possessed of a cat?
4. Was that cat the source of his wealth.

Sir M. Mite held that "the cat, Gentleman, is the Gordian knot to untie," and he proceeded to explain that a cat is a "vessel, which, from its agility and lightness, he aptly christened a cat." "Nay, to this our day, Gentlemen, all our coals from Newcastle are imported in nothing but cats."

Page 28. *Primrose Galliez.* "Having raised some three or four hundred picked men, he (Clive) furnished them not only with arms but also with dress of European pattern, drilled and disciplined them as regular troops, and appointed a British officer and non-commissioned officers to command and instruct them. This was the earliest British native regiment known as the *Lal Paltun* on account of its equipment, but later it went by the name of *Gelis-ki Paltun,* from Captain Primrose Galliez, who obtained command of it in 1763; and held that post for many years. It became the 2nd battalion of the 12th Native Infantry in 1796." Cardew: *Sketch of the Services of the Bengal Native Army.* Severely wounded at the capture of Patna 1763. Galliez was Cadet, 17th November 1758;, Lieutenant, 28th July 1759; Captain, 11th October 1763; Major, 29th April 1766; Lieutenant-Colonel, 2nd April 1768; Colonel, 18th January 1774. He resigned 11th November 1776. He married in Calcutta, on 7th April 1763, Mary de Noailles, widow.

Page 23. *Lord Clive and General Carnac quitted India in February 1767.* Gleig writes: "On one of the last days of January 1767 Lord

Clive, accompanied by the gentlemen of his household, and his old and valued friend General Carnac, embarked on board the *Britania* in the Ganges. On the 14th of July he landed at Portsmouth." Page 304 (Edn. 1907). His successor, Harry Verelst, assumed office 29th January 1767. Cartier assumed office 26th December 1769.

Page 30. *Raja Cheytsing, son of Bulwantsing.* See for defence of Hastings' conduct Forrest: *Selections from the State Papers of the Governor-General, Warren Hastings*, and for an account of the insurrection from local documents Hand's *Early English Administration in Bihar, 1781-1785* (Calcutta, 1894).

Page 31. *The late General Anthony Polier.* In Vol. V. of *Bengal: Past and Present*, Mr. William Irvine writes of Polier.

"The materials for his biography will be found in the preface to the work founded on his papers by his cousin Madame la Chanomesse de Polier, 1742-1817, *Mythologie des Indous*, Rudolstadt and Paris, 2 Vols. 1809, Vol. I., Preface pp. III to LXIII, *Biographie Universelle* (Michaud), Paris 1823, Vol. XXXV., pp. 181-183, *Nouvelle Biographie Generale* (Didot) Paris, 1862, Vol. XL, p. 605, and *La France Protestante* by Eugene and Emil Haag, 9 Vols. Supp., 1846-1858, Vol. VIII, pp, 274-283. Madame Polier's account is chiefly from Polier's autobiographical notes.

"Antoine Louis Henri Polier belonged to a French Protestant family which had emigrated to Switzerland in the seventeenth century. His autobiography says he landed in India in June 1753 at the age of seventeen, thus he was born in 1736. Haag, on the contrary, gives the date of birth as February 1741 and of arrival in India as 1756. He went out to join his uncle Paul Phillipe Poli-r (born 1712) who after serving in Sardinia and Berne, entered the E. I. Company's service and rose to be commandant of Fort St. George, dying in December 1758 from wounds received in a sortie from Madras (R. Orme, *Military Transactions*, Ed. of 1861, Vol II., p. 395). The younger Polier entered the service as cadet and in 1762 was Chief Engineer at Calcutta, but in 1764 was superseded by an Englishman. Clive re-instated him and added the office of [town] major and commandant of Calcutta. Under a rule introduced by the Company forbidding the promotion of foreigners to field rank, Polier resigned and entered the service of Shuja-ud-daula in Oudh. Forced in 1775 to leave by the English, he transferred himself to the Emperor's service; quitting him again in a few years for the Company's service. Warren Hastings, who liked him, procured him the honorary rank of Lieutenant-Colonel with permission to reside at Lucknow. Mention of him will be found in Miss Grier's *Letters of Warren Hastings*, pp. 295, 309, 312, under the year 1784. Polier's "*Moracka*" on p. 295 is for *muragga*, a scrapbook, an album.

"In 1789 Colonel Polier returned to Europe and married (20th January 1791), bought a property near Avignon and settled there. During the revolution the country became disturbed and some robbers assassinated him on 9th February 1795. A fine collection of pictures was sold to W. Beckford, and forty-two manuscripts, Arabic, Persian and Sanskrit, were acquired by the Bibliothéque Nationale at Paris. Polier presented to the British Museum (22nd May 1789) his copy of the Vedas in eleven volumes. The Bibliothéque Cantonale of Lausanne contains a manuscript catalogue of 120 Oriental works with annotations by Colonel Polier. This volume is thus catalogued: "A 392, Poller (le Colonel Antoine Louis Henri) catalogue d'une collection de manuscrits orientaux apportés de l'Inde en 1788, manuscrit in fol." Some of the Persian manuscripts in the British Museum are from his library. Many incidental mentions of Colonel Polier could be gleaned from the parliamentary papers and the records, English and Persian, of the Warren Hastings' period. For instance, there is a short note by him on the distillation of rose-essence in the *Asiatic Researches*; and General de Boigne received his hospitality at Lucknow for five months in 1783, see Victor de Saint Genis, *Le General de Boigne, 1751-1830*, Poitiers, 1873, p. 50."

Page 32. *The placid Mr. Cartier.* Cartier, who came to the chair, after a long career at Dacca, was a favourite of Lord Clive's. Cartier did not approve of Shah Allum's alliance with the Marathas, but took the step of sending Barker to accompany the Emperor, when he saw that it was impossible to prevent him leaving for Delhi. To Cartier is due the honour of having appointed the supervisors, a measured, which has been ridiculed by superficial writers, uch for instance as Sir J. W. Kaye, but was in reality one of the best steps ever taken by any English ruler before Warren Hastings.

Page 33. *This meritorious act.* Contrast the language of Macaulay. As a matter of fact the charges in regard to Hastings' conduct in regard to Shah Allum were withdrawn in 1790 by the Managers of the Impeachment. See Sydney Grier: *Letters of Warren Hastings to his Wife*, p. 464. G. W. Hastings: *A Vindication of Warren Hastings*, pp. 175-6.

Page 33. *The "Marquis of Nottingham."* See Introduction, p. .

Page 35. *Governor Vansittart.* Assumed office 27th July 1760. For the history of his rule see *The Three Surgeons of Patna*, Introduction.

Page. 37. *The "Aurora."* Grand does not mention that upon this ship was young Robert Pitcairn, who is supposed to have been the first to catch sight of Pitcairn's Island (named after him) on 2nd July 1767. The island was subsequently lost to knowledge, but it is now identified with the island on which the mutineers of the *Bounty* found a home. See article in ("Pitcairn") *Dictionary of National Biography.*

Page 35. *Scrafton Luke.* Arrived Sept. 25th, 1746. Third at Dacca in the troubles of 1756, when he negociated through the French the surrender of the Factory. Entertained by the French at their Factory: reached the refuge camp at Fulta, 26th August. After the restoration of the English at the Factory at Cosimbazar, where he corresponded confidentially with Clive, conducted intrigues for the removal of Siraj-uddaula. Submitted a plan for the punishment of the persons responsible for the 'Black Hole.' Expelled from Murshidabad by the Nawab, but sent back by Clive with a letter from the Mahrathas shewing that they were likely to assist the English. Brought Amir Chand (Omichand) down to Calcutta. It was Scrafton who broke to Amir Chand the fact that he had been tricked by the fraud copy of the treaty. He received Rs. 200,000 from Mir Jafar for his share in effecting the revolution. After Plassey he became Resident at the Durbar of Murshidabad, in which post he preceded Warren Hastings. Sub-Export Warehouse-keeper and Secretary to the Select Committee; Paymaster to the Army, 1759. Appointed to Council, 23rd Nov. 1759. Apparently left

Bengal about that time. Author of *Reflexions on the Government of Hindustan with a Sketch of the History of Bengal*—1770.

Page 35. *Colonel Ford* (Francis Forde). The conqueror of the French in the Northern Circars. Fought the decisive battle against the Dutch at Biddera (Bedarra) on Nov. 25th, 1759, apparently at the bidding of a laconic note presented by Clive at the card table; "Dear Forde, fight them immediately, I will send you the order of Council to-morrow."

Page 35. *Famine in only part natural.* Sir William Hunter writes: (*Annals of Rural Bengal*, p. 33) "Two years after the dearth, Warren Hastings wrote an elaborate report on the state of Bengal. He had made a progress through a large portion of the country, instituting the most searching inquiries by the way, and he deliberately sets the loss as 'at least one-third of the inhabitants.' This estimate has been accepted by all official and by the most accurate non-official writers. It represents an aggregate of individual suffering which no European nation has been called upon to contemplate within historic times. Twenty years after the famine the remaining population was estimated at from twenty-four to thirty millions; and we cannot help arriving at the conclusion that the failure of a single crop, following a year of scarcity, had within nine months swept away ten millions of human beings." The elaborate report to which Hunter refers is included in Vol. II of Forrest's *Selections from the State Papers of the Governor-General, Warren Hastings*. Hunter contends that "in 1770, the Government by interdicting what it was pleased to term the monopoly of grain prevented prices from rising at once to their natural rates. The province had a certain amount of food in it and this food had to last nine months. Private enterprise if left to itself would have stored up the general supply at the harvest, with a view to realising a larger profit at a later period in the scarcity. Prices would in consequence have immediately risen, compelling the population to reduce their consumption from the very beginning of the dearth. The general stock would have thus been husbanded, and the pressure spread over the whole nine months, instead of being concentrated upon the last six. The price of grain, in place of promptly rising at three-half pence a pound as in 1865-66, continued at three-farthings during the earlier months of the famine." (P. 43.) Another view is given by Colonel T. D. Pearse writing from actual observation in 1772 (*Bengal: Past and Present*, Vol. II, page 317) where he refers to Bulwant Sing's refusal to export grain, so that "on his shores were well supplied villages, when thousands starved at Buxar." "That the native Government would have made a scarcity by the same means is certain, provided we had not been in power; but had the country been in its former state, and scarcity had been occasioned, we, by our power, would have opened the magazines and saved the multitude. But when the tyranny was in our own hands—when we alone profited by the miseries of others; we could not find it, our hearts to do good, because our purse must have been lighter. Had every man been free to sell, and had been protected by us from oppression of the Native Government, every man who had a surplus would have carried it to the market for a better price; but as the matter was, each man concealed as much as he could, and what was not concealed, he was compelled to sell to those who could and did lock it up to retail to the destruction of others. The very orders given at the Durbar, to buy up the grain that could be got, and send it to Murshidabad were the destruction of this country; for they were obeyed. The inhabitants could get no food in the country; they fled to the city after grain; but the grain was too well secured for them to get a mouthful, and the unfortunate people died by thousands. The Governor [Cartier] erred from want of judgment and bad counsel; he did not share in the horrid plunder; he is a man of good character and amiable in the extreme; but there never was a Governor less capable, less active, less resolute. Much I fear the distress of the country is beyond even Mr. Hastings' abilities to restore." *Cf.* Appendix B. to Hunter's *Rural Annals* (1768). It must be remembered that the charge against "monopolising Europeans" made by R. Becher and Mahomed Reza Khan, was never examined, nor did the accusers specify the names of the offenders. The evidence is really not to hand, but it may be said that the mofussil records so far as they are known afford no support to the charge. The Supervisor's reports are by no means untouched by human feelings. Capt. J. Price (*Five Letters from a Free Merchant in Bengal*, 1777) writes: "In short, if Englishmen have nothing more to answer for this being, as has been said, the causes of that dreadful calamity, they having nothing to fear in the next world on that account."

Page 39. *Colonel James Morgan.* See references in Sydney Grier: *Letters of Warren Hastings to His Wife* and Forrest: *Selections from the State Papers preserved in the Foreign Department.* He was a brother of Frederick James Morgan, the Commandant at Fort William.

Page 39. *The disgrace of this great minister.* The Duc de Choiseul has been well described as "a brilliant adventurer rather than a sagacious statesman." *Vide* J. B. Perkins' *France under Louis XV*, Vol. II., p. 245. The Duc de Choiseul had owed his advancement to Madame de Pompadour, and to the enmity of Madame du Barry was very largely due his dismissal. On 24th December 1770 a *lettre de cachet* ordered him to resign his office and retire to Chanteloup. *Vide* Gaston Mangras' *La Disgrace du Duc et de la Duchesse de Choiseul.* Mr. Perkins reports an episode which illustrates the times. "In a curious letter, which reached Paris just after Choiseul's disgrace, the French envoy at London repeats a conversation with Lord North, who, he says, had been dining with Lord Sandwich and was as drunk as a hackney coachman. Francès was convinced that the English minister was sincerely anxious for peace and was greatly impressed by the lucidity of his mind even when hopelessly drunk. 'In the most complete intoxication,' he writes, 'there were the same principles, the same ideas, which you will find stated in my last dispatch, for these gentlemen preserve their logic in their cups from force of habit.'" The Duc de Choiseul died on 8th May 1785.

Page 40. *Married at the age of 14.* Noel Catherine Verlée was about four months short of the age of 15 when she married Grand. Her father (a "Capitane du Porte") at the age of 23 married (the first wife not C. N.'s mother) Marguerite da Silva, aged 14. Mrs. Carey, who survived the Black Hole, could not have been more than 15 at the time, and another married woman who is said also to have survived the same trial, must have been no more then 14 at the time. Mrs. Beame, in her *Heroines of French Society* writes of the time: "Girls at fourteen and fifteen or even younger, who, with us, wear their hair down their backs, their petticoats half way down to their feet, and spend their times in lessons and play, were wives, mothers, Court beauties, and distinguished members of society at the French Court of those days."

Page 44. *Sir Francis Sykes.* Arrived 9th July 1751, aged 25. Made prisoner, but escaped to French Factory. A member of the Factory at Cosimbazar in 1756. Escaped with W. Watts from Murshidabad before Plassey. Resigned the Service 1760. Took home with him Hastings' infant son. Returned to India with Lord Clive 1765. Member of the Select Committee. Chief of Cossimbazar. His wife (Catherine Ridley, married 7th February 1766) is buried in the South Park Street Cemetery, Calcutta. He was created a Baronet in 1781.

Page 44. *Sir Thomas Rumbold.* After serving under Stringer Lawrence, he served as a volunteer under Clive 1757. Voted for immediate action in the Council of war before Plassey. Third at Chittagong 1760. Chief of Patna. Council 1766-1769. Returned to England 1770. M.P. for New Shoreham. Governor of Madras, 8th February 1778 to 6th April 1780. Died 1791. The story that he began life as a waiter (Carey: *Good Old Days of Honourable John Company*) is an absurdity. He was the youngest son of William Rumbold, second at Tellichery, and his uncle Henry had been Secretary at Fort William. He had married a Miss Berriman at Madras 22nd June 1756. This lady died in child-bed, 22nd August 1764, aged 26. (Her tablet at St. John's churchyard has disappeared, but is mentioned in the *Bengal Obituary*). Of the two sons born of this marriage, Mr. H. E. A. Cotton writes: "The eldest, who died in 1786, was aid-de-camp to Sir Hector Munro at the seige of Pondicherry and carried home the despatches and colours of the fortress for presentation to the King. The second son and second baronet, Sir George Berriman Rumbold, whose birth cost his mother her life, was seized by the order of Napoleon while Minister Resident at Hamburgh in 1804, and conveyed as a prisoner to the Temple. He died at Memel in 1807. Two of his sons came to India and joined the banking house of Palmer and Company at Hyderabad, where they both are buried. George died in 1820, and Sir William, the third Baronet, in 1833, the latter leaving five sons, each of whom succeeded in turn to the baronetcy, which is now [1909] held by the youngest, Sir Horace Rumbold, the well-known ex-Ambassador." Cotton: *Calcutta: Old and New*, pp. 548-9.

Page 44. *To triumph against old established families.* The *Calcutta Gazette* of 16th August 1784 records: "We are sorry to find that may private letters mention the great disrespect in which East Indians are held in England, so much so that they are driven to associate almost entirely with each other." Setcn-Karr: *Selections*, Vol. I, p. 204.

Page 44. *Fewer men.* The passage seems to refer to General R. Smith. The attribution of inferior birth to persons of influence seems to have been a fashion among Anglo-Indians of the times. Lady Monson, according to Francis, used to assert that Warren Hastings was the natural son of a steward on her father's estate. According to some accounts Sir T. Rumbold had once been a fiddler at the opera, or according to others (*e.g.*, Carey's *Good Old Days of Honourable John Company*) "a waiter or boots at Arthur's Club in London." The legend has it that the head writer at Arthur's was one Robert McGrath and so when Rumbold returned from the Governorship of Madras, the following lines were coined, it was asserted, by Charles Lane Fox—

When McGrath reigned o'er Arthur's crew,
He said to Rumbold, 'Black my shoe,'
And Rumbold answered 'Yea, Bob.'
But now returned from India's land,
He proudly scouts the base command:
And Rumbold answered 'Nea, Bob.'

Sir Thomas was the son of William Rumbold of the Madras Civil Service and nephew to Henry Rumbold, Secretary at Fort William, who died in Bengal in 1743. Although the scandal Francis reports of Hastings' birth has long since been exposed, yet recent writers still follow Macaulay in characterising Hastings' father as a "boy" and a lazy and worthless one into the bargain. As a matter of fact the father of the Great Proconsul was a country clergyman of ancient lineage and by no means the poverty scapegrace lad of 15 years when he married a lady with a little independent fortune of her own—Miss Hester Warren of Twining. In a contemporary pamphlet, a satirical "Vindication" of General R. Smith, he is said to have been the son of a cheese maker—a statement which only agrees with Grand's in intentional malice.

Page 53. *Last Marquis of Lindsay.* Not "Lindsay" but "Lindsey." Admiral Robert Bertie, created Earl of Lindsey in 1629, died of wounds received at the battle of Edgehill.

Page 54. *The Duchess.* Mary (wife of the 3rd Duke of Ancaster, married 1750, died 1793) was the daughter of Thomas Panton, Keeper of the King's Running Horses at Newmarket. She was Mistress of the Robes to Queen Charlotte.

Page 55. *The Cardinal of Toulouse was the Minister of France at that juncture.* This was in March 1774. Choiseul was succeeded by the Duc d'Aiguillon, who after the accession of Louis XVI. was succeeded by Maurepas. Is Grand referring to the Cardinal de la Roche Aymon, who, as Grand Almoner, administered the last Sacraments to Louis XV? This Prelate, a favourite of Mme. du Barry, was Archbishop of Reims. Or is Grand thinking of Lomenie de Brienne, Archbishop of Tolouse, who become Controller General in 1787? This was the Dignitary to whom, when it was suggested that he should be translated to the Archbishopric of Paris, Louis XVI. made objection: "Il faut au moins que l' Archeveque du Paris croie en Dieu."

Page 57. *Lord Pigot, a civilian, in his memorable defence.* Malleson writes: "The Governor was Mr. George Pigot, afterwards Lord Pigot, a man of ability and discrimination, and who had the good sense to make over all the arrangements of the defence to the veteran Colonel Lawrence, who found himself within the walls. Under Lawrence were Lieutenant-Colonel Draper, the conqueror of Manilla, Major Cailland of Trichinapalli renown, Major Brereton and other good officers." (*History of the French in India*, p. 536.) Lally reached the plain in front of Madras, 12th December 1758. The seige was raised 17th February 1759.

Page 61. *Rapine.* The person referred to is Paul de Rapin. He came to England as a refugee after the Edict of Nantes and fought in the cause of William of Orange in Holland and Ireland. In 1768 he was tutor to the Duke of Portland's eldest son. Died at Wesel in poverty in 1725.

MARY, DUCHESS OF ANCASTER.
(From a Mezzotint by J. McArdell after Thos. Hudson.)

Page 65. *Captain Robert Carr.* I do not know whether this person is to be identified with the Captain who in 1777 commanded the *Barwell* and who was a brother of the Rev. Robartes Carr, who got into well deserved trouble for selling at St. Helena a slave whom the Captain had brought to that place in 1777. (*Bengal: Past and Present*, Vol. V., p. 172). Captain Robert Carr often appears in the Society's Barwell Letter Copy Books. The following letter throws some light on the times :—

CALCUTTA,
22nd November, 1775.

TO MRS. MARY BARWELL.

MY DEAR SISTER,

Every instance of your affection cannot prove otherwise than grateful to me, and it is of very little signification whether the object of it is mistaken : I am still equally indebted to the principle which influences testimony of your regard ; and am now to return you thanks for what calls a blush to my face. Had I intended to introduce to your knowledge the boy I sent to England under the care of Captain Carr, I would certainly have mentioned his name to my brother. Whether he is my natural child or not is apocryhal—most probably he is not. Be that as it may, the infant was so far adopted by my humanity as to be protected from want. I rear'd him and prepared to have had him educated in a stile suited to the character in which I intended him to appear in life. I made known to Captain Carr these my intentions, and flattered myself he would have strictly adhered to them ; instead of which, I understand from my brother James, the boy is educated after a manner by no means suitable to a dependent and servile condition, that he has been introduced to you under my name and as my son, and that you have recd. and treated him as such. Now I never meant he should behold himself in that light, nor me in any other than that of his patron and friend. To rectify this error of Captain Carr's the first step necessary is to restore to him the name by which I called him, Richard Hunter ; and, that this may be effectually done, I must positively insist on his being rebaptised by that name. The next thing I mus insist upon is, that the charge of his education, including cloaths, etc., be limited to £ stg. 50 *per annum*, that he regard his birrh as low and his expectations as nothing beyond what his own talents as a merchant's clerk may entitle him to, and that he may be able acquit himself in that sphere of life, I would have him made a perfect master of accounts and a good penman ; and, as soon as he is perfected in these particulars he is to be sent back to his native country, where he will naturally chose to spend his days, respecting in that degree which may be due to his merits and good qualities, if he has any ; and if he has not talents to push him forward he will here, as a merchant's clerk, be both happy and easy in his situation.

Though these are my sentiments and this the sphere of action I have chosen for him, yet I would not for a little expence check his education, if powers of his mind do already unfold and promise any extent of capacity. In that case I would wish to make him a master of the classics and master of the Arabic and Persian tongues and give him a knowledge of the French language ; but whatever he is taught, let it be strongly inculcated on his mind that he is an orphan brought up by the hand of charity, and is to depend on his own talents to facilitate his future fortunes. The rudiments of Arabic and Persic are much better and much sooner learnt in Europe than Asia, if I may judge from the works of Mr. Jones.*

I have mentioned to you in the first part of my letter what I intended and meant by giving the boy introduced to you as my child his education in England. The time he has already prosecuted studies so superior to a mere merchant's clerk may possibly have been happy for him in a country like this. Superior talents prove a certain independency to those who possess such. If the boy's mind does not promise to expand itself, all he has learnt is useless, and he will regret for his life mistaken zeal of my friend Carr to send him a gentleman, without giving him the means necessary to support that character. James will give you more particulars of my sentiments touching the education of my little black orphan.

I am, etc.,

R. B.

* *i.e.* The future Sir William Jones.

Page 65. *Mr. and Mrs. Floyer.* Charles Floyer had been one of the Madras Civil servants brought up by Lord Clive in 1765 to supersede those of Bengal. See *Bengal: Past and Present*, Vol. V., pp. 194 *et seq.* Military Paymaster 1767, Mint Master 1769, Secretary to the Select Committee 1769, Buxey 1770. Charles Floyer married Mademoiselle Catherine Carvalho, who was sister to Jeanne Carvalho who married Jean Law of Lauriston, Governor of Pondichery, and perhaps sister to Mary Carvalho, who married Hugh Grant (Captain H. Grant who raised the *Grant-ki-pultan*, afterwards IVth Native Battalion in September 1760?) Two Miss Carvalhos had been among the refugees at Fulta after the seige of Fort William in 1756. I do not know whether Floyer married more than once.

Page 65. *Willes* (John). A Madras Civil servant afterwards brought (1783) to Bengal to succeed the Hon. Robert Lindsay as Collector of Sylhet. See the present Editor's forthcoming volumes of Sylhet Records. Though probably an exceedingly able revenue official, Willes does not seem to have possessed the character necessary for the ruler of a turbulent frontier district. After Lindsay's energetic rule, the instances of Willes' inability to act on his own responsibility and his extreme mildness in dealing with marauders are extremely provoking. One of the most interesting incidents in his career as Collector of Sylhet is the attempt of M. Foquet de Champigny to secure a footing for the French on the southern border of the Khasi hills. In this matter Willes did exhibit some firmness of decision, with the result that M. de Champigny retired to Chandernagore.

Page 71. *Death of Colonel Monson.* Died at Hughli 25th September 1776, seven months after his wife, Lady Anne Monson. Barwell in a letter to his sister notes in regard to the death of Clavering: "He died on a Saturday, a day become remarkable in the annals of Bengal, and to which the superstition of the people has given a most malignant influence to his cause and a happy one to Hastings. Yes, says the Hindoo, Mahraja Nuncomar was committed to prison on a Saturday, he was condemned to death on a Saturday, and he was hanged on a Saturday. Colonel Monson died on a Saturday, and General Clavering died on a Saturday, and what is all the more remarkable they all three died in the month of Bhadoo (between the 15th of our August and 15th September). Whether it s so or not, I have not examined. The idea in general, and, being universally received, I take it for granted." Inscriptions have recently been placed on the graves of Colonel Monson and his wife by the Government of Bengal at the request of the Calcutta Historical Society.

Page 71. *Colonel Macleane* (Lachlan). Had served with distinction in the Northern Circars and Bengal, 1759-63. Agent to the Nabob of Arcot. For the famous struggle for possession of the Governor's chair on 20th June, see an article by Mr. A. P. Muddiman, C.S., "A Governor-General of a Day" in *Bengal: Past and Present*, Vol. I. The Society's *Barwell Papers*, when published, will throw some new light on the subject.

Page 73. *Major William Palmer* (1740—1814). Received a Cadetship in the Bengal Army (into which it is said he exchanged from the King's Service) in 1766; joining the next year the 23rd Native Infantry. About 1776-7 became Military Secretary to Warren Hastings, holding that appointment until 1782 when he left to take up the post of Resident at Lucknow. The dates as given in A. T. Pringle's Official List and Buckland are not exactly the same. He subsequently represented the Government at Sindhia's Court until 1798 and from that year until 1801 at Poona. His last appointment was to the Monghyr command. Died at Berhampur, 20th May 1816, after a short illness. The years of his commissions, according to Dodwell and Miles' *Army List*, are as follow:—Cadet, 1766; Ensign, 1767; Lieutenant, 1769; Captain, 1777; Major, 1781; Lieutenant-Colonel, 1794; Colonel, 1798; Major-General, 1805; Lieutenant-General, 1813. He was the father of John Palmer, "Prince of British Merchants" and "The Friend of the Poor," and of William Palmer, the famous Hyderabad banker.

Page 73. *Mr. Bogle.* The Tibetan explorer. Died in Calcutta 3rd April 1781. Buried in the South Park Street Cemetery.

Page 74. *Mr. Auriol.* (James Peter). Secretary to the Governor-General and Council. For his houses at Alipur, see Seton Karr: *Selections from the Calcutta Gazettes*, Vol. I, p. 217. Hastings was charged at his Impeachment with corruptly appointing Auriol to be agent for the supplies for the relief of Madras—a charge rejected by

22 votes against 4. There were two brothers of the name of Auriol in Bengal at this time. See Mrs. Ritchie's Introduction to Vol. XIII of the *Works of William Makepeace Thackeray*, (Biographical Edition), p. xii. and also Sydney Grier. *Op. Cit.*

Page 74. *Sir John D'Oily.* The name is D'Oyly. A descendant of the family who held Oxford Castle on the feudal tenure obliging them to present a tablecloth each year to the King. Hence the word "doily" for an ornamental cloth. For Sir John Hadley D'Oyly see Sydney Grier: *Letters of Warren Hastings to His Wife*, p. 218 *et seq.*

P. 74. *Mr. Cator for Mr. Barwell.* To judge by the Barwell Letter Copy Books Joseph Cator would be Barwell's paid Private Secretary, but as a matter of fact he was in 1780 a Factor in the Company's Service. Cator married on 31st October a Miss Diana Bertie, to whom Richard Barwell on his departure from India assigned for two years (1st May, 1780 to 1782) the free use of the house and furniture of "the house now occupied by Mr. Robert Sanderson in Calcutta, fronting the Esplanade." This was in acknowledgment of Barwell's "gratitude and esteem flowing from a sense of her attachment to my wife and infant children." Robert Saunderson was the father of the beautiful Miss Elizabeth Saunderson, Mrs. Richard Barwell. A Miss Ann Birtie had married North Naylor, the unfortunate victim to the fury of the Supreme Court against the Supreme Court in the Cossijurah case. She died while her husband was in prison.

Page 74. *Mr. Addison for Sir John Clavering.* This is probably the gentleman whose marriage occurs on September 8th, 1784, "John Addison, Esq., Junr. Mercht in the Hon. Co.'s Service, a Batchelor and Lucy Clark of Calcutta, by License. Present Nathaniel Brassy Halhed, Esq. and Mrs. Halhed, his wife." Addison married Miss Lucy Clark of Calcutta on September 8th, 1784. He was Judge of the Dewani Adalat at Nattore in 1782.

Page 78. *Mr. Halhed.* (Nathaniel Brassey). Born 25th May 1751, the son of William Halhed, Director of the Bank of India. Educated at Harrow and Christ Church, Oxford. Probably one of the earliest of Oxford men in the Company's civil service. See Buckland: *Dictionary of Indian Biography.* Bengal Service 1771-1778 and

1784. Up to the time of the Hastings' trial he had been an intimate friend of R. B. Sheridan: he then severed that friendship. A number of amusing letters of his to Warren Hastings will be found in an article (by J. Grant) "Warren Hastings in Slippers" in the *Calcutta Review*, No. 28, May, 1883. Died 18th February 1830. His wife was Miss Helena Louisa Ribaut, daughter of the Governor of (Dutch) Chinsurah.

Page 81. *Gall* (Lawrence). See *Bengal: Past and Present*, Vol. IV., p. 504.

Page 81. *Mr. Croftes.* Charles Croftes was Sub-Treasurer 1774. Accountant-General, Revenue Department, 1777. Chief of Chittagong, 1st February 1785, to death, 1786. Satirized in *Hicky's Gazette* as "Idle Charley the Bankrupt Merchant." The XI of the Impeachment charges against Hastings was that in 1779 "he annulled the existing contract for the provision of bullocks and concluded another with his friend Charles Croftes, Esq., upon wantonly extravagant terms." Hastings was found guilty by three and acquitted by twenty-three. He arranged for the voyage home of Mrs. Hastings in 1754, the sum of £5,000 to be paid to Captain Cooper of the *Atlas*. Croftes induced the Captain to receive some "muzlins" of his own manufacture, promising that as no commission would be charged, the Captain would make a further profit of 25 per cent. The "muzlins" sold for less than £600 of the sum expected, and in the meanwhile Croftes had gone bankrupt. *Vide* Sydney Grier. *Op. Cit.* The appointment to Chittagong would have been a loss of pay and position, but the place was then regarded as a health resort, and Croftes went there with a private medical attendant, Mr. John Williams. Sir H. J. S. Cotton writes: "The character of Mr. Croftes' work is laborious and conscientious, although it is not altogether such as might have been expected from his experience and his own ability. His letters are a marvel of circumlocution, and his deference to authority and respect for the Revenue Committee are remarkable even in age when official self-abnegation and abasement were more practised than they are in the correspondence of modern times. It was doubtless his bad health that affected the outturn of his work. He died at Chittagong on the 12th of September (1786), just a twelvemonth after his appointment."

Sooksagur Ruins.
(From Colesworthy Grant's *Rural Life in Bengal.*)

There was a nemesis in that from 1783 to 1786, the financial exigencies of the Presidency were so great that even the payment of salaries were suspended, and Croftes who, as a member of the Revenue Committee, had dealt out hard measure to a former Collector of Chittagong, in 1786 protested against economies to which he had himself been a party. It was during the time of his chiefship at Chittagong that Sir William and Lady Jones made a long stay in the place. At Sooksagur Croftes contracted for the rum supplied to the Company's ships. He also had been the owner of the *Charlotte* or *Royal Charlotte* with which and the *Resolution* Captain J. Price joined Sir Edward Verner's Fleet in 1778.

Page 81. *The plantation of Sooksagur.* Sukh Ságar = Ocean of Delight—a name frequently given to ornamental tanks attached to Mahomedan houses. Colesworthy Grant (*Rural Life in Bengal*) says "it was built by Warren Hastings as a country residence for himself and three other civilians, and for the purpose of their having an English Farm there, where experiments in the growth of coffee and other products of that nature could be tried." My friend Mr. R. Dunbar has called my attention to the following circumstance. George Forster in his *Journey from Bengal to England*, etc., (Vol. I.) writing from Benares on the 31st August 1782 says: "On the 23rd of May I left Calcutta, and on the next day arrived at Sooksagur, a valuable and rising plantation, the property of Messrs. Crofts and Lennox. These gentlemen have established at this place a fabrication of white cloth of which the Company provide an annual investment, of about two lacks of rupees. They have also founded a raw silk manufactory, which, as it bears the appearance of increase and improvement, will, I hope, reward the industrious and estimable labours of its proprietors. In this plantation a large quantity of spirituous liquor is made, resembling in an inferior degree the American rum, which, since the commencement of the Dutch war, has become in great demand. Being applied to all the uses of the Batavia arrack, a considerable benefit is expected to arise to the Bengal province from a current sale of this commodity. . . . . It must not be omitted that this new establishment hath been noticed by the particular attention of the Government of Bengal, which on many other occasions has evinced a zealous disposition, in encouraging and promoting useful undertakings."

The business connection of Hastings with the Sooksagar plantation is, therefore, a mystery: but his delight in the place is obvious. It was a favourite retreat of his wife, "the elegant Marian." In 1784 Hastings writes: "Poor Croftes, with the gent in his head, is, in defiance of it and my entreaties, hurrying after me, to make my reception at his house most welcome and salutary." On 28th February 1784: "I am, on the contrary, as well as I have been for many years, for when I landed at Sooksagar on the 19th my health failed me, and my knees trembled with the walk to Croftes' bungalow." The property passed into the hands of the great Calcutta merchant, Joseph Barretto, who added a chapel, which the next occupant, a Spaniard, M. Laruletta, is said to have turned into "an abode for *mahouts* and fighting cocks." See *Bengal: Past and Present*, Vol. II., p. 367. The house and estate, on the Hughli on the opposite side and some away above Bandel, have long since been washed away.

In the *Calcutta Gazette* of April 19, 1792, we read "three royal tigers were killed last week at Sooksagur by Mr. Baretto, one of which having seized a man very near his elephant, he shot him dead on the spot; the other two were taken in nets." Heber mentions in his journal (1824). "I saw a sign of a civilized country, a jibbet with two men in chains on it, who were executed two years ago for robbery and murder in this neighbourhood," and he adds that recently Archdeacon Corrie had observed the tracks of tiger's feet at the place. Long in an article "The Banks of the Bhagirathi" (*Calcutta Review*, Vol. VI.) speaks of "the magnificent house of the Revenue Board at Sooksagar," and says that it was the County Seat of Lord Cornwallis. This is probably mythical.

The *Asiatic Journal*, February 1839, records that "the splendid house at Sooksagur, occupied by Mr Laruletta, has been nearly washed away by the river. It was one of the most magnificent edifices in the country, and was formerly in possession of the late Joseph Barretto, who built a chapel at the back of it, which was occupied and defiled by two elephants."

Page 81. *Ghirety*, a large strip of ground lying between the Grand Trunk Road and the river, belongs to the French, and is known to history as Ghirety and to the native as Farashganj. At the North end of this strip are the ruins of the Garden Palace of the French Governors of Chandernagore. The French estate here, to be accurate, consists of 120 bighas between the Trunk Road and the Hughli, and a small plot on the West of the Grand Trunk Road.

"If there be any one place in Bengal, after Gour with its ruined palaces and mosques, which presents an air of the most melancholy desolation, heightened by the remembrance of its former beauty and cheerfulness, it is this country house of the French Governors of Chandernagore. Whether we pass it from the riverside, or look at it from the road, it wears the appearance of thickest jungle of the Soondurbuns, where the imagination pictures to itself the footmarks of the tiger and wild deer. At the northern extremity of the grounds are the remains of its once splendid mansions, which has become so entirely dilapidated as to be scarcely even picturesque. In this house, seventy years ago, were assembled the beauty and fashion of Chinsurah, Chandernagore, Serampore and Calcutta. The walls of the saloon, which was thirty-six feet in height and of proportionate width and length, were adorned with paintings and when in all its splendour, and filled with company, most have carried the mind to some of the public rooms in the Chateau of Versailles. Here the Governor of Chandernagore entertained Clive and Verelst and Hastings and Sir William Jones, with a degree of magnificence little inferior to that exhibited in the Old Government House in Calcutta. The long alley of magnificent trees to the north of the house was formerly filled with the carriages of guests to the number, it is said, of more than fifty. Captain Stavorinus tells us that, on the 22nd of February 1770, the Dutch paid a national visit to the French Governor, and as these visits were accompanied with much ceremony, when the guests were received at the chief factory, the Dutch Director preferred paying it at the country seat of Ghirety. The party set off from Chinsurah at four o'clock in six carriages, and reached the Château at six, where they were received at the bottom of the steps and conducted into a large saloon, in which the principal ladies and gentlemen of Chandernagore were assembled. At seven, the Dutch guest were invited to witness a play in a slight building, which had been erected for the purpose. The play was over at ten, when they were led into a large room, in which a hundred ladies and gentlemen sat down to an elegant supper. The party broke up at one, and returned to Chinsurah." J. C. Marshman. *Calcutta Review*, Vol. IV, 1845.

In the June of 1824 Bishop Heber visited Ghirety and it is worth while to cite his description of what he saw :—

"There is a large ruined building a few miles to the south of Chandernagore, which was the country house of the Governor during the golden days of that settlement, and of the French influence in this part of India. It was suffered to fall to decay when Chandernagore was seized by us; but when Mr. Corrie came to India, was, though abandoned, still entire, and very magnificent with a noble staircase, painted ceilings, etc. and altogether, in his opinion, the finest building of the kind in this country. It has at present a very melancholy aspect, and in some degree reminded me of Moreton-Corbet [a ruined building in Shropshire], having like that, the remains of Grecian pillars and ornaments, with a high carved pediment. In beauty of decoration, however, it falls far short of Moreton-Corbet in its present conditton. This is the only sign of declining prosperity in this part of the country."

Page 81. *Miss Noel Catherine Werlée.*—[" Put it down a we, my Lord, put it down a we "—said old Mr. Weller, but it seems unnatural to spell a French name with a W., and the more usual spelling is Verlée, Verlé, or Varlé.] Born at Tranquebar 21st November 1762. Died at Paris, 10th December 1835. A good deal of fresh light has been thrown of the period of her life since her departure from Bengal and her becoming Madame de Talleyrand by Dr. Busteed in the fourth edition of the *Echoes from Old Calcutta* (1908). In the Act de Marriage between Talleyrand and Madame Grand, 10th September 1802, she is described as the divorced wife of G. F. Grand, by an Act pronounced in Paris in April, 1798 (le 18 Germinal, An. VI.) She was scarcely fifteen when she married Grand, but nearly forty when she married Talleyrand, the Ex-Bishop of Autun. The portrait by Madame Vigée la Brun it does not give any idea of Noel Verlée's glory—'la plus belle chevelure blonde qui ait peut etre jamais existé." According to the description given by Francis to his second

The Traditional Birthplace of Madame Grand, Tranquebar.

wife, Noel was "tall most elegantly formed, the stature of a nymph, a complexion of unequalled delicacy, and auburn hair of the most luxuriant profusion; fine blue eyes, with black eye-lashes and brows."

Page 81. *Monsieur Werlee* (Pierre Jean). That he was a Chevalier of the Order of St. Louis as Grand states may be doubted. It is on record (*Bengal: Past and Present*, Vol. III., p. 147) that his pay as Capitane de Port was Rs. 2,200 a year, but he had been a shipowner on his own account. The following shows the relationships of Noel Catherine.

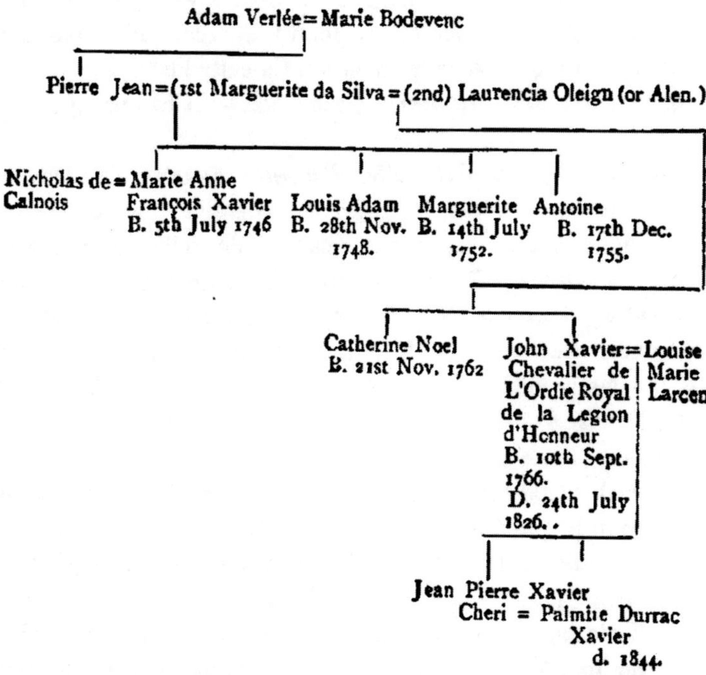

After the outbreak of the war in July 1778, Piere Verlée had obtained a license to reside in India and he seems to have been at Balsore when trouble and disgrace befel Noel on December 8 1779.

Page 82. *By the removal of Mr. Coates.* Here, I think, Grand's memory is at fault. According to Cotton's *Revenue History of Chittagong* (p. 23) William Cotes (*sic*) was Commercial Resident of Chittagong and acting Chief in February 1775. William Coates married on 19th January 1774, a Miss Diana Rochfort, who in 1779, 19th March, married Sir John D'Oyly, Bart. See *Bengal: Past and Present*, Vol. IV., p. 506 and Sydney Grier: *Op. Cit.* p. 195. Cotton characterises Coates as "a pompuous and punctillious functionary, and a very involved writer of English."

Page 82. *Mr. Charles Grant*, 1746-1823. The father of the future Lord Glenelg and Sir Robert Grant (Governor of Bombay, 1835) A life of him by Henry Morris was published in 1904.

Page 82. *The Rev. Dr. William Johnson.* He was not a "Dr." His career is given in detail in Hyde's *Parochial Annals of Bengal.* His portrait hangs on the walls of St. John's Vestry Room. He was practically the founder of St. John's Church. His wife, the "Begum Johnson," is equally famous in Calcutta history.

Page 83. *On 8th December.* Grand was at Chandernagore on duty on the 4th.

Page 84. *My benefactor Mr. Barwell's Society.* The name of Grand does not appear in the comprehensive Barwell Letter Copy Books, but it was in the house of Barwell's father-in-law, Robert Saunderson, Grand and his wife made their first home in Calcutta. *Vide* Busteed's *Echoes.* (4th Edition), p. 257. It was also under Barwell's too friendly patronage a certain Mr. and Mrs. Thomson made a home in Calcutta. See Appendix VI. of Busteed's *Echoes.* See also *Bengal: Past and Present*, Vol. V, pp. 178-9. There is an entry in Francis' Journal (February 17th, 1780) which would lead one to suppose that Barwell offered Francis a passage to England for Mrs. Grand. Vide *Echoes*, pp. 268-9.

Page 84. *Mr. Barwell's supper.* Not at Barwell's house, but, as the evidence shows at Le Gallais' Tavern. In the Note Books of Justice Hyde there is on March 30th 1776 the curious entry "An action to recover from Mohun Persaud Legallis the Cook's bills for dinners and other entertainments provided by his orders for the Council, attorneys and those they should invite during the trial of Nundcomar, Rs. 629 for eight dinners and nine suppers for 16 persons each." Le Gallais was Tyler of Lodge *Industry and Perseverance.* He is buried in the South Park Street, Cemetery, Calcutta, 1791.

Page 84. *My house.* Mr. H. E. A. Cotton favours the idea that the house was at Alipore, but this seems unlikely. We do not even to-day at the present day speak of "streets" in Alipore, but the "red house" in which the Grands lived was near to a "street" and almost overlooked by Mr. Keble's house.

Page 84. *Sir George Shee.* One of the worst things about the trial was the attempt of Shee to make himself scarce. See below, Appendix No. 11. Shee married a famous Calcutta beauty, Miss Eliza Crisp, at Hugli in 1783.

Page 84. *Jamadar* (Jemadar.) In the sense used here a servant over the other servants generally or over the camp servants. In the military sense (dating from 1768) the Jemadar is the officer next in rank to the Subadar. At the present day our native servants call the *bhisti* jemadar, and even sometimes the sweeper!

Page 85. *Mr. Shore, now Lord Teignmouth.* Reached Calcutta in 1769 and was a member of the Revenue Council, 1775-1780.

Page 86. *Mr. Dacarel* (George Gustavius). For his letter separating himself from the civil servants who signed the protest against Lord Clive's action in bringing up civilians from Madras (January 1726) see *Bengal: Past and Present* Vol. V., pp. 201-2. Supervisor of Purniah 1770. Succeded Alex. Elliot as Superintendent of the Khalsa Records, 1778. See Hunter: *Rural Annals*, pp. 410-11. Francis writes from Paris in 1784: "Dacarel has found his uncle and aunt, or rather they have found him. He was forced to get on a chair to put his arm round his uncle's neck; and he has worn my blue box to rags to keep his feet from dangling in the chaise."

Page 86. *I wrote to Mr. Francis.* The letter and reply is printed below. Appendix No. 11.

Page 86. *Mrs. Grand's sister and brother-in-law.* Her half-sister and her husband Nicholas de Calnois. The latter had been Notary Public of Chandernagore. He had a brother Nicholas de Merliere, who was afterwards engaged in indigo in John Prinsep's employ. These brothers were sons of Monsr. Nicholas, a senior Council in the French service. This will elucidate an entry in Francis' journal "27th June 1779 at Chandernagore curious explanation with La Meliere *à ce que par ait on ne demande par mieux, etc.*" Nicholas de Calnois and his brother, as prisoners of war, were among the first prisoners to be confined in the Presidency Jail in 1781.

Page 87. *Mr. Shee, the principal witness.* Grand perhaps gives Shee's evidence somewhat of a turn. Shee stated that he tried to disuade Francis. The ladder was made in Shee's yard but he swore he did not know for what purpose; he admitted that he gave directions for making the ladder. The Chief Justice concluded not too severely:—"I shall ask no more questions, as I see we do not agree upon the point of honour, for I confined honour to morality."

Page 88. *Hookabadar.* Hakka-burdâs. A servant employed to attend to his master's hooka (Indian pipe or "hubble-bubble"). See the curious and interesting quotations in *Hobson Jobson.* The deathknell of these ancient Anglo-Indian institutions is struck by Thackeray in the *Newcomes.* "Their livers are not out of order any more; as for hookah, I dare swear there are not now two kept alight within the bills of mortality; and that retired Indians would as soon think of smoking them, as their wives would of burning themselves at Kelsall Green, near to the Tyburnian quarter of the city which the Indian world at present represents."

Page 88. *Gold Mohur.* The official name of the chief gold coin of British India. In 1766 it was declared to be legal tender for 14 sicca rupees, in 1769 a new mohur was declared to be tender for 16 sicca rupees. Thackeray in the *Book of Snobs* introduces a "Colonel Goldmore, the rich widower from India."

Page 90. *Mr. Elliot (Alexander), a younger brother of the Lord Minto and Hugh Elliot.* I have discussed his career and printed a number of hitherto unpublished records relative to it in "Leaves from the Editor's Notebook" in *Bengal: Past and Present*, Vol. II. A Elliot was born 8th April 1754, arrived in Bengal, aged 18, and was appointed Superintendent of the Khalsa when that post was created by Hastings. Acted as Persian interpreter in the Nuncomar trials and sent home at the conclusion in charge of the official reports, which was published in London in 1776. The letters relative to the search for the French secret agent and Elliot's mission to Nagpur have been printed *in extenso* in *Bengal: Past and Present.* Grand, however, reveals the source of Elliot's information.

Page 90. *Lord Stormont.* David Murray succeeded his father as Viscount Stormont in 1745. Ambassador at Paris, 1772-1788. Succeeded his uncle as second Earl of Mansfield, 1793.

Page 91. *The Chevalier de St. Lubin.* See Beveridge*: Comprehensive History of India,* Vol. II., pp. 266-7, for an earlier (1768) appearance of this adventurer. Mrs. Fay (*Original Letters*) p. 65 *et seq.* met him at Mocha in 1779. See also Forrest *Selections from the Letters, Despatches, etc., preserved in the Bombay Secretariat* (Maratha Series), Vol. I. *Bengal: Past and Present,* Vol. II., p. 246, 399 *et seq.*

Page 92. *Selection of Mr. Elliot to conduct this negotiation.* See the Original Papers, *Bengal: Past and Present*, Vol. II., pp. 235, 406 *et seq.*

Page 93. *Colonel Dow (Alexander).* Having reached Bencoolen as a Sailor, he became Secretary to the Governor. In 1760 he entered the Company's military service. Captain 1764. In 1765 he commanded the 18th Sepoy Battalion (later the 45th N.I). Concerned in the European officers' mutiny, 1766. He is well known on account of his translation from the Persian of Firtisha's *History of Hindustan.* One of his plays, *Zingis,* was produced at Drury Lane in 1769. He died at Bhagalpur, 31st July 1779. His letter announcing the capture of Chandernagore and the escape of M. Chevalier was printed in *Bengal: Past and Present,* Vol. II, p. 391. He was apparently a brother of William Dow one of the earliest English Merchant trading with Assam.

Page 93. *Fell in with Mr. Chevalier. Vide* Original papers in *Bengal: Past and Present,* Vol. II., p. 391 *et seq.* 412 *et seq.*, and see *Ibid.*, Vol. VI.

Accompanied by Mr. Louis Moneron. This is a mistake. The Frenchman accompanying Chevalier was a M. Sanson, the Chief at Balasore. For Moneron see *Bengal: Past and Present,* Vol. II., p. 416 IV., p. 440 *et seq.* The name as usually written Monneron. He sat in the Constituante Assembly as Deputy for the French Indies. Died about 1797—apparently wrecked off the Arabian Coast. See Seton Karr's *Selections from the Calcutta Gazette:* Vol. II., p. 488. Monneron was by far the most important merchant of old Chandernagore.

Page 93. *Mr. Elliot travelling alone.* He died at Sarangah on 12th February 1778. A monument, still well cared for, was erected to his memory by Warren Hastings, who alludes to this in a verse of his inimitation of Horace, Bk. 11, ode 16.

An early death was Elliot's doom ;
I saw his opening virtues bloom
And manly sense unfold ;
Too soon to fade, I bade the stone.
Record his name midst hordes unknown
Unknowing what it told.

Page 94. *Defeat of Sir Hector Munro.* Probably refers to the defeat of Colonel Baillie 10th September 1780, which was followed by Munro's retreat to Chingleput, after sacrificing his guns and military stores.

Page 96. *Captain Price.* See Sydney Grier : *Op. Cit.*, p. 349 *et passim.*

Page 96. *Colonel Pearse.* (Thomas Deane.) His memoirs are in course of re-appearance in *Bengal: Past and Present.* He served Hastings as second in the duel with Francis. Died 15th June 1789 and buried in the South Park Street Cemetery. "The Father of the Bengal Artillery."

Page 98. *Colonel Carnac.* General Carnac, the veteran Bengal soldier, had been dismissed for his share in the Convention of Wargaum, 14th June 1779. Grand must be alluding not to Carnac, but to Camac. See Forest : *Selections from State Papers preserved in the Foreign Department, 1772-1785*, Vol. II. p. 700 *et seq.*

Page 99. *Mr. Markham, the late Archbishop of York's son*—William Markham had originally come out under Wheler. He was appointed to replace Francis Fowke at Benares in 1780. See a number of interesting notices in Sydney Grier. *Op Cit.* Died 1815 after suffering long from paralysis. The Archbishop, a keen supporter of Hastings, died in 1807.

Page 104. *Rajah Beemsing's lattee.* Is this the lion pillar of Asoka, known as the Bakhrā pillar at Kolhua? The height of the monument above the ground is 22 feet, but persons who have attempted to dig down to its base have failed in their attempts. One of the first to set the evil habit of carrying their names on this pillar was Reuben Barrow, the mathematician, in 1792.

Page 104. *Reynell.* This is, of course, Major Jas. Rennell, "the Father of Modern Geography," to whom there is a monument in Westminster Abbey. He married in Calcutta on 13th October 1772 Miss Jane Thackeray, the great aunt of the novelist.

Page 105. *The only one of the Chasseurs.* Probably refers to the 14 men of the Company of French Rangers who had been left sick at Mirzapore when the remainder of Popham's detachment marched under the command of Captain Mayaffre to Ramnagur. Hastings refers to this in his *Narrative of the Insurrection.* (Forrest's *Selection 5 of the Governor-Generals.* Vol. II., p. 176). "They were made prisoners, and sent to Lutteefpore.........They were all butchered on the spot, and almost in the immediate presence of the Rajahs except one man, who made a shift to crawl with a mangled body to the neighbouring woods, where he subsisted for a few days, retiring to the fort, received money, and is still living, and in our camp."

Page 107. *The Nawab Vizir, Azop-ul-Doulah visited Mr. Hastings.* See Sydney Grier. *Op. Cit.* p. 151 and p. 161.

Page 108. *The following are the names.* This list differs from the official one given by Forrest: *Sele.tions from State Papers in the Foreign Department*, Vol. III., p. 20. The name of J. Willes does not appear in the official list.

Page 109. *John Edmund Grand.* The official list has "Lieutenant Zimooker Grand." On p. 115 we meet with Robert Edward Grand.

Page 109. *Mr. Sumner.* Richard Sumner, Chief of Chittagong. Survived the wreck of the *Dartmouth.* Present with Hastings in the Benares troubles. See article by Miss E. M. Drummond in *Bengal: Past and Present*, Vol. III.

P. 109. *Charles Chapman, Esq.*, Sydney Grier writes: "Charles Chapman was another of the young civil servants who attached themselves to Hastings with an affection that bordered on idolatry. At the beginning of his service he appears to have acted for some time as Private Secretary. . . . In 1778 Hastings employed him to explore the coast of Cochin China and penetrate as far inland as he could. At the beginning of 1781 he was sent to Nagpore as agent at the Berar Durbar." He suceeded Clevland at Bhagulpore. On February 4th 1784 he married Miss Macy Williams, whom Miss Mary Barwell had sent to India to the care of the Hastings. Salt Agent at Contai, 1794. Returned to England with a fortune of £70,000 but lost the bulk of it by gambling. M.P. for Newton Devon. Died 1809.

Page 111. *In the fields next morning.* The various accounts of this duel are given in an article "The Barwell-Clavering Affaire d'Honeur" in *Bengal: Past and Present*, Vol. III. For the alleged malversation in salt, see Beveridge: *History of the Backergunge District*, p. 138. Sir F. J. Stephen's *Nuncomar and Impey*, Vol. II, pp. 289 *et seq.* This question will not be cleared up till the Barwell Papers in the possession of the Calcutta Historical Society are published.

Page 112. *Miss Clavering.* See Busteed: *Echoes* (4th Edition), p. 158, which is faced by a portrait of Maria Margaret, daughter of Sir J. Clavering, wife of the 7th Lord Napier of Merchiston. She died at Enfield in 1821, aged 65.

Page 112. *Returned to Benares.* This was on 28th September 1781. Mrs. Hastings joined her husband there in October. See Sydney Grier. *Op. Cit.* p. 163.

Page 112. *Mr. Hastings' Birthday.* According to Grand this would have been 6th February. Warren Hastings was born 6th December 1732.

Page 113. *Administration of Collector.* In the *Bengal Gazette*, February 1782, Hicky records: "Mr. G.——, who has lately been much employed in reading and digesting Milton on divorce, will, we hear, in a few days be appointed Collector of Turott (*sic*) in Behar province." It was a new appointment. Hand: *Early English Administration of Behar.*

Page 113. *Mr. Charters.* One of the earliest Collectors at Jessore. (*Vide* Westland's *Jessore*). A member of the Committee of Revenue, 1771. Died when Senior Judge of Appeal, 1795, at Patna.

Page 117. *Sir John Macpherson.* For his relations with Hastings see Sydney Grier. *Op. Cit.* pp. 212-16.

Page 117. *The late John Stables, Esq.* From 1759 to 1769 had pursued a distinguished military career in India, defeated the Rajah of Kurrackpore, 1760; commanded a battalion at the Battle of Buxar; Town Major at Fort William August 1765; Retired 1769. Sent out as Member of the Supreme Council in Francis' place and took his seat November 11th, 1782. In March, 1783, Hastings complains of Stables opposing him with "a rancour so uncommon that it extends even to his own friends." "In Council he sits sulky and silent waiting to declare his opinion when mine is recorded." Both Stables and Macpherson had been selected for their places in the Council in consideration of their supposed friendship for Hastings, so later on Laurence Sullivan expressed his regret for having sent snakes into Mr. Hastings' bosom. Stables was one of the original Building Committee of St. John's Church, Calcutta. Resigned his seat on the Supreme Council, January 19th, 1787.

Page 117. *Introduced the manufacturing of indigo.* Nicolas de Merliere, a relation of Mrs. Grand by marriage, was one of the pioneers of the European indigo manufacture, and it was probably from this connection Grand derived his knowledge of indigo concerns. Dr. Busteed (*Echoes*, p. 278) refers to a report of a suit in Equity in 1794 in the *Calcutta Chronicle*, in which it is said: "Mr. Grand by very extensive works having laid the foundation of that valuable manufacture in Behar." Readers interested in the history of indigo factories in Behar should consult the Index of Sir Wm. Hunter's *Bengal MS. Records.* Sir Wm. Hunter's four volumes are only a selection from a catalogue of documents, and he has deprived it of much value by abstaining from giving the names of the officials whose letters are catalogued. Some of the letters are undoubtedly Grand's.

Page 118. *Temporary Charge.* 8th February 1785 to September 1786.

Page 121. *Henry Colebrooke (Henry Thomas) 1765-1783.* See Buckland: *Dictionary of Indian Biography.*

Page 121. *Robert Bathurst.* See Hand *Op. Cit.* p. 26. Apparently a son or relation to Baron Apsley.

Page 125. *My Brother-in-Law Mr. Ledlie.*—My friend Mr. E. W. Madge has kindly obtained this extract from Marriage Register at St. John's Church, Calcutta: "Marriage, 1786, January 3rd, Robert Ledlie, Esq., Bar.-at-law, and Miss Susannah Grand. T. Blanshard, Chaplain." From a most interesting pamphlet *The Memoirs of the Ledlie Family* kindly lent me by Mr. J. S. Davidson, J.P. of Mozufferpore, I learn that Ledlie came out to India on the same ship as Lord Cornwallis in 1786. The pamphlet continues: "Robert at once distinguished himself as a lawyer, and ultimately became Jdgeu

Advocate-General of the Supreme Court in Calcutta. This is a splendid appointment at that time, as I am told—worth £10,000 a year, but both L and his wife were of very expensive habits and squandered their revenue as fast as it was received. They died without family. A curious anecdote is told of this pair. They had come out in the same vessel and naturally became intimate on the passage. On the arrival of the new Governor-General a grand ball, etc., etc., was given to his Lordship and suite at Calcutta, to which Ledlie and his future wife were invited—he as a matter of course, she from courtesy. During the course of the evening, whilst they were dancing together, a dispute respecting precedence arose between Miss Grand and another lady as to places in the dance, each claiming a high situation near the top of the room. Miss G. refusing to give way the altercation arose to '*unpleasantness*' between the ladies. On Ledlie being applied to by the other lady's partner he told that gentleman that he always left such matters to the ladies, and as he presumed that his partner *must, of course, be in the right*, he could not think of interfering in the matter. This nonchalance and refusal to yield only made matters worse. The wordy war between the ladies (?) increased, and at last the stranger lady fell on the floor in fits. Her partner being much irritated, came up to where Ledlie was standing enjoying the scene, and with much warmth of manner sternly informed him that, in consequence of the misconduct of him and his partner, the lady, his (the gentleman's) partner had fallen into hysterics. Ledlie replied with great gravity and apparent concern, 'My dear Sir, I regret the unfortunate circumstance most exceedingly, and sincerely hope that you are not about to full into the name situation yourself.'" The result was a duel in which Ledlie shot his adversary—whether with fatal result we are not told. It will be observed that if R. Ledlie and Miss Grand were married on January 3rd, 1786, they cannot have come out with Lord Cornwalis, and they must have been man and wife at the time of the ball incident. Mr. Madge traces R. Ledlie in the *Annual Directory* up to 1809 when he appears as Master in Equity, Accountant General, and Keeper of Records in the Supreme Court. The *Bengal Obituary* gives the following epitaph from the South Park Street Cemetery.—

Sacred to the Memory of
SUSAN LEDLIE
Wife of Robert Ledlie, Esq.,
Barrister at Law. She died in Calcutta
On the 33rd of her age.

In the same Cemetery.—

Sacred to the memory of Robert Ledlie, Esq.,
Barrister at Law,
Who died 24th November, 1809, aged 65 years.

This disposes of the idea that Ledlie was a "young barrister" in 1786.

As to other relations of Grand in Calcutta, the Registers at S. John's show:—

1799. 6th July. Lieutenant Reed to Jane Grand, Spinster. Witnesses R. Ledlie, etc.

1800. 8th March. Philip Hunt to Harriet Hyde. Witnesses Mary Ashe, Eliza Grand, etc.

Mr. E. W. Madge informs me he has found the name of William Grand, Indigo manufacturer, Lelaulgur, "in Bengal Directories for 1800 and 1801."

Page 125. *Mr. Cockrell's house at Belvedere.* In Seton Karr's *Selections from the Calcutta Gazette* several public notices will be found signed by C. Cockerell, Postmaster-General.

The *Calcutta Gazette* of 8th October 1789, records "On Monday evening after a long and melancholy illness, died the wife of Charles Cockerell, Esq. Those who had the pleasure of being acquainted with this lady need not to be told of her worth and amiable character. To others, a conspicuous testimony of the general esteem she had acquired was afforded by the numerous and respectable assemblage of ladies and gentlemen who attended her funeral.

If beauty, youth, and worth could save,
She had not met an early grave."

She was a daughter of Sir C. W. Blunt, Bart., who died and was buried at Pultah (a few miles above Barrackpore) on 29th September 1802. Of her sisters:

Lydia married Sir Alexander Seton, Bart., B.C.S.

Anna Maria married the Hon'ble Charles Andrew Bruce, Governor of Prince of Wales Island and brother of the seventh Lord Elgin.

Charlotte married Warren Hastings' step son, Sir Charles Imhoff. The "Sweet Charlotte" of Mrs. Hastings' letters. Sydney Grier writes: "She nursed Hastings in his last illness and a letter of hers 'blistered with tears,' says Gleig conveyed to David Anderson the details of his friend's last hours."

Dorothea married Edward Fletcher, B.C.S.

Of her brothers:

William died at Madras in 1860, aged 81 years. Appointed to succeed Sir Charles Metcalfe as Governor of Agra, 20th March 1835.

Sir Charles Richard Blunt, 4th Bart. One of the chief mourners at Warren Hastings' funeral in 1818, appointed to Bengal Civil Service, 1793. Out of office in 1813. M.P. for Lewis.

Sir William Blunt, 8th Bart. An Advocate of the Supreme Court at Calcutta.

A cousin, Sir William Blunt, 7th Bart, I.C.S., 1846-1875. Mrs. Cockerell's father, after having run through his fortune, came out to India late in life, leaving his wife at home: the daughters came out in 1792 on the same ship as Marian Brisco, who had been born in the Hastings' house and derived her Christian name from the second Mrs. Hastings and returned to India under the care of Lady Shore. Sir C. W. Blunt had a share in the Post Office (Postmaster-General in 1795) and this connection with Cockerell, the Postmaster-General, explains how Grand, a *protegé* of Warren Hastings, was able to get employment in connection with the daks after the loss of his post at Patna. Mrs. Charles Cockerell's grave is in the South Park Street Burial Ground. The inscription according to the *Bengal Obituary* runs:—

MARIA TRYPHENA CAROLI COCKERELL.
Ux or Ob. October 5. Anno. Dom. 1789

There is a monument to her father in St. John's Church. It may be added that Cockerell was created a Baronet in 1809. His son and successor assumed the surname of Rushout instead of that of Cockerell.

Page 125. *Mr. Mercer.* Died in September, 1791. The eldest son of a respectable family at Perth: entered the Company's service in 1773. After serving at the Presidency was appointed an Assistant at Dinagepore. An eulogy of his services will be found in Seton-Karr: *Selections from the Calcutta Gazettes*, Vol. II, p. 301. Mr. R. J. Hirst writes that Mr. Lawrence Mercer joined Burdwan as Collector on December 30th, 1788, after having been for a while on special duty in Kuch Behar in company with Mr. Chouvet. See article. "The Early Collectorate Records of Burdwan" in *Bengal: Past and Present, Vol. VI.*

Page 127. *Henry Douglas.*—Behar seems to be distinguished by longevity of some of its British Resident, *e.g.*—

1. William Augustus Brooke. Died at Benares but the greater part of his services was spent at Patna. Died July 10, 1833. Aged.
2. Samuel Denton. Died at Patna, where he had resided for 56 years, 6th January 1831, aged 85.
3. John French, entered the C.S. 1764, died in it November 1856 after 60 years actual service. See *Bengal: Past and Present*, Vol. I, p. 27.
4. Henry Douglas, arrived in 1780, retired on annuity after 56 years service in May, 1836; died at Patna, aged 77. November 1839.

Neither in the *Bengal Obituary* nor in Wilson's Lists of *Inscriptions* is there any mention of Douglas' grave at Patna, but Mr. H. Beveridge in the *Calcutta Review*, April 1883, refers to "Henry Douglas, who was buried in this (the Patna) Cemetery, and who is recorded to have died in 1839, at the age of 78."

Page 128. *William Augustus Brooke.* Sydney Grier writes that Brooke owed both his first appointment to the Civil Service and his post at Patna to Edward Wheler. Much interesting information in regard to his work at Patna will be found in Hand's *Early British Administration of Behar.* Hastings stopped at Brooke's house at Bankipore in March 1784. Bishop Heber, in 1828, was his guest at Secrole, near Benares. The Bishop describes him as "a very fine healthy old man, his manners being singularly courteous and benevolent; and his tone in speaking Hindoostanee and Persian such as marks a man who has been in the habit of conversing much with natives of high rank." In 1794 Brooke was Julius Imhoff's superior in the Court of Appeal at Calcutta, and at this time he seems to have resided at Belvedere. See Sydney Grier's *Letter of Warren Hastings to his Wife*, p. 199; Cotton, *Calcutta Old and New*, Chapter XVI. Brooke died at Benares after 56 years of Indian service. The epitaph on his grave runs :—

Sacred to the memory of
WILLIAM AUSTIN BROOKE,
Senior Judge of the Court of Appeal, and Agent
to the Governor-General at Benares,
Who died on the 10th July 1833,
in the eight-first of his age.
His amiable character endeared him alike to the
Hindoo, the Mussulman, and the Christian
inhabitants of this city.

Page 128. Thomas Law. For the Law family in Bengal see *Bengal: Past and Present*, Vol. III., pp. 370-71. This member of the family must, I think, be a son of Edmond Law, Bishop of Carlisle and a brother of the first Baron Ellenborough and the Bishop of Elphin and Bath and Wells. In 1793 he went to America to endeavour to establish a national currency and died at Washington in 1759. He would, in this case, be the uncle of the Governor-General, the first Earl of Ellenborough and great uncle of the famous Jesuit Missionary on the Zambesi—Augustus Henry Law. A portion of Gaya, originally known as Elahabad, was renamed Sahebgunj, in memory of improvements made there by T. Law.

Page 135. *Beeknapahree.* Bhikna Pahari. To the N.-W. of the site of Asoka's Palace at Patna there is an artificial hill known as Biknapahree "over 40 feet high and about a mile in circuit, now crowned by the residence of one of the Nawabs of Patna and has been identified with the hermitage hill built by Asoka for his brother Mahendra." O'Malley: *Patna*, P. 205, (Bengal District Gazetteers).

Page 141. *Manick Shah.* In Patna was born in 1666 Guru Govind Singh. The place of his birth is marked by the Har Mandir temple, where, besides the Guru's cradle and shoes, is preserved the holy book of the Sikhs, the Granth Saheb, containing his name written by himself with the point of an arrow. The temple is one of the four great pilgrimage places of the Sikhs. The small Sikh community at Patna is remarkable for its orthodoxy and strict adherence to the original injunctions of the founder of their religion. See O'Malley: *Patna (Bengal District Gazetteers).*

Page 142. *I reached Patna in five days.* In ordinary the journey would be made by river. The rates fixed for dâk bearers in 1796 amounted to Rs. 400 from Calcutta to Patna, and Rs. 500 from Calcutta to Benares. Seton Karr. *Selections from the Calcutta Gazette,* Vol II. p. 185.

Page 147. *Dewanny Adawelt. Adālat*—Court of Justice. Under the Moghul rule there were three adalats named by the titles of their presiding officials.

Nizamat Adālat—the Chief Criminal Court
Dewani Adālat—Civil Court.
Fawjdari Adalat—a Police Court.

For a sketch of the history of these Courts see the extract from the regulations of 1793 in Seton Karr's *Cornwallis* (Rulers of India) pp. 89-92, or Field: *Introduction to the Regulation of the Bengal Code.* It must be remembered that the Jurisdiction of the Supreme Court established in 1774 was limited to British subjects and the native servants of the Company. The Criminal Judiciary over natives remained in the hands of native Courts until 1790, and it was not until 1862 the Sudder Dewany (*Sadr' Dewani Adalat*) was united the Supreme Court. and the present High Court organised. This arrangement had in a sense been anticipated in 1780 when Warren Hastings appointed Sir Elijah Impey as head of the Sudder Dewanny—a measure afterwards denounced as a bribe. The alternative to Hastings' policy was to make the Executive Government the Supreme Judiciary in all native cases.

Page 147. *Provincial Courts of Appeal.* These were established in 1793 by Lord Cornwallis at Murshidabad, Patna, Dacca and Calcutta, each consisted of three Judges. From them lay an appeal to the Sudder Dewany Adalats at the Presidency, which on the breakdown of Hastings' plan of 1780 was practically to the Executive Government until at least 1805.

Page 148. *Zillah Courts.* Zila=A rib, hence a district. See *Hobson Jobson.* Grand's idea that the Cornwallis Regulations were designed to meet his own special case is perhaps one of the most superb instances of the "Fly on the wheel" obsession to be found on record.

Page 149. *Until June 1798.*—After losing his post as Judge at Patna, Grand must have spent a long time in Calcutta. Dr. Busteed notes: "His name turns up occasionally in old Calcutta newspapers. Thus in December 1793, he is found serving on the Grand Jury. In June, 1794, he is the officer employed to despatch the Mail Packet for Europe from Diamond Harbour. In November of the same year he is one of the Commissioners for the scheme of a general lottery." *Echoes*, p 280. The *Calcutta Gazette* of 17th December 1795 reports briefly a case in the Supreme Court of *C. Grant and W. Pope* versus *G. F. Grand.*

Page 152. *Beoparies.*—"Following the course of trade as it flows into Calcutta, we find that between the cultivator and the exporter there are: 1st the BEPPAREE, or petty trade; 2nd the AURUT-DAR, and 3rd the MAHAGUN, interest in Calcutta trade. As soon as the crops are cutt, Bepparee appears upon the scene; he visits village after village, and goes from homestead to homestead, buying these, or at the village marts from the ryots; he then takes his purchases to the Aurut-dar, who is stationed at the centre of trade, and to whom he is perhaps under advances, and from the Aurut-dar the Calcutta Mahagan obtains his supplies . . . . for eventual despatch to the Capital. There is also a fourth class of dealers called *Phoreas* who buy from the Mahagan and sell to the European exporter. Thus, between the cultivator and shipper there are so many middlemen, whose participation in the trade involves a multiplication of profits, which goes a great way to enhancing the price of commodities before they reach the shipper's hands." Letter from Baboo Nobokissen Ghose cited in *Hobson Jobson.*

158. *As Mr. Shore had opposed the inversion of property.* Sir John Shore's views are stated in three famous minutes (June 18th,

September 13th, December 21st, 1789) which are incorporated in the *Fifth Report from the Select Committee on the Affairs of the East India Company*. In June 1789 Shore certainly held that the Zemindars and Talookdars "are the proprietors of the soil," although of course, subject to removal in case of inability or unwillingness to fulfil the duties of their stations or pay the land tax. I do not know of any evidence to show that Shore ever, as Grand puts it, "completely changed his principles." It is not clear what Grand means when he says Lord Cornwallis "revolted at the new doctrines." Grand holds that the Sovereign was "Lord of the Soil." In a learned work *The Zemindary Settlement of Bengal* (Calcutta 1879) it is contended that the Ryots were the proprietors of the land. This is not the place to review an ancient discussion, which really turns on failure to appreciate what is meant by property in land. Hastings, with his intimate knowledge of Bengal, in his *Review of the State of Bengal*, very wisely wrote: "The public in England have of late years adopted very high ideas of the rights of the Zemindars in Hindoostan; and the prevailing prejudice has considered every occasional dispossession of a zemindar from the management of his lands, as an act of oppression. I mean not here to enter into any discussion of their rights, or to distinguish between right, and fact and form as applied to their situation. Our Government, on grounds which with more scrutiny may, perhaps, find at variance with the facts, had admitted the opinion of their rightful proprietorship of the lands. I do not mean to contest their right of inheritance to the lands, whilst I assert the right of Government to the produce thereof. The Mahommedan rulers continually exercised, with a severity unknown to the British administration in Bengal, the power of dispossessing the zemindars on any failure in the payment of their rents, not only *pro tempore* but in perpetuity. The fact is notorious; but lest proof of it should be required, I shall select one instance out of many that might be produced; and only mention that the Zemindary of Rajeshay, the second in rank in Bengal, and yielding an annual income of about twenty-five lacks of rupees, has risen to its present magnitud during the course of the last eighty years, by accumulating the property of a great number of dispossessed zemindars, although the ancestors of the present possession had not by inheritance a right to the property of a single village in the zemindary." The great advocate of a permanent settlement was Sir Philip Francis, but he probably derived his views and information from John Shore. The story is told that Hastings, having guessed at the dependance of Francis on Shore, sent the latter on a journey, during which Francis found it necessary to plead sickness as an excuse for non-attendance at Council.* Shore owed his appointment to Hastings' opponents, and was a thoroughgoing partisan of Francis. He writes in his early days, "Mr. Francis is my friend, and will, I believe, give me proofs of it, whenever time shall put it in his power." See an article "Lord Teignmouth" by Sir John Kaye in the *Calcutta Review*, May, 1844.

Page 160. *Ceremony of the Porneah. Punya*, corruptly *Puneah* or *Pooneah*. Wilson defines: "In the lower provinces the day on which the revenue for the ensuing year is settled or an annual meeting of the revenue payers at the office of the chief collector, or of the cultivating tenants at the court of the zamindar, to determine the amount of the assessment, the assemblage of the rent payers forming a kind of festival or holiday: the term is also applied to the day on which the first instalment of the annual rent or revenue is paid." After the concession of the *Dewani*, Lord Clive as Dewan and the Nawab as Nazim sat side by side on the Musnud at the Moti Jheel, Murshidabad, on April 29th, on the occasion of the first English Punya. See the most excellent work of Purna Chunder Mazumdar, *The Musnud of Murshidabad*, 1704-1904.†

Page 160. "*Tuccavey*", *Takávi*. "Advances of money made by the Government to the cultivators at the time of sowing, especially in the South of India, where the Ryotwari settlement prevails, to be repaid when the crop is gathered : similar advances are made in

* See *Some Observations and Remarks on a late Publication entitled Travels in Europe, Asia and Africa, London 1782* (Probably by Captain J. Price). P. 119.

† Copies of this work being in ordinary rather difficult to obtain, it may be mentioned that they are procurable through the Secretary of the Calcutta Historical Society. The price is Rs. 5 or seven shillings and sixpence.

bad seasons and the like or sometimes made to the cultivators to enable them to extend their cultivation." Wilson *Op. Cit.* (1855).

Page 161. *Melancholy reflection.* The best account of the failure of the Permanent Settlement will be found in Sir William Hunter's too little known introduction to his *Bengal M.S. Records* (1894). Seton Karr in his *Cornwallis* ("Rulers of India Series") points out that in the Great Mutiny "the silent loyalty of the zemindars of Bengal was a great asset." "In other provinces the system of village communities afforded no bulwark against the tide of anarchy. In Bengal public tranquillity hardly suffered. The rebellion of Koer Sing in Behar was a solitary exception." He also shows that the co-operation of the zemindars in times of famine has been most valuable. Seton Karr is clearly in favour of Shore on the plea for a delay in making the settlement permanent, but he most candidly urges everything that can be said in defence of Lord Cornwallis' policy.

Page 162. *The Rev. Dr. Buchanan.* This is a curious confusion between the Rev. Dr. Claudius Buchanan, who was Chaplain at Barrackpore in 1797, and Vice-Provost of the College of Fort William from 1799 to 1807, with Francis Buchanan, M.D., who about 1814, on succeeding to his mother's property became Buchanan—Hamilton. The *Statistical Survey of Dinagepore* was published in 1833: how is that it is quoted here?

Page 163. Sir John Shore's declared policy was "to adhere as literally as possible to the strictest possible interpretation of the restrictive clause in the act of Parliament against entering into hostilities." It is not too much to characterise the result of this policy as extreme pusillanimity, but in criticising Sir John Shore it must be remembered that he ruled in the spirit of instructions from superior authority, and that Hastings' impeachment was an ever present deterrent to rulers in Bengal from acting on their own initiative. It has been remarked that "nowhere so much as in India is timidity provocative of aggression," and that "Sir John Shore could not have taken a more effectual method of stimulating the Mahrattas to attack the Nizam" than by his declaration of neutrality. His argument was that "as the union of the three allies was the basis of the treaty, the continuance of that union or friendship is essential to the performance of the obligations imposed by it, and a war between two of the parties totally changes the relative situation of all." Most unfortunately Sir John did not confine himself to explaining away the obligation, but went on to discuss the question of expediency. In this part of his minute he practically admits that he is deciding in favour of peace at the cost of "the British reputation throughout India for good faith, firmness, and moderation." The incident affords a curious illustration of the principles of Machiavelli adopted in public conduct by a man whose private life was moulded by stern and unbending evangelical principles.

Page 163. *Monsieur Raymond.*—A sketch of his career will be found in the Appendix to Mr. H. Compton's *European Military Adventurers in India.*

Page 164. *De Boigne*—See Compton *Op. Cit.* and also for Perron.

Page 164. *Dhoulah Rao Scindiah* [Daulat Rao Sindhia.] For the worthless character of this person see H. G. Keen *Madhava Rao Sindhia* ("Rulers of India"). P. 198.

Page 165. *Meditated attack by Zemann Khan.* The grandson of Ahmad Shah Abdali, who in 1796 actually reached Lahore, but returned on the news of the rebellion of one of his brothers. This alarm led to the cession of the Fort of Allahabad to the Company on the occasion of the elevation of Sadat Ali to the throne of Oude. (21st January 1798.)

Page 165. *Vizier Ally.* For his grave in Calcutta, see Thacker's *Guide to Calcutta.* The condition of this Mahomedan graveyard (opposite the Bamun Basti Police Thana in the Lower Circular Road) is a disgrace to the city. The inscription on the grave (*Vide* Vol. X of the *Asiatic Journal*, 1828) has long ago disappeared. It is said that 30 lakhs of rupees were expended on the festivities connected with his marriage: his funeral cost seventy. For the graves in this place see *Bengal: Past and Present*, Vol. II., p. 100.

Page 166. *Horrid Massacre at Benares.* 14th January 1799. "It had been previously intimated to Mr. Cherry that his (Vizier Ally's) appearance was hostile, and that he ought to be on his guard, but he unfortunately disobeyed the caution. Vizier Ally made many complaints of the Company's treatment of him, and having continued his strain of reproach against them for some time, he finally gave the dreadful signal to his attendants who rushed in at that moment and litterally cut Mr. Cherry to pieces."—*Asiatic Journal*, February 1818, p. 191. From Cherry's house, the frantic prince went on to that of Mr. Davis, killing Captain Conway and Mr. Robert Graham on the way. Davis' defence of his house until the arrival of the Cavalry from Secrole is one of the finest chapters in the annals of British gallantry. When the Vizier had been brought from his asylum with the Rajah of Berar on the stipulation that his life should be spared "he was brought down to Calcutta, and confined at Fort William in a sort of iron cage, where he died at the age of thirty-six years, after an imprisonment of seventeen years and some odd months." A little while before his death (of "water in the chest,") it had been arranged that he should be sent to Vellore and allowed "comparative liberty and comfort." Vide *Calcutta Gazette*, May 22, 1817. Grand's account implies that Sir John Shore was in Benares at the time of Vizier Ally's attempted general massacre. Cherry had been Persian interpreter to L ord Cornwallis in 1790. For a biographical notice of S. Davis, the companion of S. Turner in Tibet, and the compiler of the famous Fifth Report, see Clements S. Markham's *Narratives of the Mission of George Bogle*, p. lxxi. He was grandfather (on mother's side) of J. H. Rivett-Carnac. See the latter's *Many Memories*. P. 2.—Davis was the father of Sir J. Davis, Bart, K.C.B., who was three years old when his father defended his family at Benares.

Page 166. *Sir John Shore gave over charge.* This was on March 12. The Earl of Mornington (created Marquis Wellesley, December 2, 1799) landed in Calcutta on May 17 and assumed charge on the following day. In the interim Sir Alured Clarke, K.C.B., had officiated.

Page 167. *Peter Speke.* Collector of Rajshahi Assumed place on Council September 17, 1789. Resigned October 2, 1801. He died in Calcutta 30th November 1811, aged 66 years, when President of the Board of Trade and of the Marine Board. He is buried in the North Park Street Cemetery. *Vide Bengal Obituary*, p. 184. Sudder Street in Calcutta was originally Speke Street. From Grand we learn that the Councillor was a son of the Captain Speke and a brother of the heroic "Billy" Speke. See Hunter: *The*

Thackerays in India, pp. 29-31, or *Thacker's Guide to Calcutta*, p. 137.

Page 166. *William Cowper.* Assumed place in Supreme Council, November 6, 1790. Resigned February 25, 1801.

Page 168. *Chubdar.* Chubdar=a stick-bearer. Maria Graham wrongly suggests that the word is derived from *Chup-dar*—a silence keeper.

Page 170. *Admiral Affleck.* See *Dictionary of National Biography.*

Page 171. *Lord Kaine's Essays.* Henry Home, Lord Kaines 1752. See article in *Dictionary of National Biography.*

Page 172. *Mr. Charles Purling.* Assistant at Dinagepore or Rungpur, 1771. Negociated treaty with the Raja of Cooch Behar, 1772. Acting Chief of Dacca, 1773. Collector of Rungpur, 1777-1779. Resident in Oudh, 1781. On Board of Commissioner for Management of the Dutch E. I. C. possessions at Chinsurah. Was one of the witnesses at the Trial of Warren Hastings. Returned to India. Collector of Rungpore 1790. Died January 31, 1791, aged 44, and buried in South Park Street Cemetery.

Page 175. *Mirza Aboo Taleb Khan.* This person published an account of his *Travels* in three Volumes in which he describes "Mr. Grand—in the next cabin, a very passionate and delicate gentlemen." During a storm "Mr. Grand, who was of enormous size and whose cabin was separated from mine by a canvas partition, fell with all his might upon my breast and hurt me excessively; what rendered this circumstance more provoking was that if by any accident the smallest noise was made in my apartment he would call out with all that overbearing insolence which characterises the vulgar part of the English in their conduct to Orientals 'What are you about? You won't let me get a wink of sleep,' and such other rude expressions." The Calcutta Historical Society possesses a copy of the *Travels* presented to it by Dr. Busteed. Mirza Abbo Taleb Khan seems to have died in 1807. See Sandeman: *Selections from the Calcutta Gazettes*, Vol. IV., p. 181, and the *Asiatic Journal*, Vol. xix., N. S. 1836, pp. 102-4.

Page 176. *La Forte.* See Captain R. W. Eastwick. *The Adventures of a Master Mariner.*

The *La Forte* was captured by Captain Edward Cooke of *La Sybelle* after a severe fight February 28—March 1, 1799. In the South Park Street Cemetery his monument will be found—

Sacred to the Memory of
Edward Cooke, Esq.
Captain of H. M. Ship "La Sybelle,"
Who received a mortal wound
in a gallant action
With the French Frigate "La Forte,"
Which he captured in Balascre Roads,
March 1st, 1799, and brought to this port,
where he died 23rd May 1779,
aged 26 years.

The East India Company placed a monument to Cooke's memory in Westminster Abbey. Dr. Busteed's *Echoes* (p. 280) and Mr. Julian Cotton (*Calcutta Old and New*, p. 578) assert that he was the son of the great navigator. Dr. Wilson on the other hand (*List of Monumental Inscriptions*, p. 78) says he was "the son of Colonel Cooke of Harefield and brother of General Sir G. Cooke, Commander of the First Division at Waterloo." For the arrival of the *La Forte* at Calcutta see Seton Karr: *Selection from the Calcutta Gazettes*, Vol. III, p. 224. For another sea fight off the Sandheads. *Ibid.*, pp. 270-1.

Page 180. *Bengal friend, Colonel Brooke.* Robert Brooke arrived in Bengal in 1764, shortly after the battle of Buxar, and greatly distinguished himself as a soldier. Governor of St. Helena, 1787. Died at Bath, January 1811. A memoir will be found in the *Asiatic Journal*, Vol xix., New Series, 1836.

Page 183. *The Bellerophon.* The only English ship entirely dismasted in the battle of the Nile: her hull was almost shattered. Her loss was estimated at 49 killed and 148 wounded. The *Bellorophon* conveyed Napoleon to England in 1815.

Page 184. *Admiral Sir Roger Curtis* (1796-1816). See *Dictionary of National Biography.*

Page 184. *Sir George Yonge*, 1731-1812. See *Dictionary of National Biography*, Governor of the Cape, 1779-1801.

Page 186. *Sir Thomas Williams.* See *Dictionary of National Biography.*

Page 189. *The late Lord Melville.* Henry, first Viscount. President of the Board of Control, 1793-1801. There was a nemesis in regard to Dundas' motion for Hastings' recall in 1782. In 1805 Dundas was struck off the roll of Privy Councillors, and in the following year impeached for malversation. He was found guilty of negligence, but acquitted of the serious charge. He was restored to the Privy Council in 1807; died 1811.

Page 193. *Mr. Barrow*, created Baronet 1832. See *Dictionary of National Biography.* It is not revealed in what work Barrow made the allusions to which Grand takes exception.

Page 195. *Sir George Prevost, Bart.* (1767-1816.) See *Dictionary of National Biography.* His only son died as late as 1893—the Rev. Sir George Prevost, the pupil and disciple of John Keble, Perpetual Curate of Stinchombe and Hon. Canon of Gloucester.

Page 196. *Colonel Swiney Toone.* Commander of the Governor's Horse Body Guard, which was received in 1773, but first of all used on service against the Sanyassis. Toone was invalided home in 1775, and returned in 1782, and left India in 1785 with Hastings. See Sydney Grier, *Op. Cit.*, p. 202 *et seq*, and Mr. V. Hodson's *History of the Governor-General's Body Guard.*

Page 196. *Sir Thomas Theophilus Metcalfe.* Dodwell and Miles record:—"Ensign, 31st July 1767; Lieutenant, 23rd September 1767; Major, 28th July 1781. He married in Calcutta, on 2nd February 1778, Miss Susanna Sophia Selina Templer. This is, I believe, the marriage which Mrs. Fay (*Original Letters*, p. 173) tells us she was present at, although on this supposition Mrs. Fay is astray with her dates. Charles Theophilus, Baron Metcalfe, the provisional Governor-General, was the second son of this marriage and was baptised in Calcutta on 18th April 1785.

Page 203. *Kelladar.* Kilàdār, the commandant of a Kila or fort.

Page 231. *Edward Ephraim Pote.* See a biographical notice of him by Mr. Irvine in *Bengal: Past and Present*, Vol. VI., p.p. 174-6. Son of Mr. Pote of Eton and a scholar of King's Cambridge. Elected a writer in 1771, but did not reach India till July 1773. After various appointments at Calcutta, he was sent to Rungpore and

Kassim Bazar, and in 1778 was Commercial Resident at Rungpore, Commercial Resident at Patna 1787. Returned home 1800. He presented a large collection of Persian manuscript, half to Eton and half to King's College.

Page 247. *A miserable author denominating himself the Modern Plutarch.* Dr. Busteed has pointed out that "the anecdote is not in the *Modern Plutarch*, which is a poor collection of brief biographies published at Berwick in 1811; but in the *Female Revolutionary Plutarch*, which must be the book that Grand referred to."

Page 247. *I never saw the first Mrs. Grand, neither in India nor in Europe from that melancholy day.* In the introduction we have noticed that Sir Elijah Impey's son asserts that he himself was present when "Mr. and Mrs. Fox, Sir Elijah and Lady Impey, M. and Me. de Talleyrand, Sir Philip Francis, and Mr. Le Grand (*sic*) met beneath the same roof in Paris in 1892." The question, however, is not, so far as Grand's honour is concerned whether he actually met his real wife, but if he had dealings with her, and played the ignoble part of blackmailer. Mirza Abu Taleb Khan remet Grand at Paris at this time. He writes: "I was much surprised to meet here my shipmate Mr. G—d. He had come to Paris to improve his fortune through the interest of Madame Talleyrand to whom he had once had the honour of being husband. I understand she has since procured for him an appointment under the Dutch Government at the Cape of Good Hope." To back this up here is a letter from Madame Talleyrand, dated September 20, 1802, ten days after her civil marriage with Talleyrand; and addressed to M. Van der Goes the Minister for Foreign Affairs of the Batavia Republic.

Monsieur.

Je ne veux pas tarder davantage à vous remercier de votre obligeance, et de tout ce que vous avez bien voulu faire pour M. Grand à ma demande.

L'empressement et la grâce que vous y avez mis, me prouvent, Monsieur, que l'on ne compte pas en vain sur votre amitié, et cela m'autorise à vous demander un nouveau service. C'est celui de faire enjoindre à M. Grand de s'embarquer sans délai, étant tout á fa inconvenant qui'l prolonge son séjour à Amsterdam, où il est déjà depuis un mois, fort mal à propos.

Talleyrand-Perigord, nee Werlee.

In a work entitled *Relations Secretes des Agents de Louis XVIII a Paris sous le Consulat*, it is a asserted that Grand got 8c,000 francs from Talleyrand. This sum added to the 50,000 sicca rupees (£5109-2-11) obtanned from Francis in 1778 would suggest that Grand, if in lucre only, made a very nice thing of the little woman he had picked up at Chandernagore; but the Secret Agents, if their "relations" are indeed genuine, probably only repeat the same sort of gossip we find detailed by Madame de Remusat.

Returning to the younger Impey's assertion, Dr. Busteed writes: "It may be observed that on his showing he was only in Paris during the visit he alludes to for a portion of December 1801 and January 1802. Now as we have seen already, there was no Madame de Talleyrand till September 1802, and Francis was not Sir Philip till 1806." (*Echoes*, p. 296) It is true that the younger Impey describes the re-union of inconveniently assorted folk to the period of that visit, but he, an Oxford undergraduate at the time, simply went home to keep his terms, and "Early in the summer of 1802, I returned to my old quarter at Monsieur le Comte's, in the Rue Vielle Estrapade, and remained there during the ensuing vacation—dined with the three consuls, and renewed my acquaintance with Mesdames Talleyrand, Recamier, and de Stael." The *Memoirs of Sir Elijah Impey* were not published till 1857, although the introduction is dated September 1846. In the course of forty-four years it is but likely that the writer, an old man, may have assigned to an earlier visit to Paris an event which occurred on a later one. The *Francis Papers* show that Philip Francis was in England in the winter of 1781-2, but in Paris in August 1782. Francis, however, (*Memoirs of Sir Philip Francis*, Vol. I, p. 151) records that Madame de Talleyrand wrote expressly to ask him not to attempt to see her, sending him a few elegant books by way of a personal reminiscence, and that he did not see her. Francis was in Brighton on October 21, 1802. Grand was at Amsterdam in August and *en plein mer* Africa-bound a month later. It may have been that the Philip Fancis whom the younger Impey met was the *younger* Philip Francis.

Page 212. Fussily *Fasli* relating to the harvest, a solar calculation of the year introduced for purposes of revenue collection to avoid his inconveniences of the lunar system of calculation from the Hija.

Page 233. *By a Soonthael.* Súrat-i-hal, Surat = form, fashion and *hal* condition. A representation of facts made by an individual before a witness, or a report by a subordinate to a superior officer.

INDEX TO GRAND'S NARRATIVE.

EDITOR'S ERRATA AND ADDENDA.

Page 72. Line 3 from top, for "cautions" read "cautious."

Page 186. For "Chapter IV" read "Chapter XIV."

Page 277. To note on Colonel Forde, add "A memoir of Colonel Francis Forde" has recently appeared :—*Lord Clive's Right Handman*, by Colonel Lionel Forde.

Page 279. Line 16 from top, for "Mangras" read "Maugras."

Page 282. Line 18 from top, for "Tolouse" read "Toulouse."

Page 282. Line 9 bottom, for "Cailland" read "Caillaud."

Page 287. To note on J. Addison, add "He was one of those who attended Clavering, Francis and Monson on their visit to Nuncomar."

Page 289. To note 11 from top, for "Verner" read "Vernon."

Page 292. To note 3 from bottom, for "la Brun" read "le Brun."

Page 293. To note 11 from top, for "Bodevenc" read "Bodeveuc."

Page 293. To note 5 from bottom, for "Balsore" read "Balasore."

Page 296. To note 15 from bottom, for "the Lord" read "the "first Lord."

Page 299. To note on Charles Chapman, add "Chapman was a member of the Board of Revenue in 1790. Governor of the Calcutta Free School, 1790."

Page 300. Line 10 from top, for "Merchiston" read "Merchistoun."

Page 301. To note on Robert Bathurst, add "He married Miss Maria Leister, Spinster of Patna, on 23rd January 1784, Grand being one of the witnesses."

Page 301. To note on Ledlie, add "From Capt. Eastwick we learn that Ledlie was an early friend of the Great Duke of Wellington, Cf. Compton : *A Master Mariner*. Page 124 "On our arrival at Garden Reach, Colonel Wellesley asked me to land with him at the house of his friend Mr. Ledley, whose beautiful mansion was built close to the river bank."

Page 314. Line 2 from bottom, for "Captain R. W. Eastwick" read "H. Compton."

Page 319. Line 4 from bottom, for "his" read "the."

Page S5. Mr. Archdekin, Salt Agent. *Vide* Stephen's *Nuncomar and Impey*, Vol. I., p. 82.

FROM GRAND'S LIST OF ERRATA.

Page 123. Of present Edition. Appendix K. This document referred to is wanting. It relates to Appendix H, wherein will be seen in the Board of Revenue's letter, that they thank me for it, as comprising an essential detail of the customs and usages of Tirhoot, and indeed those prevailing in Behar.

Page 124. For "Rochefancoult" read "Rochefoucault."

Page 129. Appendix L.M. relates in its reference to Appendix H. being a part of the contents of the above letter described.

Page 146. For "*vide* memorial, 30th June, Appendix P" read "30th June, Appendix L."

Page 149. "For *vide* Appendix Q" read "*vide* Appendix L."

Appendix. For "prescribed" read "proscribed."

For "speedy justice" read "speedy injustice."

Postscript, fourth line from end, for "at once" read "an omen."